Social Deviance

Social Deviance

SOCIAL POLICY, ACTION,
AND RESEARCH

LESLIE T. WILKINS

Visiting Professor of Criminology
University of California at Berkeley

TAVISTOCK PUBLICATIONS

PRENTICE-HALL, INC.
Englewood Cliffs, N.J.
1965

PRENTICE-HALL SOCIOLOGY SERIES

Herbert Blumer, Series Editor

First published in 1964
by Tavistock Publications (1959) Limited,
11 New Fetter Lane, London E.C.4
Printed in Great Britain
in 10 point Times by
C. Tinling & Co. Ltd.,
Liverpool, London & Prescot
© *Leslie T. Wilkins, 1964*

Published in the U.S.A.
by Prentice-Hall, Inc.
Englewood Cliffs, N.J.

Contents

Acknowledgements

Any attempt to address an audience which does not possess a common language is unlikely to succeed. Yet there are problems which involve different professional skills and different viewpoints that need a common understanding and a joint effort to provide any form of solution.

Since this book attempts to draw together the social scientist, the social administrator, and the social worker, it may be expected to fail at least in some degree. If the average social worker is to find the book easy to read, the average social scientist may find parts of the writing insufficiently rigorous. If the scientist is addressed, the problems which can be discussed with the required sophistication might seem somewhat superficial to the social worker. The choice in this work has been to make the book as readable as possible and to hope that the meaning is clear to those specialists who may feel that important concepts are given cavalier treatment. To those who may think that much of the material is 'old hat' I express my sympathy; but perhaps if they persist in their reading the restatements in a new context may throw light from a different angle on the subject.

Intentionally avoiding jargon whenever possible has meant that words like 'responsibility', 'culture', 'class', and so on, have been used in ways which may seem semantically unsatisfactory. In particular the term 'responsibility' is used to mean 'charged with' in the sense in which a civil servant is 'responsible' within the bureaucratic structure for certain actions; it has been used as an ethical concept related to the legal meaning of responsibility for actions, and also with other shades of meaning. It is difficult to assess whether the contextual material has always been adequate to separate the different common usages where rather more than common-use concepts are under discussion. To overload the text with footnotes setting out the precise sense in which the word is used with detailed annotations might only have led to a false precision and an inconsistent style.

I doubt whether I have succeeded in the attempt to present material regarding social problems in a common language, but I hope that in my failure I may have stimulated others better qualified than myself to try to develop ways for different disciplines to examine problems together. The problems of the present-day society are big enough, if we can get them into focus, to make differences between skills and disciplines look very small indeed. The scientist should not attempt to contract out of society, of which, whether he likes it or not, he is a member. Society is one! Social administrator, social worker, and social scientist must get together and make a concerted attack upon the problems of the one world.

It was through my association with an attempt to involve administrator, social worker, and scientist together in the President's Committee on Juvenile Delinquency and Youth Crime that much of this book came to be written. But it would not have been possible to have had this experience if the Ford Foundation had not generously provided a Research Fellowship to enable me to spend a sabbatical year in the United States.

Many other persons have helped in many different ways. I am indebted to the faculty and students of the Department of Sociology at Temple University, Philadelphia, who first suffered my discourses on many of the topics in this book and who provided me with 'feedback' and research data. The faculty and students of the Department of Criminology at the University of California at Berkeley also influenced improvements in the text.

Special mention must be made of the help I received from Dr. Israel Gerver, the Chief of Research of the President's Committee on Juvenile Delinquency; at least one chapter has been completely redrafted and much improved on the basis of his suggestions.

Permission to reproduce material from published work is acknowledged, and particularly the following:

Dr. D. L. Marples for permission to reprint two diagrams and other matter from his paper published by the Institute of Engineering Designers;

Dr. Calvin F. Schmid and the Editors of the *American Sociological Review* for permission to reproduce tabular data and comment;

Dr. J. I. Kitsuse and Dr. D. C. Dietrick also for material originally published in the *American Sociological Review*;

Dr. D. J. Bordua and the Editors of the *Annals* of the American Academy of Political Science;

ACKNOWLEDGEMENTS

Dr. Gwynn Nettler and the Editors of *Sociometry*;

The Editor of the *Guardian* (previously the *Manchester Guardian*) for permission to quote from their material as noted in appropriate references;

Stevens and Sons and the Editors for permission to reprint charts and reports from my paper originally published in the *British Journal of Criminology*.

None of the views expressed in this book is to be interpreted as representing any official view or opinion either in this country or in the United States of America, unless the source is noted as an official document.

L.T.W.

Department of Sociology
Temple University
Philadelphia, Pa.
June 1963

Introduction

Everybody is concerned in some way or other with human behaviour, and few, if any, are not aware of problems in interpersonal relationships. Everybody can claim valuable experience which guides him in his dealings with other people. From the small child who finds ways to manipulate the school situation, to the top business executive, we may all refer to our experience of the ways in which people are likely to behave in different situations and we adjust our behaviour in accordance with our predictions.

Everybody is concerned with the behaviour of physical substances, and everybody can claim valuable experience which he uses in deciding how to handle or select materials. From the small child piling up bricks until they fall, to the designer of a modern office block, we may all refer to experience of the ways in which different substances behave under different conditions and we may select materials according to our needs and adjust the stresses we place on them according to qualities we have noted from experience or learned from theory.

In the world of social relationships, no less than in the physical world, our success in dealing with problems depends on our ability to make reasonable predictions of likely responses to probable situations. In some cases the behaviour to be expected under a set of given conditions may be stated with apparent complete certainty, but in others the level of specification of the conditions, or other factors, reduce the degree of belief in the predicted outcome. Degrees of belief may be related to different considerations. We may give greater or lesser weight to the evidence of others according to our beliefs regarding their competence or our understanding of their explanations.

In the physical world the relationship between experience and theory seems generally to be agreed. Few would doubt the value of theory here. In the physical sciences the engineer can be considered to stand between the experiences of the layman and the theoretical physicist, mathematician, or chemist. The engineer can translate the needs of the layman into problems which he himself may be able to solve or which he must refer to others. The needs of the layman or the community may be expressed in everyday language, and then translated by the engineer into a language which he shares in its essentials with the related sciences. The language of *need* is thus translated into the language of *problem-solving*. The necessity for a different language for stating problems in the physical sciences is generally recognized, as is the role of the specialist. The 'problem-solving structure' is integrated.

There are specialities in the social sciences, and there are roles which may be similar to that of the engineer standing between the theoretical and the practical. The social administrator and the social caseworker represent, perhaps, such a role, but the problem-solving structure is not well integrated. There are difficulties of communication between persons orientated to social action and the theorists and research workers. There are considerable difficulties in moving from the language of 'need' to the language of 'problem-solving'. The special strengths of the specialist disciplines are not known throughout the field.

This book is an attempt to assist in the task of facilitating the communication between problem-solving persons and social administrators and others concerned with social action. Those whose special skills are based on their experience of dealing with people and with personal problems can be helped in their work by the results of social research, and the social research worker who is concerned with problem-solving should find both assistance and a challenge in the experience of the practical man. Too often the social scientists concern themselves with experiments and elegant measurement, and it is seldom possible to apply such methods to evaluate the action which the social administrator and social caseworker consider to be necessary to meet the needs of society.

It is the author's belief that it is not desirable for social science and social action to be separated by a gulf of misunderstanding, where the scientist may solve elegantly problems which either do not exist or are trivial, and where the persons concerned with social action are content to 'do good', but never to know whether any good results are achieved.

Scientific methods may be concerned with the advancement of knowledge, but this does not restrict the range of the problems to which they are applied. To some extent all rigorous analysis can help towards this end. It is no longer possible to draw a fine line between 'pure' and 'applied' problems and methods. Whether the term 'social engineering' is or is not an acceptable one (and there are difficulties with any analogy), there is a need for understanding between the different disciplines concerned with human behaviour, whether in terms of action or abstraction.

The major difficulties in communication between those mainly concerned with social action and those concerned with social research seem to be related to the distinction between action and abstraction. But problem-solving in all fields of human endeavour has been facilitated by the derivation of suitable abstractions. When we are dealing with materials we see few difficulties in abstracting factors and applying theoretical solutions, but we are more reluctant to convert human problems into abstract concepts. The stress in a metal may be expressed by a mathematical function, and no one feels particularly concerned so long as the answer is correct. Yet the *very fact* of relating human stress situations to mathematical functions meets with resistance – and few people are content to evaluate the outcome by its results alone. The damaging effect of this difference in attitudes is increased by the absence of a common language – the language of needs used by the social administrator and the social worker is translated by the empirical research worker into a language of problem-solving, but most inadequately. The inadequacy is twice confounded, because the translator is only partly aware of the language from which he is translating, and tends to be impatient with those who know only the language of social action, while the representatives of social action are unable to consider the adequacy of the translation.

Yet two languages are essential. A language which is adequate for communication of concepts of needs is not adequate for problem-solving. To convey a sense of need it may be necessary to use language that also conveys some emotional elements, but such elements cannot be carried into a logical process of evaluation. A language which is optimal for communication must contain a large amount of re-dundancy, but redundancy must be removed before techniques of problem-solving can be applied.

But two languages do not mean two worlds.

The social administrator and social worker should not find it difficult to communicate with the social research worker, and the social research worker should not be unaware of the real-life problems faced by those concerned to get something done as well as it can be done. Whether we like it or not, we live in one society, and a society where beliefs and feelings are not regarded as the only criteria of action. In social evaluation the social research worker and the social administrator can and should both meet together and think together.

The need today for evaluation of social action means that thinkers and doers, social administrators and social scientists, theorists and empiricists, should learn the skills of collaboration. In this belief, the present book attempts to relate research methods to some 'real' down-to-earth problems of current society with particular reference to deviant behaviour and juvenile delinquency.

This is not another textbook in research methodology nor is it a book on statistical procedures. It is not concerned with how data are to be collected or analysed so much as with why they are collected and how different methodologies may be selected to be appropriate to different types of task. We will consider some of the important issues that the social administrator has to have in mind in policy decisions concerning social research and action.

Some aspects of statistical techniques and research methodology may be a source of misunderstanding between those concerned in team projects. It is these sources of misunderstanding and difficulties of communication which it is hoped some of the discussion will help to simplify. What questions ought the user of statistics to ask? When must the non-specialist rely upon the specialist, and when is it better to use his own skills? While the layman may fail to appreciate the value of the specialist's role, the specialist may be too closely concerned with the technicalities of his profession to observe how his special skills fit into general problems of social administration and policy.

It will not be possible to deal specifically with all the different applications of research methods in all the possible fields of social administration. However, as will perhaps become more evident later in this work, the different fields of application are concerned with problems which are basically extremely similar. The problems of measuring sickness and ill health are very similar to the problems of measuring crime. Both sickness and crime may be considered as deviations from normality. Problems in the field of social administration concerned with the educationally sub-normal, problems in the field of youth or old age, will have different terminologies, but where the basic concern is with human behaviour, the problems of measurement, classification, and analysis are easy to transpose from one field of application to another.

It would, of course, be possible to develop the discussions by use of abstract symbols like x and y, and thus to underline the generality of the issues considered, but it is probable that the general applications might be more interesting to read, if not more simple to follow, if the translation from one field to another were left to individual readers. Problems of behaviour disorder are of interest to many fields of social administration. Health, education, and welfare as well as law become involved in different ways with the problems of the youthful offender. The layman, too, is interested in crime. Crime is a subject about which most people have strong views, and from their readings of various levels of literature tend to be informed (or misinformed) perhaps more fully than are non-specialists in other fields of social problems. For this reason, the illustrations given will, in the main, be orientated towards problems of deviant behaviour. As illustrations of deviant behaviour, data related to crime and criminals will serve as the major subject-matter for the examples.

Social Deviance

CHAPTER 1

Scientific Evaluation of Social Policy – Is it Needed?

The social services in all countries are hotly debated. No matter what level of provision is or is not made for the socially vulnerable groups within a culture, some persons regard these as totally inadequate while others see them as excessive and as waste of taxpayers' money. Neither side in this debate is at present able to produce in support of its beliefs much evidence that is sufficiently 'scientific' to withstand critical analysis. But the 'scientific approach' is now being demanded from many quarters.

What is a Scientific Approach?

What is meant by a scientific approach? What is generally defined as 'science'? It is easier to define the 'scientific method' than to define 'a science'. Perhaps 'a science' might be defined as a discipline which made use of the 'scientific method' and 'science' as a body of knowledge obtained by means of this method. The scientific method is completely independent of the subject-matter, in all its essentials; it is a coherent plan for investigating complex systems and states of affairs including great organizations involving men, materials, machines, and money. The method ensures that the results are reproducible, valid, and efficient, and that departures from any of these requirements can be stated and measured. Sometimes 'science' is defined as an organized body of knowledge (acquired by the rigorous scientific method) of the workings of the world of systems and institutions as well as of things and people. T. H. Huxley (1872) remarked, '. . . by science I understand all knowledge which rests upon evidence and reasoning of a like character to that which claims our assent to ordinary scientific propositions . . .'

There is something unsatisfactory about all definitions of 'science', and even the 'scientific method' is not immune from philosophical questioning. None the less, while people's ideas of what science is differ, and not all scientists or even philosophers of science are completely agreed, it is both a term and a methodology to which people react strongly. Some people look on what they believe to be science as something remote and treat it with far too much respect or even fear. Others, dismissing what they cannot understand as, therefore, invalid, say that they are 'not going to be blinded by science'. Both methods of rejection of the scientific method are unsatisfactory and unnecessary.

Another view is that there are some areas of human activity that are outside the scope of the scientific method. This may be true of the creative arts, but the scope of the scientific method, as well as its power, has been rapidly and relentlessly increasing. Matters which were outside the province of science a few years ago are now being studied by scientific methods, and there is little doubt that the province of science will continue rapidly to increase.

There are some who would think of themselves as scientists who would take the view that their ability to understand a phenomenon or process was a satisfactory criterion of the degree to which science had been able to explain it. But clearly there could be few advances in knowledge if every advance were tested by the ability of the majority of people, or even the majority of scientists, to understand it and to feel subjectively satisfied with the evidence. Democratic evaluation of this kind has a place, indeed an important place, in the scientific method, but its place is limited. There are, of course, rules for the acceptance of evidence other than democratic evaluation and the subjective satisfactions of the scientist.

Human Science and Ethics

It was at one time thought that 'human' problems were outside the scope of the proper functions of scientific inquiry, but few today would take this view in any general way, although they might select specific areas as improper for application of the scientific method. The problems of human behaviour and of social administration and management are well within the range of known scientific methods of analysis. The tools of science today can be applied to problems of evaluating social action.

In the past most social agencies claimed support for their activities

2

from voluntary or government funds on the grounds that they were 'right' (i.e. ethical) and therefore it must be more effective to do what they proposed than to continue with less humane systems. For example, it was argued that treatment in 'open' penal institutions must be more effective in reforming criminals than punitive detention in secure prisons. It was also argued that provision of after-care for discharged prisoners was right, and therefore *must* be more effective than merely leaving them alone to find their own ways back into society. These and all similar arguments confound two factors: it may be right (ethical) to provide certain facilities such as after-care of prisoners and to use 'open' institutions, but these are matters of a different order from the assumption of effectiveness, which is a matter of fact that can be ascertained. Indeed, ethical considerations cannot be soundly based unless they are based on evidence which is itself independent of ethical considerations.

It may be believed that it is wrong to flog offenders, but it is difficult to make such a claim unless it is known whether or not those flogged tend afterwards to commit more or fewer offences than those not flogged. It could be that flogging resulted in fewer reconvictions by offenders so dealt with, and yet it may still be held that it would be wrong to flog. But suppose that *all* those flogged subsequently lived good lives and *all* those not flogged returned to a life of crime, could flogging then be considered to be unethical? It might be so argued if other aspects of flogging could be found which were relevant to the issues, but these other factors would need similar assessment. Again, some would argue that flogging is ethical – the offender, they believe, must be given a taste of his own medicine. But if *all* those flogged returned to crime, and *all* those not flogged lived good lives, it would be difficult to sustain the view that flogging was right. The extreme views on either side of the controversy regard the outcome of flogging as irrelevant. But can such a position be regarded as reasonable or ethical?

If we have no information of the outcome, how can we make sound ethical judgements? Clearly such judgements are possible only in limiting cases. It cannot be argued that scientific considerations are independent of ethical considerations, since it is highly probable that the scientific method will be necessary to provide the basic evidence upon which sound ethical judgements can be based. The scientific method, as we shall subsequently see in more detail, is not concerned with ethics, nor is it concerned with the arts, but the arts cannot (and generally do not) ignore science. Similarly, ethical arguments cannot avoid considerations of scientific data.

Uncertainty

It is often believed that science deals with things about which we can be certain, and that areas of experience where uncertainty and the philosophy of indeterminism are relevant are not fields for scientific inquiry. This was at one time true. Uncertainty was once a topic that science knew nothing about, but modern science has made notable successes in dealing with uncertainty. The scientific method can now deal with uncertainty both within the atom and within the human brain, both in the individual and in the human and animal group.

Uncertainty is dealt with by modern probability theory. Chances can be measured, risks can be calculated and strategies assessed. Measurements in these terms relate directly to problems of social administration and individual casework and real life.

But there are areas where science is not important – even aside from ethics. There are areas where human insight and creative art are by no means out of date. Indeed, the scientific method has been used to provide information regarding situations in which human creativity may be increased.

In the complex and costly business of social action we should not leave to chance any area of decision-making or any aspect of any situation that can be properly studied. By properly, we mean rigorously and powerfully and in such ways that other people may verify any results for themselves – in fact, we mean scientifically.

The scientific method can lift issues completely out of the area of controversy. It provides a court of appeal.

Method: The Criterion

If two scientists disagree on any issue, and the issue is within the ambit of science, then it must be *possible* for them to agree on a procedure which they *can both accept as a critical test* of their points of difference. For reasons of personality they may not be able to get together to work out such a test procedure, but it must exist as a possibility. If such a critical test cannot be imagined as possible, then the issue between them is not a scientific issue. The scientific method does not vary with the subject-matter, but is the same irrespective of its results and basically the same in all the sciences.[1]

[1] This does not hold where the difference of opinion may relate to the scientific method of inference itself.

Destruction and Construction

The different social agencies which operate in most societies today have many functions – some preventive, some constructive, some preservative, and some remedial. All have, perhaps, one feature in common: they aim to make groups or individuals more effective members of society, by direct or indirect means. They are concerned with social change. There seems to be no reason why agencies whose objectives are to build up society should be content with less powerful tools than those whose job is destruction. The problems are often similar but reversed. We can even refer to the 'war on want' and the 'war on crime'. These phrases are more than picturesque terms, they refer to the idea of a *strategy* which underlies both planned actions in war and actions in social administration. The use of scientific method in war was proved of extreme value in terms of effective destruction, and it can be applied equally to social construction in peace.

What did the scientific method achieve in war? A few examples have become generally known. The effectiveness of radar was doubled by means of a scientifically planned strategy. The Royal Air Force stated that by the use of certain analytical procedures the strategy for submarine attack was improved to the extent that the number of 'kills' increased by 700 per cent. The mining strategy used against the Japanese was credited with the loss of 1,200,000 tons of shipping. Much was learned about flying safety, and many lives of friendly forces were saved.

It may be easier to measure the damage done in war than the productivity or constructive work achieved in peacetime by social agencies, but there is no inherent reason why this should be so. When we are fighting for our country and motivated by patriotism we may be more willing to try scientific methods and to be a little more 'hard boiled' about our problems, but we can find ways of evaluating our socially constructive strategies as well if we try. Indeed it is our duty to try to do so.

Any social agency supported by taxpayers' money or voluntary funds has a duty to study and evaluate its effectiveness and to seek continuously to improve the methods it employs to achieve its objectives. It is not enough to believe, however sincerely, that we are doing good. It is not enough to invoke 'experience' or to collect meaningless and misleading information. It is not completely honest to spend money on giving attention to people who do not need such

5

attention, or to those who might be better integrated with society if they were not disturbed by unsought ministrations of well-meaning people. It is not enough to rely upon the support of colleagues and those in the same professional group and to accept their endorsement of our work as proof of its effectiveness. Professional in-group support does not measure effectiveness and does not absolve us from accountability for our decisions. The effectiveness of social agencies, it is claimed, is a question to be determined empirically by methods which can be repeated and verified by others.

Experience and Knowledge

The need for evaluation of social action is not completely agreed. To some it seems an absolute and obvious necessity, but others would claim that even if it were possible, which they doubt, it is still not necessary specifically to plan evaluative routines. The money so spent, they claim, would be far better spent in doing more of the particular work which the agency has as its commitment.

Perhaps the argument most frequently put forward against the demand for rigorous evaluation of social action is that of experience. It is 'obvious from experience' that the system is doing good, that patients are getting better, and that clients are profiting from the work of the caseworker. The experience to which defences of this kind usually refer is the experience of colleagues or an élite. 'No one can test my methods unless they have been trained in them,' is a frequent assertion. Let us examine the nature of this kind of proposition.

Interesting personal experiences can certainly be cited to defend almost any policy or system or action. The testimonials received by various patent medicine companies are not fakes, yet in many cases it is known that the 'cure' could not possibly have been due to the effect of the 'treatment'. Large proportions of patients given a placebo in medical clinical trials are convinced that the 'medicine' did them good – they know from their experience. In fact, in many cases they are definitely better.

There may be many cases where the most desirable action is to do nothing. But there are many ways in which nothing may be done. A placebo is a way of administering 'nothing' to a patient, and indeed to do 'nothing' in any other way would defeat the objectives of the trials. If the patient knew or believed that nothing had been done, his reactions would not be comparable with those of the experimental group. It may defeat these objectives if the patient believes that nothing is being done, even if action is taking place, and, conversely, belief that something is being done may be sufficient to be 'effective'. But the decision to do nothing, in no matter what way it may appear, should always be recognized for what it is by those responsible. Where we know nothing, it may be preferable to do nothing, *but if we do not know that we know nothing, we shall never learn any more.* One word can always be said in favour of doing nothing (or perhaps in favour of the use of a suitable placebo): unlike many other things we may do, this course of inaction is likely to do no harm; it will leave room for spontaneous recovery.

Time, it has been said, in another connection, is a great healer! Spontaneous recovery is often the fastest known form of recuperation. Time, indeed, may be said to be such a great healer that its effects may even cancel out the harmful effects of inappropriate action. In all evaluation work it is essential to separate out the effects of chance and time. In human subjective integration of 'experience' the effects of chance or of the probability of spontaneous recovery are not likely to be well assessed.

It is not long since medical experts 'knew' from experience that leeches and bleeding were effective cures for many complaints. Had they not bled many patients who recovered? Grant (1962) has wittily asked when a person claimed eighteen years of experience whether he had had eighteen years' experience or one year's experience eighteen times! Of course, there is nothing wrong with experience as a means of making good decisions or as a basis for advance in knowledge. Everything depends upon how the experience is organized. Experience is, in fact, the basis for the scientific approach. The problem of effective and efficient evaluation of any process is largely a problem in ways of organizing the available experience, or in ways of specifically seeking new experience relevant to the process.

Experience directed towards one objective may not be the best kind of experience for a different purpose. Experience gained in one way may not be organized in the best way for different end-products. The type of organization of experience that facilitates some decisions is almost certainly not optimal for guidance to different decisions. The effective evaluation of a social agency or a specific social action project requires the optimum organization of the existing experience plus, perhaps, some new data. It is in suggesting these procedures that the scientific method is necessary to provide effective evaluation. Perhaps some business firms are successful in making a profit or avoiding bankruptcy and yet do not make use of an accountant or costing procedures. The taxation officials, however, are rather suspicious of an absence of records or of accounting procedures that are not in accord with accepted practice. Perhaps it is surprising that the general public pay with so little complaint for so many social agencies and social services without demanding an accounting procedure that measures the effectiveness of the different types of enterprise. But there is now beginning to become evident some demand to be shown results in terms of reduced delinquency and other specific outcomes of social action. None the less the demand should not have to come from outsiders. The social agencies themselves should be the first to seek rigorous evaluative procedures as a means to helping them towards improved services. The agencies claim that they are doing good and that it is their aim to do more good. They should be as interested to do more good by becoming more effective in their tasks as by being allocated more trained staff or more money. Efficiency is something which cannot be achieved without effort expended in the appropriate ways, and measurement is one of the ways towards improved efficiency. It is difficult to see how efficiency can be improved without some basis in measurement.

Instruments and Feelings

Many do not seek to challenge the need for evaluation of social policy, but argue that such evaluation is not possible. It is, they claim, from their experience, known that such evaluation is impossible because the human intelligence alone can correctly assess any situation involving human emotions. Evaluation, they correctly point out, involves some form of measurement, and human situations cannot be measured. Perhaps these arguments should be examined before the power and limitations of some of the methods which are available for evaluation purposes are discussed.

In recent years, the division between research and action has led to those who seek to use measurement being attacked as inhuman; as reducing men and women to mere numbers. Fink (1962) claims that there is no substitute for human judgement and human feelings. 'I am inclined much more to the judgement of a judge who is wise, humane and just than I do to the efficiency of prediction tables,' he says, and Teeters (1962), discussing parole prediction, writes, 'the parole petitioner is a person, not a mere digit, and this presents a hazard of losing sight of him as a living personality'. These and

8

similar comments miss the basic issue. The issue is, of course, not *how* the task is done, but *how well* it is done, and, of course, what the task is. These writers and others sharing their views are claiming that because they disapprove of the *means*, the *ends* must also be wrong (i.e. inefficient).[1] This is the same type of argument as has been used to support social action – it is right (ethical), therefore it must be true. If, in fact, measurement systems do not do better the particular task required, they should be rejected, but measurement should not be rejected as such without reference to the specific objectives of the agency. If measurement itself is rejected, the claim seems to reduce to 'we have the right to do good, and we reserve the right to do it only in our own way, whether it is effective or not, and whether it achieves the ends we claim we wish to achieve or not!'

Ends and Means

There is confusion of ends and means in this type of attack upon measurement in principle. Perhaps if medicine threw away the thermometer, the encephalograph, the X-ray, and all other technicalities, medicine would become much more human! How much more preferable the tender hand on the brow than a nasty piece of glass in the mouth – how inhuman! But is it sympathy and fellow-feeling that we want from the physician or a technical competence to identify the condition and give us the cure? The bedside manner still has a place in the cure, even although the hand on the brow has been replaced by the thermometer.

Measurement in human investigations is not inhuman.

Who, it may be asked, shows the greater concern for the sanctity of human life – the scientist who devotes himself to discovering step by step, always ready to submit to facts, always aware that even his boldest achievement will never be more than a stepping-stone for those who come after him, or the 'mystic élite who reject measurement and thus are free to maintain anything, because they need not fear any rigorous testing of their beliefs'? (Popper, 1954.)

Why do Research?

Those who wish to evaluate social action and test the effectiveness of social agencies want to do so for the *very same reasons* as those who plan the work of such agencies and carry out their work in the field of their choice wish to do the active part. The work of social rehabili-

[1] For further discussion of means and ends, see p. 191.

tation, reconstruction, preservation, and preventive action is a joint enterprise for action and research. The one can never be a substitute for the other.

Measurement is a tool to help us to do the job which we, social scientist, social administrator, and social worker want to do and want to do well.

Of course there are problems in any joint enterprise. One of the major problems in this field is communication, and problems of communication are largely due to the separation of social action from policy and social research. This rift did not exist a century ago; indeed, it is a recent development that ought to be reversed. We shall examine some of the possible reasons for this separation of science from action and policy, and consider also the related division between 'pure' and 'applied' research.

REFERENCES

FINK, A. E. (1962). Current Thinking on Parole Prediction Tables. *Crime and Delinq.*, vol. 8, no. 3, p. 227.

GRANT, J. D. (1962). It's Time to Start Counting. *Crime and Delinq.*, vol. 8, No. 3.

POPPER, K. (1945). *The Open Society.* London: Routledge & Kegan Paul, p. 231.

TEETERS, N. K. (1962). Current Thinking on Parole Prediction Tables. *Crime and Delinq.*, vol. 8, no. 3, p. 237.

CHAPTER 2

The Divide – Action and Research:
' Pure ' and Applied

Early social research and action – Operational research – Science becomes 'other-directed' – The problem of objectives – Scientist: scapegoat or tool? Rationality – The problem of responsibility – The role of ethics – Change: a challenge – The 'power structure' – Cooperative teams – Communication and operationalism – The language barrier – Democratic science?

It may be valuable to examine the nature of the division between social action and social research by relating it to the division between pure and applied research in other fields of study. In the physical sciences a unity linked pure and applied research in past times although the division began somewhat earlier than the separation between social action and social research. Neither the distinction between pure and applied research in the physical sciences nor the separation of social research from social action can now be retained in a meaningful way for similar reasons.

Early Social Research and Action
Perhaps the earliest attempts at evaluation of social action were the forerunners of modern statistical procedures. One fact is both certain and important: the early social accountants were not divided from the social reformers or from social action and policy. Their philosophy seems to have been something like – 'if only the people knew what was happening they would do something about it, or allow us to do something about it'. Their recording and description of social events had the purpose of stimulating action and of alerting the public to take action to remedy what they saw as social evils.

It is usual to credit Adolphe Quetelet (1796–1874) with the beginnings of social statistics and attempts to evaluate social policy by some form of social accounting, but it is not our purpose to discuss the history of social investigations. None the less, it is interesting to consider one very early claim to priority in relating data to social action. That much maligned character in British history, Thomas Cromwell, may have at least this one thing to his credit. During Tudor times England suffered very considerably from plague, and various precautionary measures – perhaps an early form of social medicine – came to be deemed necessary. The main action was in terms of quarantine and isolation, and certainly these seem to have been the most important in obtaining any measure of control. But to carry out these measures successfully it was necessary to have early warnings of the existence of plague in specific areas, and even in particular houses. In order to obtain this information, *searchers*, usually women, were appointed under the Parish Clerk, to whom they were required to report the causes of each death occurring within the Parish. The Clerk in his turn sent these reports to the Parish Clerks' Hall. These returns were known as the *Bills of Mortality*. They were summaries of the data collected by the *searchers* and showed the areas in which plague was current and the Parishes which were free from plague. It is generally believed that the *Bills of Mortality* date from 1538, when the Parish Registers were first established by Cromwell, but there is extant a Bill which dates from August 1535 and even one which is possibly earlier. It is certain that the Bills were systematically compiled in a standard form in December 1603, and they continued regularly until 1842, when the Registrar General's Office took over the implementation of the Births and Deaths Registration Act of 1836, and the Registrar General's returns were published instead. It was, however not until 1728 that the ages at death were recorded. This was a very important fact leading directly to the *life tables* on which life insurances were based, and probability became a commercial proposition. However, previous to this in 1662, a John Graunt had published his work *Natural and Political Observations*, which made use of inductive methods based on the data of deaths in London from 1632 to 1661.

Another very important social statistician and philosopher was Thomas Robert Malthus (1766–1834), one of whose most sophisticated works was *Inquiry into Rents*. But, of course, it is Quetelet who is most usually credited with the extension of statistics to 'moral' factors.

Operational Research

The separation of the social scientists from those concerned with social reform seems to have been a progressive influence, that became noticeable after the 1914–1918 war, but gained great momentum after the 1939–1945 war. Indeed the impact of the 1939–1945 war on science and scientists may have been an important factor in the separation. The developing division of responsibility and difference of basic philosophy is doubtless useful and in accord with the general philosophy of science, but it raises many problems. The scientist could detach himself from value judgements, he could enter his ivory tower, and, once he had entered it of his own volition, certain people attempted to turn the key on him and confine him there. The scientist wanted to explore and to try to understand the phenomena which he could observe. He was inclined to be content with acquiring knowledge. But it is now more apparent that the problem is not *what* we know, but how we know that we know what we believe we know.

The pursuit of knowledge for the sake of knowledge, although the basic philosophy of the early scientists, was never a realistic one. The concept of 'pure research' has been shattered with the atomic bomb. The non-utilitarian nature of research, even of the 'highest' forms of mathematical analysis, can no longer be expected to be more than a temporary phase. Perhaps the splitting of the atom was the pursuit of knowledge for the sake of knowledge, perhaps the early investigations of set theory were carried out solely as an exercise in art and to discover the beauty of number; but it is no longer possible to assume that even the most remote investigations will not at some time have a great impact upon our society or even upon the future of mankind. We may say that we are ignorant of the likelihood of any such impact when we carry out our research, but by this we are stating an area of ignorance which itself should be a challenge to our intelligence to investigate. There is no longer any meaningful dichotomy between pure and applied research – there is a continuum from long-term to short-term research. But inherent in this time factor is a qualitative difference. If we take our motivation from the current problems in society and develop our research inquiry along the lines these suggest, we have applied research, and we have some measure of control over the objectives of our inquiry. There may be by-products of the investigations which are unknown, but it is our initial belief that our results, if they are sound, will be applied in the solution of an existing problem of which we have direct knowledge. We may, however, begin an inquiry in a different way. We may have in mind no particular problem except that we, as scientists, are curious regarding a certain phenomenon. In the course of our inquiries, beginning in this way, we may be solving problems which do not as yet exist, or which cannot now be made explicit.

Science Becomes 'Other-Directed'

Perhaps the major factor changing the role of scientific inquiry in recent years was the 1939–1945 war. Whole nations were mobilized. The scientist was conscripted from his tower to be on tap – but not on top! The relationship between the scientist and the power structure, never an easy one, became a very difficult problem. Many aspects of the difficulties of these relationships are still undisclosed. There was a tendency for any scientist who became too closely identified with the power structure to be rejected by his peers. The reasons for this were never studied in terms of their social and psychological implications. The sociology of science, and the psychology of men of science are still under-developed areas, and, during the war, any such inquiries would have been perceived as unnecessary luxuries. It may be speculated that one of the reasons for the peer rejection of scientists accepted by the power leaders was the fact that such scientists had accepted a major change in their perceived roles. What had determined the direction of scientific inquiry had, in the main, until that time been decided by considerations of science, whereas then the main considerations were non-scientific. Previously a line of investigation had been followed without too much consideration for its potential applications, now application became all-important, and was decided by non-scientists. Instead of science determining its course, and applications being coincidental, applications determined the course of inquiry.[1] The consequences of this change of orientation have not yet been worked through. The relationship between the scientist and the power structure which developed and modified the role of scientists during the war has continued its trend. Yet the problems of science and administration in peacetime are different from those of wartime. In war it could be taken as axiomatic that the society, of which the scientist was a member, had to defend itself, and this meant finding ways to win the war. The social system would allow of no doubters of this philosophy. Even the sub-problems and solutions of interim questions presented little or no difficulty. It was easy for the scientist to accept, for example, an end-objective which specified that the lives of fellow-citizen soldiers should be saved or used as

[1] For a description of some of the problems of relationships between scientists and the power structure, see *Brighter than a Thousand Suns* (Jungk, 1958).

sparingly as possible. Quite often the scientists were aware only of the sub-problems which they were studying and not of the total problem of which they formed a part. Nor were they informed of the final use intended for the sum-product of their labours. The general strategy of science was under the general command, and served the general command's objectives. But should the scientist in peacetime be asked to yield the direction of research strategy to the 'general command' in the same way? Clearly the total situation is different, and certainly more complex.

The Problem of Objectives

Who has the right or duty to say whether what we know should be applied in specific ways? Or if we do not know how to do certain things, or do not know how to do them well, whether we should apply scientific methods to find out how? And with what priority should we select these questions for answer? Should the social scientist place the responsibility for utilizing his results upon those responsible for social action and social policy? Are they to be expected, without his involvement, to specify the problems he should attempt to solve?

The scientist claims that he has the right to inquire into material and human systems and problems, but he usually rejects responsibility for the applications of the knowledge he acquires. He is often glad to claim ignorance of the utility and applications of his work. He leaves this responsibility to others. When he has been forced into a different role, and has had to relinquish his right to investigate things just because things are there to be investigated, when he has been instructed to investigate a problem in order that a specific purpose may be achieved, he has often objected that such instruction has restricted the scientist's sacred freedom to investigate whatever he pleases. Of course, freedom is a quality which most people appreciate – it is very nice to do what you want to do in your own way without interference, no matter what you are doing. But is this the only reason for reluctance to accept purposeful direction from external authorities? Perhaps not. It may be that the scientists who take this view believe that no ethical questions arise if they merely pursue knowledge for its own sake. If the knowledge obtained can be used for almost any purpose, for good or ill, the ethical questions relating to the applications of the results do not fall to the scientist – the choice is up to others to determine. Other scientists have been quite ready to accept instructions to investigate particular problems for

15

particular purposes, and quite willing to accept the rewards for their work, leaving the responsibility for the applications with the employing authorities. But has the scientist the right to shelve the responsibility for applications of his work in this way? Are others to be expected, without his involvement, to specify the problem he should attempt to solve or to determine the application of the results of his 'pure' research investigations? Can there really be absolution from all ethical considerations for scientists when the applications follow his endeavours, that differs from the absolution afforded him when the applications are specified first?

Scientist – Scapegoat or Tool?

Certain sections of society have turned the blame for what they fear or regard as unpleasant in modern living against the scientist. 'They ought not to have made the things!' says the man on the Clapham bus. 'Science is devilish!' 'If only we could go back to the good old days . . !' It is true that these kinds of attack, in many different forms, are directed mainly against the physical sciences, but this may be because the layman has more evidence of the effects of research in these fields. The same line of thinking is beginning to develop with respect to the social sciences; as evidence of this trend are films like *A Face in the Crowd*, and the book *The Hidden Persuaders* (Packard, 1957) and some novels by the 'angry young men'. Of course, the issues raised by the H-Bomb are more clear-cut than those raised by the application of social science, but it may be doubted whether the basic problems which these comments reflect are inherently different.

Gunther Anders (1962), for example, claims that it is not merely the bomb itself which threatens the existence of mankind, but the fact that the power of mass destruction is in the charge of a bureaucracy of such a kind that the participants in any mass destruction have no sense of responsibility for their actions. As he remarks, 'the specialized worker is not conscious of the fact that the conscientious efforts of a number of specialists can add up to the most monstrous lack of conscience; just as in any other industrial process he has no insight into the process as a whole'. 'No one can speak here of "agents". The men who carry out such actions are always co-agents: they are either half-active and half-passive cogs in a vast mechanism, or they serve merely to touch off an effect that has been prepared in advance to the extent of 99 per cent. *The categories of co-agent and "touching off" are unknown in traditional ethics.*' Anders considers that the concept of collective guilt used in the war crimes trials was inadequate although indispensable. He regards this inadequacy as due to the fact that situations where all perpetrators are merely co-perpetrators, and all non-perpetrators are indirectly perpetrators, require entirely new concepts, and also to the fact that the nature of the actions performed was outside the realm of moral appreciation. As he states, 'one can repent one murder, not a million murders'. In the case of an individual murder 'man's emotional, imaginative and moral capacity are congruent or at least commensurable with his capacity for action'. This is a sort of collective fatalism leading to a total anomie. It ignores the concept of the 'power structure' discussed by Merton (1957) and Wright Mills (1956).

Anders claims that because 'they know not what they do' the monstrousness of the act makes possible a new, diabolical innocence. Perhaps there is true individual ignorance, but is there also innocence and a collective ignorance? How sound is the connection between innocence and ignorance? Is Anders's assumption that the actions of mass destruction are possible only or mainly because they differ qualitatively as well as quantitatively from individual murder soundly based?

Recent research would seem to suggest that the dimensions of innocence and ignorance cannot be confounded, and that the basic dimension may be that of information and the ways in which information is perceived. It has been shown in laboratory research situations that, provided the individual subject can be thoroughly persuaded that he is in no way responsible for the consequences of his actions, he will go to almost any lengths in applying tortures to other human beings within his full view. In other words, the information which he obtains from the person being tortured, i.e. the results of his own actions, is treated by him as irrelevant to the actions. That is, because he is not responsible for his actions, the information which is relevant to his actions is *perceived as irrelevant*. The information set is, as it were, turned orthogonal to the problem. It would seem from these results that all human beings could behave in the same or similar ways to the concentration camp guards if they were placed in similar situations involving similar 'information sets' (Millgrim, 1964).

Christie (1952) in his study of Quisling concentration camp guards found that most of their attitudes could be described as normal, but they did not perceive the prisoners as normal human beings. The guards did not identify with their prisoners. It is not that the informa-

17

tion necessary to condition their actions was not visible to them, but that it was treated *as though* it were absent, because there was no concept of responsibility to consider it – those matters were being looked after by others.

It is convenient at this stage, in order to develop our analysis of this problem, to ignore for the moment all considerations of ethics involving the concepts of innocence or guilt and to consider only the nature of rational decisions.

Rationality

It would appear that three basic dimensions are involved in relationship to each other in the concept of rationality. These are:

(a) information
(b) room for manoeuvre (possible decisions)
(c) purpose or 'pay-off'.

Clearly, if we do not know what we wish to achieve there is no meaning in any information; similarly, if we can make only one decision (a rare situation), there is no point in discussing the other two dimensions; again, if no information can be available, one cannot discuss rationality. A rational decision may, it seems, be defined as the decision which, having regard to the information available, maximizes the likelihood of obtaining the purpose we wish to achieve or minimizes our probability of loss. But ethical considerations, including the concepts of innocence and guilt, are not included in the three-dimensional structure of rationality. For these considerations a fourth dimension is required. Ethical considerations may determine what it is that we should try to maximize using our rational framework, or may impose other boundary conditions, perhaps on the 'room for manoeuvre' within our decision set.

Ethics has nothing to do with the *way* in which the three-dimensional structure of rational decisions is resolved. As long ago as 1872, Huxley came very near to making this point in his essays on Mr Darwin's critics. He wrote, '. . . they are unable to allow that reason and morality have two weights and two measures . . .'. Huxley's 'two weights' would perhaps tend to suggest the idea of resolution into one dimension, whereas the concept here is of two dimensions – reason and morality, where rationality is broken down into three essential dimensions or sets.

Anders (1962) seems to be collapsing the four-dimensional model into a three-dimensional structure by equating the absence of information (ignorance) with innocence. He seems to have much public support for this. It is quite a common claim that innocence is established by a plea of ignorance, although no such plea is acceptable in law. The legal fact of innocence is not established by demonstration of ignorance. Innocence is established only by means of an external criterion, namely the law itself, as interpreted in relation to the action performed. The law is thus another dimension which is used to establish guilt where there may well be present the factor of ignorance. If any individual is in ignorance of relevant matters, he will not, perhaps, *feel* guilt unless he has specifically avoided obtaining such information, but such avoidance presupposes some small quantity of knowledge, at least knowledge that knowledge could be obtained that was relevant. Thus it may be possible to avoid *feelings* of guilt by adopting the way of ignorance (i.e. by rejecting 'information') as a conscious or subconscious defence.

It seems possible to suggest a theory integrating the concepts of 'information', decision, purpose, and the ethical factors of innocence and responsibility.

A politician (in any social system) may reject a proposal for research into certain substantial social issues on the logically sound ground that 'any information on this subject could only be an embarrassment'. This could be, given certain conditions, a very sound reason for the rejection of research – the possibility of finding relevant information. If no information is available, any decision, either right or wrong, cannot be challenged as irrational. In other words, there is no restriction on the politician's room for manoeuvre in his political decisions if they are not encumbered by data! If all information relevant to the issue were absent, the question of whether or not the decision was functionally sound could not arise. As Tocher (1962) remarks, '. . . the concept of a system about which we know nothing is as meaningless as the idea of "complete ignorance" so beloved of the exercise-solvers who confuse the whole field of inductive reasoning'. Thus if no information were available, the opposition would have no grounds to claim that the decision (any decision) made by the politician was not the most appropriate one to achieve a stated objective, even where the same objective might have been shared by the two opposing parties. Immediately information becomes available, it becomes possible to put forward arguments in favour of some decisions rather than others, and, indeed, the number of rational decisions will tend to diminish as information increases. It is possible that if information could ever be complete with respect to any subject, there would be only one optimum and rational decision to achieve any one given objective. In the sense in which information is discussed in the argument here, it is information relevant to the *objective* – the objective is *given*, and the discussion of the issue turns on its relationship to the information. If a politician knew what decision he wished to make (on political grounds), and the objective to be achieved by any decision was not in question, he could reject information. The decision set then becomes the objective and is thus *fixed*, and hence the only way to ensure that the decision cannot be challenged in respect of its rationality (the remaining dimension) is to avoid the collection of specifically relevant information; since rationality concerns the power of the decision to achieve the objective.

It will thus be obvious that Anders's dimension of ignorance is not a general factor of ignorance, but ignorance with respect to some specific dimension or criterion which he does not specify in detail. Information which is irrelevant to a criterion is the same as no information. There is no meaning to information in itself. Thus it is possible for a person to be led to believe, or to claim, that information which is available to him is not relevant to the action, but, if he fails to examine its relevance for himself, it could be asserted that he was behaving in an *irresponsible* manner. It may, in fact, appear that any questioning of rationality may be avoided by collapsing the dimensions required in the rational decision set, and ethical considerations may be avoided if they can be treated as identically equal to any of the other dimensions.

It is necessary to invoke the concept of responsibility and to require that four dimensions are considered together, and to relate the concept of responsibility to a concept of functional or perhaps ethical behaviour. Let us examine this statement in a little more detail.

The three-dimensional model for rational decisions imposes three sets of boundary conditions. These conditions interact. If, as in the example of the politician, I have made up my mind to behave in a certain way, and I do not wish to be proved irrational, I must either reduce the information to zero or leave the objectives unstated. If the objectives are ambiguous, the relationship between my decision and the information cannot be tied down. Thus there is an interdependence between decisions, information, and objectives. Similarly, if ignorance (absence of information) is associated with innocence, there is a relationship between innocence and information, decisions and objectives. If guilt and innocence are opposite poles of the same dimension, it must also follow that there is a relationship between guilt and the three dimensions involved in consideration of rational decisions. One effect of this relationship is that if I wish to remain innocent, and also to fix my decisions so that they may fit the requirements of rationality, I may choose ignorance; alternatively, I may still claim to be rational and innocent if I remain ignorant of the objectives or do not influence the decisions. Thus the politician in our example was able to reject guilt by rejecting information, while the 'pure scientists' reject guilt by rejecting concern with the decisions made on the basis of the information they provide. The one limits responsibility in one way and the other in a slightly different way.

The question of guilt or innocence, however, seems in this regard to turn upon the degree of ignorance. If we specifically seek ignorance of information in order to claim rationality we may be considered to have sufficient indication of the nature of the information to impose some boundary conditions. Thus, if the politician claimed ignorance in order to claim rationality, he may have been selecting guilt by the rejection of responsibility. The rejection of responsibility may be seen either as an acceptance of guilt or as a rejection of rationality. A similar argument applies if we retain our claim to rationality by pleading an ignorance of the objectives or fail to concern ourselves with the decisions, that is to say, with the uses made of the information. All dimensions must be considered together. We cannot reject only decisions or objectives or information according to personal preferences and remain responsible individuals. To throw out any one set is related to throwing out the others.

The definition of the concept of guilt does not affect the fact of the relationship, but it gives rise to a different model if the consideration of guilt is limited to either ethical or functional terms. The functional definition of guilt must be related to our concept of our society. If we believe that our society, and particularly our own culture (or sub-culture), is ethically good, then anything which is perceived as dysfunctional for this 'good' society involves 'guilt'. Only the concept of guilt as an ethical and independent dimension permits the scientist and politician to claim that the three dimensions of rational decisions do not apply to any particular case or types of case. The politician may be prepared to accept the charge of irrationality, justifying his irrational decisions by claiming that he is doing what is right – that

21

ethical considerations override everything else. He could not accept the charge of being dysfunctional, since this would mean accepting a charge of being incompetent and require apology and rectification of the 'error' and possibly resignation. The society which the politician represents must be identified with 'right' and 'good' and 'functional', otherwise he should not be in power. The definition of guilt in functional terms is again similar to a reduction in the set of dimensions. For the politician what is 'right' is functional even if irrational, while for the scientist rejection of ethics as an independent dimension can be achieved by equating truth (information) with 'goodness' (right), since for the scientist what is correct is perceived as right, whereas for the politician the proposed action is equated to right ('good'). For the scientist information is right (ethically right and correct) independent of the decision made upon it, and he contracts out of concern for the decisions. For the politician, his decision is right, no matter what the information. If society is good, then what is functional is right; if society is bad, then what is dysfunctional is right. The politician sees society as right, because it is his decisions that make it that way! The scientist sees society as right, because he is measuring it that way!

The Problem of Responsibility

It would seem that the 'pure scientist' would claim to avoid responsibility by being no more than a provider of information with which society can concern itself in whatever ways it wishes – for cancer cure, for electric power, or for destruction. He ignores the interaction between information and decisions because these are matters with which he, in his view, is not concerned. But his innocence or guilt does not turn only upon his rejection of responsibility, but also upon the degree and quality of his ignorance of possible applications.

While the 'pure scientist' avoided responsibility for the applications of research by the rejection of considerations of its use (objectives and decisions), the social and applied scientists have sought and found refuge in a scientific fallacy. What is right is good! Thus their work has *become* their ethic. This fallacy springs directly from the Platonic philosophy that goodness, truth, and beauty are closely related to each other and are to be pursued as the ultimate goals. 'Beauty is truth, truth beauty, that is all we know . . . and all we need to know.' Nettler (1961) points out that Platonism is part of the culture in which most social scientists are steeped. The assumption that all deviation is evil and all evil is based on incorrect, that is unscientific, information, is fairly general. The psycho-analysts make an almost one-to-one identification between badness and sickness. Nettler suggests that if 'bad behaviour' is a symptom of sickness, and if a symptom of the sickness is a perverted picture of the world, then the equality of morality with correctness seems established, and as he remarks 'certain happy consequences may be inferred, for example,

(a) that truth and utility are not at war as Pareto and the inconsistent Plato believed

(b) that science can "prove" values and thus give them the underpinning they lost with the decline of religious authority

(c) that since evil-is-sickness-is-error, therapy remains what some like to think it is, truth-giving

(d) that we good people are also more factually correct.'

It will be recognized that this is the reciprocal of the social reformers' argument that what is right (ethical) must be good (functional). Thus both the social worker and the social scientist are operating with an identical philosophy, and applying it from different angles.

Nettler examines empirical data and concludes that the assumption 'that evil action is sickness is doubtful and the assumption that a prime symptom of the illness that generates badness is a false picture of the world is particularly doubtful'. He suggests that the notion that bad people must be sick is the result of 'American pragmatic optimism, bred with the classic values of goodness, truth and beauty'. He points to the danger of this '. . . it must be considered that while as scientists we protest our preference for truth over error, as culture bound thinkers we may favour lies when their credentials are of the right sort'. In other words the social scientist has found it possible to avoid the concept of values by equating them to his science. But is it not better to suppose that truth and good are orthogonal? The fact of the atomic structure is neither good nor bad, what is good or bad is how the information is used. But if the desired 'good' – the end-objective – is not correlated with truth in such a way that one dimension can be ignored, an optimum strategy for society cannot be achieved by the reduction of either set of dimensions. A scientist is as 'wrong' (dysfunctional) to equate evil and error as the politician to regard information as irrelevant to ethical judgement. Let us examine one or two examples.

How does this type of reasoning fit the problem of flogging, for which it was earlier claimed that information was necessary for ethical decisions? Whether flogging is right or wrong may be discussed independently of considerations of information relating to its outcome (reduction of set), but such discussion does not take into account enough dimensions to be regarded as functional. Any decisions made without reference to relevant information in this particular case, and, it is suggested, in general, amount to substitution of truth (right) for information (correctness), or to ignoring the objectives. The argument may be, 'I do not want to know whether they recidivate or not, they *deserve* a taste of their own medicine!' This represents a substitution of the objective (deserve) together with a rejection of information. Alternatively, the argument may be, 'Flogging is wrong, no matter what the apparent result'. Both arguments are of the *same* kind. Simply, these two arguments reduce to, 'I don't care whether it's functional, it's ethical (right)'. The ethic, opposing though the two cases are, is held to be superior to information, and itself adequate to determine the decision. Information is reduced to zero in *both cases*; hence nothing is known, and the scientific method can tell us nothing.

To help people to live seems to be an uncomplicated and worthy objective, but even research into matters of life and death is not a simple issue to resolve in terms of the dimensions of information, decisions, objectives, and ethics. Consider euthanasia. In this case we know the means required and the unsolved issues are not referrable to scientific inquiry. But why not? If the means were not known, scientists could soon devise a system of painless, or perhaps even pleasant, death. Suppose, then, that the means were not known, how should scientists react to the suggestion that they should investigate the problem of producing such a means? Examined from one viewpoint, euthanasia, we would conclude, raises a simple dichotomous question: whether we permit the person to continue in conditions we can specify more or less precisely, or whether we permit an ending. But what are sometimes put forward as ethical factors can be looked at in a different light. The ethical factors could be seen as matters of faith and religion which throw doubt on the completeness of the information set. It is claimed that there are essential unknowns; moreover, it is claimed that these unknowns are unknowable. If this thesis is accepted we are faced with the problem of determining the nonsense issue of what is rational action in the case where nothing is known.

24

Knowledge may be unrelated to ethics in the way suggested by Nettler, but there is no reason for assuming that we live in a simple universe. It is through a recognition of a number of possibly orthogonal dimensions that we may see the relationship between ends and means, between art and science, between social action and social research, and between science and ethics.

The Role of Ethics

Much of the raw material of ethics and art today is derived from information and experiences originating in the application of scientific methods and principles. Scientific factors are not outside the scope of ethics, but ethical considerations are outside the scope of the scientific *method*. Ethical considerations may be superior to scientific considerations. Ethics impinges on research but is not concerned with it. Ethics may be concerned with the ends desired, and even with the processes of *obtaining* information, but not with the processes of inference or the techniques of valid measurement. Ethics may discuss what is *desirable* in ends or means but not what is valid. What is valid (true) has nothing to do with what is right. The scientific method is concerned with methods of inference and deduction and thus with problems of validity; with the consistency of its *methodology*. The scientist is, of course, in common with all other human beings, a product of his time and age. If he is too far ahead he is defined as mentally ill, and if he is behind he is not a scientist!

In western democratic societies it is generally considered that society should be an evolving process which attempts to continue to expand individual freedoms through social cooperation between its members. If this sort of society is *given* as an *ethic*, both social action and scientific methods may be evolved within it. The same ethic concerns all members of the society, whether politicians or scientists or laymen; all are concerned to ensure that within this social ethic their behaviour is functional.

Change – A Challenge

If, then, we accept this ethic, what are the optimum means of working out social action and research within it? Who has the right or the duty to say whether what we know should be applied to what situations in terms of the ends stated? Or who has this right or duty in the similar case where we do not know enough to say what further factors need specification and measurement, and what priorities should be devoted to the inquiries directed at the several problems involved? This question may be seen as one of methods of research organization and administration – an area in which there are extremely few research studies. Most studies that have been attempted point to major difficulties in communication both between different research disciplines and between research and administration and policy. Sociological investigations and analyses of administrative systems, and particularly of social administrative systems, are highly critical of the bureaucratic organization and 'power structure'.

If we may interpret the philosophy of the 'power structure', from the actions we perceive, we must infer that all power systems have difficulty in dealing with the concept of progress. The safeguards, checks, and balances built into the administrative machinery seem to concentrate on inhibiting progress. Progress, as such, is not regarded as evil, but it is treated as though it were undesirable in most cases, and as if attempts to hold it back were the essential guarantee that only the good managed eventually to break through. This attitude has a parallel in another sphere – if we do not know what is 'good' music or 'good' art, we will be well advised to be reluctant to make statements about contemporary composers or painters. But if a composer or artist has been acclaimed for a large number of years, we are reasonably safe in expressing approval of his work. Perhaps it is not surprising that those who are unfamiliar with the scientific method adopt a similar approach to scientific progress.

The 'Power Structure'

Some sociologists who have made particular studies of bureaucratic systems have suggested the possibility of more problems than a mere inertia to change. The *system* of bureaucracy is, they claim, likely to be *dysfunctional* in more serious and even evil ways. C. Wright Mills (1956) states that, 'the top of modern society is increasingly unified and often seems wilfully co-ordinated; at the top there has emerged an élite of power'. Merton (1957) notes that 'more and more people discover that to work they must be employed . . . so develops the new type of scientific worker. To work he must be employed by a bureaucracy with laboratory resources.' He observes also 'the bureaucratic structure exerts a constant pressure upon the official to be "methodical, prudent, disciplined". If the bureaucracy is to operate successfully it must attain a high degree of reliability of behaviour, an unusual degree of conformity with prescribed patterns of action. Hence, the

fundamental importance of discipline which may be as highly developed in a religious or economic bureaucracy as in the army.'
Further, Merton, acknowledging Durkheim, suggests that out of, and within, the bureaucratic process 'there develop prerogatives involving attitudes of moral legitimacy which are established as values in their own right . . .'

But is there some Machiavellian force driving the bureaucratic machine to grind freedoms, including scientific freedoms, to dust? Perhaps a more insightful view is expressed not by a sociologist, but by a newspaperman, Jack White, writing in the column 'Seen From Dublin' in the *Manchester Guardian*. His favourite thesis, he says, is

'that no commentator on human affairs ever allows enough for the element of muddle. I am not talking about the accident, the stroke of fate, the cat that knocks over the test-tube. Muddle, plain muddle is something quite different. It comes from people not doing what they are expected to do or doing what they are not expected to do, or simply not bothering to say that they have not done what they were expected to do. It springs from the exchanges of memoranda in which everybody puts his position too strongly; from the conference at which complete agreement is reached, which everybody leaves with a different idea of what has been decided; from the order half-understood but instantly executed ("He'll be annoyed if I go back and ask him what he means"); from the stand on dignity. The most engaging feature of muddle at its best is that it proliferates like yeast in a warm room, and every attempt to explain it gives birth to a new and even more complex muddle . . . (If) muddle is disguised as efficiency it is the most devastating kind of all . . . The real problem is with people who think they know the facts, and persuade you that they do know the facts, when they are living in the midst of the muddle themselves. The man in the street is a veritable mine of misinformation.'

This is why we need the 'court of appeal' of the scientific method – to test what we know and to begin to fathom the depths of our ignorance; to help us to ask meaningful kinds of questions.

Cooperative Teams

The social administrator needs the social scientist, and the social scientist needs the social administrator. The business of running a society along democratic lines is a team job; a team of those who concentrate on *ends*, and those who have special knowledge of *means* and techniques. Collaboration between research and action is essential. But to collaborate, people need a common language. Those concerned with action should not divert into a language of imponderables and intangibles as a cover for carrying out the action suggested by their personal bias, and the research workers should not use the difficulties of communication to retreat once more to their university towers, concerning themselves with 'pure knowledge' and, ostrich-like, persuade themselves that by that means they are avoiding any concern with the applications of their findings.

Communication and Operationalism

Communication is the means which enables society to adjust itself to alterations of technology and education and other social changes. The scientific method can offer no grand vision, no global strategy, no panacea. It will never be possible to demonstrate that anything is absolutely right or even completely scientifically true. We must approach problems in a more or less piecemeal way. But piecemeal does not mean random, nor does it mean that we should not look as far forward as we can. We may work with current processes, and we should also take note of what is in the pipeline for the future. If rational decisions relate to

        (a) possible decisions
        (b) amount of information
        (c) the objective desired

our room for manoeuvre within this structure is clear. The more information that is available, the better the decisions that can be made, that is, the more likely it is that we *could* achieve the desired objectives. It follows that it is 'good' (functional) to try to obtain more relevant information so that the decisions have a *chance* to be improved. The objectives desired may be continually changing, indeed it would seem to be 'good' that they do change. This is the dynamism of society. *The social administrator is concerned with the decisions set; the social scientist is concerned with the information set; and the objectives are those which accord with the philosophy of the society with which both scientist and administrator are together concerned.* Any 'set' may at times lead the other, providing the evolutionary force of society through the evolutionary mechanism of society, namely, communication.

Lots of people are doing things about society fairly well. The scientist can begin by helping. Among the many things which are being done in accordance with the conscience and to the best of the ability of those concerned there is plenty of variation. It might be more profitable for the social scientist to cease to look for the 'big break-through' and to take up the task which is challenging and near at hand. If in general we are going the right way, why should we not speed up the process? We shall not make progress if laymen blame scientists for those factors in society of which they disapprove, if the politicians avoid considerations of evidence provided by scientists, and if the scientists avoid any concern or responsibility for the evidence they provide. It is clear that such a system of avoiding responsibility and laying blames can only be circular. If the layman places his fear of the consequences of the applications of scientific methods on the scientist, if degrees of certainty in expressions of opinions are related to willingness to take action but not to knowledge, the future does not look too bright. If this is the way things are going, we can only conclude that the problems of the world have come to be regarded as too hot to handle by any persons well enough informed to appreciate their temperature. If this is true, then we are destined to play a game of passing the hot potato, letting it rest with those who perceive it as a pleasant diet. If responsibility can be accepted only by those who lack information, that is, where innocence is claimed because there is ignorance, this is a situation which must be remedied. Is it true that information, and particularly the pursuit of scientific information, inhibits a concern with action? If those who know and those who wish to inquire refuse to be concerned with action, or, what amounts to the same thing, do not learn the necessary skills of communication, society certainly will not evolve, and may even perish.

The significance of this argument may be more obvious with respect to the physical sciences. But do not all scientists tend to behave in the same way when they say they will concentrate on 'pure research'? A similar situation results when scientists accept objectives for research projects and place the entire responsibility on the administration. Social scientists are as involved in these problems as are their colleagues in the physical sciences. It may be questioned whether the power of mass destruction which is due to the work of the physical sciences is the more important issue, or whether the science of social systems which 'deprive the participants of any sense of responsibility in its use' may not have to face the greater share of potential guilt or dysfunctional behaviour.

In the preceding paragraphs, three diabolical hypotheses have been raised with respect to research and action in the social field:

(a) The more subjectively certain people feel about their opinions, the more willing they will be to take action.

(b) Degrees of certainty with which opinions are expressed tend to be inversely proportional to the amount of information.

Hence (c) the amount of information tends to be inversely related to the willingness to take action, although the amount of information is related to the probability of improved action.

A search of the literature has not revealed any studies which have tested these hypotheses in any rigorous manner, with the possible exception of hypothesis (a). There would seem to be a quantity of evidence at the level of anecdote which supports the three hypotheses. For example, ask any layman what ought to be done about juvenile delinquency and he will express few doubts about the actions he will certainly propose, unless by chance he has studied the subject. A recent research carried out by the Home Office Research Unit led to the suggestion that children about five years of age were more likely to be disturbed by war or other forms of *social* upheaval than children at any other age. The same report also suggested that another critical period was in the mid 'teens. The *Daily Express* commented on this research,[1] 'Home Office research workers labour on the problem of delinquency among young children, they put forward a great many figures and arrive at a conclusion that will surprise nobody . . .' Similarly the *Daily Mail* commented,[2] 'Clever people sometimes go to enormous trouble to reach conclusions which simpler minds have already jumped to.' *The Observer*, however, remarked that,[3] 'One of the findings that disturbances around the age of four or five are particularly harmful seems to be of doubtful validity'. Thus for some the conclusions were obvious without any evidence, and for others, despite the evidence, the conclusions were still untrue! Perhaps hypothesis (b) can be sustained more readily in the field of crime or human behaviour than in any other field.

[1] 12 Jan 1961.
[2] Editorial, 12 Jan 1962.
[3] Comments, 15 Jan 1961.

Shaw and Penrod (1962) have provided some evidence related to hypothesis (c). Using undergraduate psychology students they demonstrated that information available to a group does not increase the group effectiveness in problem-solving unless the attitudes possessed by the recipients of the information towards both the information and its source can be specified. They found that moderate amounts of additional information possessed by a group member increased his influence on a group and improved the group's behaviour, whereas with greater amounts of information the reverse was true. They summarize thus, 'whatever the reasons for these results, it is clear that there are conditions under which additional task related information possessed by a group member does not improve group problem solving effectiveness and may even impair effectiveness'. They correctly counsel, 'that if theorists use the notion of amount of information as an explanatory concept, it is incumbent upon them to demonstrate that the conditions which prevail are suitable to group acceptance of the information in question'. Shaw and Penrod's concept of 'acceptance of information' is similar to the concept used here of the ways in which information is perceived. Rejection of information is a problem we shall examine further in connection with the general theory of normality – the information set is rotated by the receiver to be orthogonal to the problem set. Partial rejection seems to present exactly the same model as partial rotation to an out-of-phase position. To some extent, therefore, this research relates to the fieldwork of Christie (1952) concerning Quisling concentration camp guards.

If these hypotheses are sustained, the mechanics, the perceptual processes, the communication factors, and other variables involved call for urgent further study. It is notable that the increase in the rate of technological developments has occurred as communication between technologists has improved to the extent that there can be a division of labour and responsibility. Many minds may now interact to produce developments that would be impossible for one man in his small string-and-sealing-wax laboratory. The communication skills which have been learned in the physical and engineering sciences must similarly be learned in social engineering. If we may assume the curve representing the increase in the technological field to be a power function, it is rather disturbing to compare this with the rate of advance in the humanities and the social sciences. It may appear that these two functions represent a relationship like that suggested by

Malthus with respect to food and population. Our technological advance is like the Malthusian curve for population, while social philosophy and knowledge of man are improving at a much slower rate, like that for the Malthusian food supply. Many are concerned together to produce the sharp increase in technological facilities, and such improvements are profitable in the relatively short run, but few are engaged in consideration of the ends to which these advances might be put, and their social consequences. Moreover, the 'pay-off' associated with different forms of social organization has not been considered an appropriate field for much research endeavour.

Perhaps it is not surprising that the combined work of many minds, communicating effectively, outstrips the work of isolated groups. But Malthus's pessimistic prophecy has so far proved wrong. It would, however, appear to be a functional strategy for more of the resources of men and money to be made available for research into behaviour problems, particularly for the scientific study of decision-making processes and communication in social administration.

There is no obvious reason why these factors should not be considered in the course of operational research directed towards applications of our current social ethic in various fields where human need is perceived to exist. Decisions will have to be made, and these decisions can form the raw material for research.

It is true that at present there appears to be a powerful difference between the social scientist and the social administration. The advocates of social action philosophy seem to claim that they know what to do and what ought to be done. The social scientist is not so sure. Certain types of information possessed by certain types of people can, it seems, prove disabling. But lack of information can be dangerous, even though it may inspire confidence.

The Language Barrier

But why should the scientist not merely assist the administrator towards the ends determined by policy considerations? Why should the scientist have to take a share in the policy-making and the responsibilities of administration? Simply because he cannot do otherwise. Even if the scientist were to try to take his instructions from others, and if he were prepared to permit the questions for research to be stated by the administration, he would not be able to do so. The reasons lie in the problems of communication.

The aims and objectives of social policy may seem to be agreed by at least a majority of those concerned, but such agreement tends to be more apparent than real. There can be little to quarrel with in 'doing good', or in 'helping dependent groups', or in 'advising and befriending offenders', or in 'training of the character', and the like. But the agreement that is possible is only possible because the language in which the ends desired are stated is not precise – the terms used have a broad 'band width' of meaning. This fact soon becomes clear when we examine what different people do within the same general frame of reference. Immediately the broad evaluative terms are spelt out in any more detail, as soon as interim objectives are stated, serious communication difficulties arise between policy makers and social administrators themselves. But when this occurs the administrative art of compromise is most helpful. Compromise does not require an exact language in the same way as does research. Before the objectives can be ready for statement in research terms there may be any number of phases where the broad 'band-width' language may be the better one to use. The first statement of the objectives may lead to disagreement, the disagreement to discussion, to compromise, to restatement, to further disagreement and further compromise, during which process the 'band width' of the terms used may be progressively reduced.

The special skills of trained research workers are not without possibility of application in the process of working through the disagreements about objectives by the art of compromise. Although compromise, being an art, does not require the precise language of scientific methods, the application of the art may be inhibited by semantic and communication problems due to different ways in which basically the same concept is perceived by different people. The problems which arise in translating the language of social philosophies into research aims (the problem of research criteria) will be considered in more detail later in this work. Methods are known to social scientists which can be used to help attempts at collaborative problem-solving, for example by systems of 'translating' different 'languages'. There are methods for examining the 'band width' of concepts about which there may be disagreement owing to the lack of specificity, and there are methods for applying in a scientific manner the general principles of democracy.

Democratic Science?

The scientist should be neither on top nor on tap, but integrated into the system. Both social research and social action are concerned, for essentially the same reasons, with the same objectives, and they should be able to work together through the necessary steps. If we believe in democracy, then we should not seek to apply autocratic or dictatorship methods in the sub-world of social action, social policy, or social research.

REFERENCES

ANDERS, G. (1962). In *Man Alone*, ed. Josephson E. Dell. New York: Laurel Books.

CHRISTIE, N. (1952). Fangevoktere i konsentrasjonsleire. *Nordisk Tidsckrift for Kriminalvidenskab*, vol. 41, pp. 439–58, and vol. 42, pp. 44–60.

JUNGK, R. (1958). *Brighter than a Thousand Suns*. New York: Harcourt; Harmondsworth: Penguin Books, 1963.

MERTON, R. K. (1957). *Social Theory and Social Structure*. Glencoe, Ill.: The Free Press.

MILLGRIM, S. (1964). *Lancet*, 9 May, p. 1198.

NETTLER, G. (1961). Good Men, Bad Men and the Perception of Reality. *Sociometry*, vol. 24, no. 3.

PACKARD, VANCE (1957). *The Hidden Persuaders*. New York: Pocket Books Inc.

SHAW, N. E. & PENROD, W. T. (1962). Does more information available to a group improve group performance? *Sociometry*, vol. 25, pp. 377–90.

TOCHER, K. D. (1962). In discussion of paper by Box and Jenkins. *J. Roy. Statist. Soc.* B vol. 24, p. 333.

WILKINS, L. T. (1960). *Delinquent Generations*. London: H.M.S.O.

WRIGHT MILLS, C. (1956). *The Power Elite*. London: O.U.P.

CHAPTER 3

The Place of Theory

Scientific theory is not 'hunch' or an unattached idea, although the hunch and the unattached idea may be the beginning of a theory. Theory often starts from fact, providing a means for integrating items of information and assisting towards further progress by making a more general level of explanation possible. The construction of scientific theory is, perhaps, the art of science. But while the origination of the idea, the tying together of the facts, the forward leap of the imagination, are important art forms, the art form must be restricted within the medium of the method of science. In the concepts of social action, and even of legislation, are to be found implicit theories, or parts of theories. The perception of the 'needs' of clients on the part of social workers implies a theoretical framework. The setting down of questions in sample inquiry or census implies some basis of theory because the questions asked are not random selections of all the questions that could possibly be asked. Latent, incomplete, and unsatisfactory as scientific theories as some of these may be, some may have potential for development, reformulation, or amplification and thus prove useful tools of the scientific method. Others, if they were more completely stated, might be proved to be unsustainable in the light of evidence. The latter should be cleared out of the way to make room for advance. Some theories of the causes of crime will be examined in this chapter, mainly to test whether they are good or bad theories – whether they fulfil the function of a theory – not whether they are true or false.

Examining a Theory

The best theories are concise, elegant summaries of observations; the observations are accepted as sound, and they have been subjected to

35

replication by different workers. Theory interrelates observations in a common statement. The best way to distinguish good theories from bad is to consider ways of destroying them. If a statement, which is claimed to be a 'theory', is made, but does not contain any means whereby it may be disproved, that statement does not qualify as a theory.

The first step in testing a theory (*qua* theory) is to examine it to see what deductions can be made from it – to set up postulates which may be tested either experimentally or by observations of the 'real-life' situation. That is to say, the first step in testing a theory is to state the practical consequences of it. If the deduced practical consequences (operational definitions) are proved to be unsustained, the theory is discredited. No theory can ever be proved to be true: it is held for so long as no better theory can be found. Popper (1945, p. 210) makes this point most strongly. 'The only course,' he says, 'open to the social sciences is to forget the verbal fireworks and to tackle the practical problems of our time with the help of the theoretical methods which are the same in all the sciences. I mean the methods of trial and error, of inventing hypotheses which can be tested and of submitting them to practical tests.' And again (p. 220), '... in science we do not accept an abstract theory because it is convincing in itself, we rather decide to accept or reject it after we have investigated those concrete and practical consequences which can be more directly tested by experiments ... our decision rests upon the results of experiments ... if these confirm the theory we accept it until we find a better one.' Clearly, the greater the number and the wider the scope of the hypotheses and the practical consequences that can be deduced from a theory, and the greater the number and the wider the scope of the hypotheses that have been or could be tested, and that could have been proved false, the better is the theory.

Two Theories Examined

(a) Multiple Causation

The first theory to be considered is one which is most vigorously put forward in current criminological literature, namely, that of 'multiple causation'. This merely asserts that crime is a function of numerous factors. The examination of this theory by the criteria given above suggests that it is a statement which can hardly be dignified by the term theory. Perhaps, to some extent, it summarizes observations, but what observations is not at all clear. Proponents of the theory would claim that since research has found no single factor as the cause of crime, but rather that many different factors appear together associated with greater or lesser frequency of criminal activity, this is evidence for multiple causation. But the theory does not facilitate the deduction of any hypotheses or practical consequences that are of any help whatsoever. If it is claimed that the theory applies to all factors which are operationally found to be related to criminal tendencies as they become known, it is apparent that the theory lacks the major and essential feature of any scientific theory – it is framed in such a way that it is impossible to find any test whereby it could be proved wrong. The theory of 'multiple causation' is, then, no theory. At best it could be considered an anti-theory which proposes that no theory can be formed regarding crime. Such an anti-theory may be legitimately put forward as a kind of beatnik philosophy, but not as a scientific theory.

The implications of acceptance of this untested and untestable 'theory' as a basis for social action will be obvious. The best we could hope for would be a random strategy – try anything, it may come off!

(b) Differential Association

One theory which does meet the test proposed and which is attracting considerable attention is due to Sutherland and Cressey (1960) who state, 'A person becomes delinquent because of an excess of definitions favourable to violation of law over definitions unfavourable to violation of law'. This is called the principle of differential association. The basic assumption here is that delinquincy is learned behaviour. It means, in terms of very broad principles, that it is believed that when persons become delinquent they do so because of contacts with delinquent patterns and also because of isolation from anti-delinquent patterns: persons assimilate the surrounding culture, unless other patterns are in conflict. Whatever faults this theory may have, it has at least the merit that from it a number of hypotheses may be set up and subjected to test. An examination of it by Glaser (1960) reveals that it is a good theory, not only in that a large number of practical consequences and hypotheses may be derived from it, but also, that a large number of these have been demonstrated by other research workers to hold up reasonably well under test.

37

Theory Development

There are, however, a number of other factors known to apply at least to some criminals and some forms of criminal behaviour which it is not possible to deduce from the differential association theory. What, then, should happen to this theory? Following Popper (1945), it should not be discarded unless it can be replaced by a better theory. Is it possible to find a better theory or to modify this one? The question may be examined by reference to some further theories and other general conceptual frameworks.

Perhaps the best-known work on the problem of gang delinquency is that of Cohen (1955). The theory put forward in Cohen's work is summarized by Kitsuse and Dietrick (1959) as follows:

'(i) The working-class boy faces a characteristic problem of adjustment which is qualitatively different from that of the middle-class boy.

(ii) The working-class boy's problem is one of status frustration, the basis of which is systematically generated by his early exposure to working-class patterns of socialization.

(iii) The working-class boy's socialization handicaps him from achievement in the middle-class status system.

(iv) Nevertheless he is thrust into this competitive system where achievement is judged by middle-class standards of behaviour and performance.

(v) Ill-prepared and poorly motivated, the working-class boy is frustrated in his status ambitions by the agents of middle-class society.

(vi) The delinquent subculture represents a "solution" to the working-class boy's problem, for it enables him to "break clean" with the middle-class morality and legitimizes hostility and aggression against the sources of his frustration.

(vii) Thus the delinquent's subculture is characterized by non-utilitarian, malicious, and negativistic values as "an attack on the middle-class where egos are most vulnerable" . . . It expresses contempt for a way of life by making its opposite a criterion of status.'

Theory Comparison

Many criminologists have found difficulties in reconciling this theory with observed facts, even in the United States of America. It is unnecessary to recapitulate all the objections, since we are not concerned here with testing the theory, but only with examining it as an example of how theories may be examined. In this connection a modification of the theory is interesting, It relates in obvious ways to the theory of differential association, and hence may serve to show how theories may be developed. This modification is due to Kitsuse and Dietrick, (1959) who were concerned with the difficulty in Cohen's theory of explaining the *continuance* of the delinquent sub-culture. They postulate:

'(i) The individual learns the values of the delinquent subculture through his participation in gangs which embody that subculture.

(ii) The motivations of individuals for participation in gangs are varied.

(iii) The malicious, non-utilitarian, and negativistic behaviour which is learned through participation in the subculture is met by formal negative sanctions, rejection, and limitation of access to prestigeful status within the middle-class system.

(iv) Thus, participation in the delinquent subculture creates similar problems for all its participants.

(v) The participants' response to the barriers raised to exclude them from status in the middle-class system . . . is a hostile rejection of the standards of "respectable" society and an emphasis upon status within the delinquent gang.

(vi) The hostile rejection response reinforces the malicious, non-utilitarian, and negativistic norms of the subculture.'

No suggestion is made here that the later theory is necessarily better than the earlier. The example is given only to indicate a *method* whereby theories may be modified and 'grow'. In the two statements above, the essential similarities and differences are pleasantly obvious owing to the ways in which the statements have been set forth.

Often it is difficult to trace the similar elements in the total argument. More frequently, critics of theories emphasize the differences. This is also a useful technique, particularly if the apparent significance of the differences is assessed. Bordua (1961), commencing with the work of Thrasher (1927), contrasts the various sociological theories of the gang up to and including the work of Cloward and Ohlin (1961). He remarks, 'we must wait for a study of gangs which will approach Thrasher's in thoroughness before we know if there are new facts to be explained . . . nor do I believe that the changes in viewpoint have come about because old theories were shown to be inadequate to old facts.' Both Cohen (1955) and Cloward and Ohlin (1961) felt that older theories did not deal with the origins of the delinquent sub-cultures, but only with the transmission of the culture once developed. Bordua also remarks on an interesting difference which may arise from differences in either the observers or the observed; he notes, 'Thrasher's boys enjoyed themselves being chased by the police, shooting dice . . . it was fun. Miller's boys (1958) do have a little fun, but it seems . . . so desperate. Cohen's boys and Ohlin's boys are driven by grim economic and psychic necessity into rebellion. It seems peculiar that modern analysts have stopped assuming that "evil" can be fun,[1] and see gang delinquency as arising only when boys are driven away from "good".'

Another feature of the difference discussed by Bordua is that of the reference group. Miller would regard the main reference group as the lower-class community itself. Miller (1958) presents the focal concerns of lower-class culture as 'trouble', 'toughness', 'smartness', 'excitement', 'fate', and 'autonomy'. 'Trouble is what life gets you into' – especially trouble with the agents of the larger society. Miller sees the street group as an essential part of the general training-ground for lower-class boys; such groups are not *necessarily* delin-quent. Bordua suggests an interesting resolution of some differences between Miller and Cohen. Discussing the process by which conflict of values may arise, he says, '. . . lower-class boys will be told about them [middle-class value systems] at the very time they are being status-deprived by their teachers and others. They will likely hate it and them [teachers and values and deprivation] and the process is started. It seems unlikely that Miller's lower-class boys can spend ten years in school without some serious outcome. They should either come to accept middle-class values or become even more antagonistic or both, and this should drive them further into the arms of lower-class culture.'

Theory Completeness

These theories are interesting and valuable. Much more work will, however, have to be done to rid them of redundancies and to add essential components. Or, of course, they may all be destroyed by the failure of one common and essential element to withstand test. All

[1] It may also be remarked that delinquency may be profitable.

these theories discuss the learning of delinquent values, they do not seem to consider very adequately the mechanics of *learning*. As Bernstein (1961) has aptly pointed out, the main problem is, 'how the outside gets into the inside'. Bernstein suggests that language is perhaps the main intervening variable. It would certainly appear that there is some evidence in favour of communication factors in some aspects of delinquency. But before this idea is considered further, we should, perhaps note another way in which theories may be utilized.

The theories of delinquency which are currently attracting most attention are based on sociological concepts. There are theories which are basically psychological. It is often possible to transform a theoretical statement from, say, the language of psychology into the language of sociology, or conversely. Such transformations quite often assist both in the derivation of practical consequences and in the modification and development of the theory. As an example, consider the concept of 'anomie'. This concept was first put forward by Durkheim to explain variations in suicide rates: it was a socio-logical theory. But by use of arguments based on 'perception', Srole (1959) has been able to restate it in a different form. A good deal of research has been carried out in the field of perceptual processes, and this work has had considerable impact upon many other fields. Perhaps a short summary will suffice to indicate the means whereby the conversion of theoretical constructs may take place.

Summary of Perceptual-Process Theory

It is assumed that all 'knowing' is indirect; man constructs his know-ledge by orderly transformation of coded signals, and this process is called 'cognition'. Intuitive directness, whether in perceiving or thinking, may result from practice and predisposition, but it is achieved by inferential processes, no matter how short-cut they may become through learning and development. The attempt to identify an approaching figure, to develop an idea, to form a sentence, or any other activity involves selection or constructing a means appro-priate to some end-objective. Our perception is conditioned by experience. Social perception refers to the way in which the world of other people is seen – how people try to make sense of others. Social perception is the process of observing, recording (coding and storing), and organizing the experience one has with other people, groups, and social organizations. The same term is also used – and this is important – to refer to the way in which social factors influence observations of one's world. Work in this area is concerned with such matters as how people 'understand' other people, and how they relate this 'understanding' to adjustments to their own behaviour, how accurately people observe, describe, and judge other people and themselves. Differences in ability to perceive, and relate to, other people in social situations are often related to ideas of 'social maturity' (Grant, 1960).

Anomie Theory

Durkheim's sociological and, indeed, ecological concept of 'anomie' is stated by Srole (1959) in perceptual terms as follows:

A person having a 'high anomie score' would perceive:

(a) the lot of the average man as getting worse;
(b) the future as so black that it is hardly fair to bring children into the world;
(c) public officials as uninterested in problems of the average man;
(d) other people as untrustworthy;
(e) life to be lived very much for today – tomorrow to take care of itself.

It is not suggested that such a view of the world is necessarily 'unrealistic' in certain types of social situation. It is argued that anomie *results* when an individual is prevented from achieving his objectives, and is in this way related to the theories of 'blocked opportunities' to be developed in the next chapter.

Glaser (1960) has suggested that the differential association theory might be more powerful if it were modified to a 'differential identification' or 'differential expectation' theory. While the differential association theory stresses the factor of learning, differential identification allows not only for learning but for modifications of learning through perceptual processes interacting with personality differences. The idea of differential identification enables the theory to take account of communications and particularly of communication symbols. For example, in a Home Office Research Unit Report (Wilkins, 1960), it was shown that youths between seventeen and twenty-one years of age from 1955 onwards, who would be expected to have been exceptionally delinquent as a result of the effects of the 1939–45 war, were, in fact, even more delinquent than could be expected. Some other factor peculiarly conducive to delinquency among young men had apparently begun to operate about 1955. Although the accretion of an effect is another explanation, the most direct inference that can be drawn is that this 'other factor' had something to do with the fact that from about 1955 the young adult males in the particular subcultures which give rise to most delinquency, for some reason unknown, stumbled upon a 'communication symbol'. This particular symbol was a form of dress – jeans, drapes, black jackets, and so on. As with any other minority group, symbols of communication are powerful factors in preserving the group and in maintaining its self-identification. There is no doubt, too, that the easy identification which the dress symbols made possible to persons both inside and outside the minority group made the process described by Kitsuse and Dietrick as 'formal negative sanctions, rejection, and limitation of access' easier to apply on the part of persons outside the group, and increased the identification and solidarity within the group. Thus delinquents became more delinquent.

Theory and 'Need'

Doubtless the theory which began as differential association will continue to grow and change; it will come into contact and opposition with other theories; perhaps at some time it will be completely discarded in favour of a better theory. Theories are attractive, and they can be useful if they are highly vulnerable and their mortality or conversion rate is high. Perhaps the best theories grow out of existing theories. Occasionally there may be a clean break with the past, but breaks with the past are seldom very effective and they cannot ignore previous work.

Social scientists and those concerned with social action should have equal regard to the work of theorists and to the results of prior empirical research. Both aspects are part of the scientific method – in the same way as there can be bad and meaningless theories there can be bad and misleading data.

Theories relate to aspects of social action as they do to social research. As noted earlier the concept of the 'needs' of clients implies a theoretical framework. If the underlying theoretical constructs – the background to the concept of 'need' – could be spelt out in terms of scientific theories in the manner illustrated, the integration of research and action would be a very fruitful one. A good scientific theory is the cement which sticks facts together and enables the building to continue.

REFERENCES

BERNSTEIN, B. (1961). Aspects of Language and Learning in the Genesis of the Social Process. *J. Child Psychol. and Psychiat.*, vol. 1, p. 313.

BORDUA, D. J. (1961). Delinquent Sub-cultures. *Annals*, 338, pp. 119–36.

CLOWARD, R. S. & OHLIN, L. E. (1961). Illegitimate Means and Delinquent Subcultures. *Delinquency and Opportunity*. Glencoe, Ill.: The Free Press.

COHEN, A. K. (1955). *The Culture of the Gang*. Glencoe, Ill.: The Free Press.

GLASER, D. (1960). Differential Association and Criminological Prediction. *Social Problems*, vol. 8, no. 6.

GRANT, D. (1960). The Treatment of Non-conformists in the Navy. *Annals*, March 1960.

KITSUSE, J. I. & DIETRICK, D. C. (1959). Delinquent Boys: A Critique. *Amer. Sociol. Rev.*, vol. 24, p. 208.

MILLER, W. B. (1958). Lower Class Culture as a Generating Milieu of Gang Delinquency. *J. Soc. Issues*, vol. 14, no. 3.

POPPER, K. (1945). *The Open Society*. London: Routledge & Kegan Paul.

SROLE, D. (1959). As quoted in Meier, D. L. and Bell, W., Anomie and Differential Access to the Achievement of Life Goals. *Amer. Sociol. Rev.*, vol. 24, p. 198.

SUTHERLAND E. H. & CRESSEY, D. R. (1960). *Principles of Criminology*. (6th Edition.) New York: Lippincott.

WILKINS, L. T. (1960). *Delinquent Generations*. London: H.M.S.O.

CHAPTER 4

A General Theory of Deviance

DEVIANCE, OPPORTUNITY, AND NORMALITY

Relative nature of deviance – Legitimate and illegitimate definitions – Opportunity structures: legitimate and illegitimate - A general theory of deviance – Information modifies definitions of deviance – Types of information – Systems, individuals, and deviance – Sinners, saints, and the system – The role of the victim – Individuals as scapegoats for systems – Information loops and definitions of deviance – Progressions, good and bad – The general model – Some supporting evidence for feedback models – Some general observations in relation to the theory – Implications for action

---

Theory is related to action. What is done provides evidence from its results which interact with theory and permit of further advances in theory. To some extent a good theory should relate observations together into a common statement. If sound observation forms the basis for theoretical statements, there should be a tendency for theories to converge as knowledge increases.

It is encouraging to observe that convergence is beginning to appear in the literature of criminological research. The present chapter represents an attempt to provide for some further integration of theories and observations over a wide range of subject matter. Deviant behaviour is usually considered from the point of view of conformity as functional to society. It is usual to find 'deviant' behaviour almost automatically connoting 'bad' behaviour. But there is deviant behaviour which is 'good' or functional to society – the genius, the reformer, the religious leader, and many others are 'deviant' from the norms of society as much as is the criminal. It may assist the formulation of theory if some ways can be found to relate into common statements or models behaviour which is deviant, without reference to the direction of the deviance. Indeed, it might be that the one can be understood only if it is related to the other. It may be necessary to consider a value-free theory of deviance before the values of society may be related to social action to mitigate the ill effects of dysfunctional deviance.

In this chapter we will first consider the convergence of some theoretical models which, in their initial statement, were related to rather limited aspects of juvenile delinquent behaviour, and attempt to extend them to more general theoretical frames of reference.

Relative Nature of Deviance

In discussing deviance, whether criminal deviance or deviance of genius for good or genius for ill, there are no absolute standards. At some time or another, some form of society or another has defined almost all forms of behaviour that we now call 'criminal' as desirable for the functioning of that form of society. Different societies today define criminal behaviour in different ways. Crime, like other forms of deviance, is human behaviour, and this behaviour is interpreted by other members of the society in which it takes place in terms of the norms of the society. It is possible to throw light on the more general problems of deviance by considering a verbal or mathematical model. Human actions, even as interpreted within a society at a fixed time, do not divide into black and white, good and bad, functional and dysfunctional. The divisions into crime and no crime, into what are regarded as health and ill health, are cutting-points on a continuum. It is, then, possible to picture these concepts as forming a continuous distribution. For example, a continuum of human acts ranging from

FIGURE 1

Continuum of good and bad acts, and the cutting-points for various types of definition

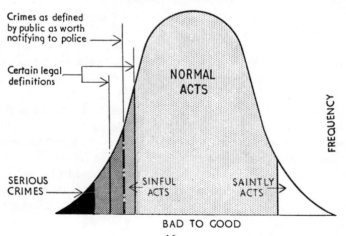

very saintly to the most sinful may be imagined. In our society there are very few acts which are regarded as extremely saintly or extremely helpful to the society, and there are very few acts which are regarded as extremely sinful or seriously criminal. The majority of actions of ordinary people in our present culture are regarded as 'normal'. If this is so, it is possible to draw a distribution very similar to that used to describe measurements of general intelligence. In the case of intelligence measurements, very few people are classified as geniuses and very few are classified as mentally sub-normal – the majority of people have an intelligence measurement within the 'normal' range. A diagram of the familiar distribution is given as *Figure 1*.

It may be supposed that the model given by the normal frequency distribution shown in this chart represents the distribution of ethical content of human action. Crimes in the main will be represented by actions at the 'bad' or 'sinful' end of the scale. It will be obvious that the number of incidents defined as 'crimes' will depend on the point of cut-off. There will be no doubt about the classification of actions which are extremely deviant, but these extremely deviant actions represent a rather small proportion of the distribution.

Legal definitions of indictable offences are quite clear, and there is no intention in this discussion to criticize them when they are used for legal purposes. But, as descriptions of human behaviour, they have a very wide range of inclusion. For example, the value of an article stolen is not relevant to the legal definition of larceny, and robbery with violence may include, at one end of the scale of the definition, cases where no lay citizen would use the term 'violence', whereas at the other end the worst possible headline story would be included. Few children over seven years of age have not been so fortunate as to find some small coin or apparently discarded article which they have retained, and in consequence are technically guilty of larceny by finding. There is a sense in which nearly all members of the population could be described as having committed some crime (indictable offence). A number of criminologists have examined what has become to be called the problem of 'white-collar crime'. They have been concerned to investigate the point at which astute business practice crosses the 'line' and becomes illegitimate. It is unnecessary to develop this point in any detail. It may be taken as self-evident that what is crime, and who are the criminals, are not easy questions. (See for example Short & Nye (1957), Reiss & Rhodes (1960).)

It is important to note that the cutting-point determined by some

47

legal definitions of some crimes may well be perceived by the majority of the population as further towards 'normal' behaviour than some other definitions. For example, damage done by vandals is not an indictable offence in England and Wales unless the damage exceeds the value of twenty pounds. To give this point some emphasis, it would appear that a person who opened the door of a parked car and took a half-used packet of cigarettes from the glove pocket would have committed an indictable offence, whereas a person who twisted off the door handles of a locked car, but stole nothing, had not committed a 'crime', but merely a non-indictable offence. The layman might well think that the latter incident was rather more serious than the former. The solid lines on the left of *Figure 1* illustrate the cutting-points for certain definitions according to the law, and the line $\cdot — \cdot$ represents the cutting-point as it might be perceived by the normal middle-class citizen. There are obviously some incidents which are technically described as crimes which the average citizen would not define as anything worth telling the police about. Martin (1962) has demonstrated this fact by survey methods. It will be necessary to consider later how his findings affect the criminal statistics as they are published in different countries, and the inferences which may legitimately be drawn from such data. At this point we are concerned only with the nature of the model afforded by the continuous distribution.

Many distinctions between what is perceived as legitimate and what is perceived as illegitimate are made culturally, but not legally. Members of one class in society will doubtless consider the expense account in one light, while those who work with metals will regard the use of certain tools and materials rather differently from those who are responsible for management.

Legitimate and Illegitimate Definitions

Related to the individual perception of actions which fall on either side of the possible cutting-points in the continuum is the concept of legal definition, which encodes a society's definitions of unacceptable acts. Some societies cut the continuum of actions at points which are not recognized in other societies. Some societies closely relate the codified illegal actions to the continuum of sin → saintliness as defined in their religious literature, others ignore actions which may be defined as 'sinful' which are not also perceived as dysfunctional to the society. In some societies, for example, certain sexual

48

deviations are not regarded as matters for the legal code, provided that the participants in the act agree together to commit it. These facts do not invalidate the model, but merely indicate the material with which the model deals within the culture to which it may be applied.

For present purposes, the base-line against which deviant behaviour is measured is not particularly relevant. A property-owning society will define deviance with respect to its property-owning concepts, beyond which action will be not permitted and, if committed, such action will be defined as illegitimate or illegal. A nomadic society will not have any such concept of deviance. A socialist society will regard deviance from its norms of collectivism as actionable when it proceeds too far outside the perceived boundary conditions of functional behaviour. A religious society will define deviance beyond certain limits as heresy and take action according to the perceived degree of seriousness of the deviance. Whether the definitions of the society which are encoded differ from the individual definitions of deviance by members of the society will depend upon the nature of the society and the nature of the deviance.

A society in which a large proportion of the population regularly practise a given form of behaviour will tend to permit the behaviour and not define it as 'deviant'. Indeed, on one interpretation of the term 'deviant' it is impossible to conceive of any action being classified as deviant if the majority of the population within a culture regularly behave that way. Owing to inertia within social systems, the official definition of deviance may fall out of line with the definitions of individuals. A ruling minority or powerful group may, for a time, be able to persuade the majority to permit the definitions to remain unamended because they reflect some idealized behaviour patterns to which the majority tend to subscribe. But in democratic countries there is little scope for large differences between the definitions of the majority of the people and the encoded definitions. The idealized pattern of behaviour, rather than the actual behaviour, will, of course, have more influence on the encoded definitions in societies which have a formal religious system. This latter point may explain the situation regarding public attitudes towards and legislation concerned with gambling behaviour. A society in which 90 per cent of the population are given to gambling will tend to permit gambling – not defining it as deviant, or may even incorporate a form of gambling (known by a different term!) into its economic system. On the other hand, a society in which a very small percentage of the population indulge in behaviour which they classify as gambling may well define it as illegal and force those who would participate into illegal opportunity structures. The concept of 'local option', whereby laws regarding the sale of alcoholic liquors are determined by local referenda, illustrates this point where it has been formalized into a system. The divergence between 'democratic' definitions and 'legal' definitions cannot be maintained at too great a distance for too long.[1] It must be noted, however, that it is not only the actual behaviour which conditions the definitions, but the attitudes of the public towards definitions, that is to say, the way in which the behaviour is perceived may be more important than the way in which the behaviour is classified in deciding the balance of time and distance. Moreover, it has been noted that religious societies would define deviance from the religious norms as deviant, and economic societies, deviance from economic norms, and this fact influences legislation also. Although Western democratic societies may be described as 'economic societies', there are vestigial traces of older religious societies within them. Certain laws which remain on the statute books derive from the religious or theological frameworks, and certain others remain from earlier economic frameworks. Taxi drivers are, within certain cities, still required by law to carry a broom and shovel, and to remain within 15 feet of their 'hack' – laws which are still applied to motor vehicles, although they derived from earlier modes of transport!

Opportunity Structures – Legitimate and Illegitimate

The greater part of crime in most societies is defined in terms of the property laws. This seems to be true whether the property is owned by the state or by private individuals. Although criminal statistics throughout the world devote nearly all their attention to describing the crime or the criminal, crime involves two parties – the victim and the offender. Both are equally important in any consideration of the activity labelled 'criminal'. What may be defined as 'criminal' may differ markedly according to the perception of the roles of either of the two essential parties. Both actors are members of the society which defines the one as the criminal and the other as the victim. The society in which the given 'criminal' event occurs determines the way in which the event is perceived and classified.

---

[1] The history of prohibition in the United States of America provides a good example of this fact.

In Western societies there is a measure of agreement, but in the U.S.S.R. crimes are defined differently because the perceived roles of persons living in the socialist society are perceived differently. If, for example, the state has a philosophy regarding property and the property stolen belongs to the state, the state, and not an independent authority, becomes the victim. The private possession of wealth may itself be seen as criminal, since it should be owned collectively. Where wealth is privately owned, crimes against such ownership will be seen as attempts to obtain by illegal *means* the wealth of another. The obtaining of wealth, as such, for oneself is not in question in such societies, but only the means of obtaining it. The means to obtain wealth both legitimately and illegitimately exist in the society. A line is drawn between legitimate and illegitimate means for the obtaining of property.

It has been represented by many writers that the line between legitimate and illegitimate means becomes, at times, quite thin, and different sub-sections of the community may not perceive this distinction in the same way. This difference in viewpoint may result in some offenders being dealt with by the authorities for actions which they did not themselves see to be criminal. Thus some 'crimes' may result from differences in the definition of 'crime' on the part of the society and on the part of the individual within that society. A very large proportion of first offenders brought before the courts do not offend again, and it may be that the main effect of being detected and proceeded against is in relating their subjective definition more closely to the definitions of their society. The workman who removes a small item of equipment from his employer may justify this by thinking, 'Oh, he will not mind!', and hence, since the victim does not seem to be involved, the 'crime' is not defined subjectively as 'crime'.

Despite problems of definition, perception, and communication, and cases of criminal activity which would be more appropriately regarded as problems of mental health, there remains a large amount of crime against property, and perhaps also other forms of criminal activity, which are not explained in this way. The rare and unusual case may, perhaps, be more easy to explain than the general level of criminal activity which causes the main concern at the present time.

The current economic phenomenon of the Western democracies, termed 'the affluent society', has given rise to much questioning of the general crime problem. It used to be claimed that poverty caused crime. The average layman could understand why a person stole if he was hungry, but today he finds it difficult to excuse or understand the motives of the thieves in a welfare state. It has been generally observed that with increasing prosperity and increasing affluence has come increasing crime. This has led social theorists to re-examine many of the easy explanations of criminality which were put forward in the past. Further theories and explanations have been sought, some of which have been considered in the previous chapter. The war, working mothers, divorce, conditions in the home, modern living conditions, child-rearing practices, and many other explanations are offered today, but not poverty. Others have given up the attempt to find a 'cause' and instead take refuge in the so-called theory of multiple causation, which, as has been shown, does not meet the requirements of a scientific theory.

Some writers have modified the earlier explanations based on poverty. Jackson Toby (1961) says, 'Poverty causes crime [today] because the emphasis on material goals threatens the self-conception of persons who are *relatively* [italics in original] unsuccessful in terms of wealth and income'. Cloward and Ohlin (1961) stress the importance of relationships rather than absolute measurements in their theory of opportunity structures. Their central postulate is that of a relationship between opportunities for obtaining desired ends by either legitimate or illegitimate means. In other words, their theory discusses the balance between two types of opportunity available to the potential offenders; a differential in access, whereas Toby discusses a differential distance. But these two theories may be related in operational terms. Cloward and Ohlin themselves point to an integration which their theory makes possible as they remark, 'The concept of opportunity structures permits us to unite the theory of anomie, which recognizes the differentials in access to legitimate means, and the Chicago tradition in which the concept of differentials in access to illegitimate means is implicit'.

Both the differential access and the differential distance concepts relate to relationships between the economic climate and conditions, and particularly economic conditions as they apply to sub-sections of the population, to criminal activity. Since the economic climate at any one time is associated with cultural factors, it is to be expected that it will prove difficult to disentangle economic, cultural, and criminological factors. This will certainly be so if we accept the relationship between legitimate and illegitimate means as an explanation of criminal behaviour. We have to invoke cultural factors for our definitions of crime, economic factors for the availability of means (legitimate plus illegitimate), and socio-economic factors for the evaluation of illegitimate means. If the total number of 'means' increases within a society, the *relationship* between legitimate and illegitimate means may not be expected to change unless there is a change in the social system at the same time. The greater availability of legitimate means may result in a greater distance between the rich and the poor, or the distance (in relative terms) may remain constant. This formulation makes it possible to test some of the assumptions underlying these two theories by observations from existing data. In any stable social system the increase in economic activity and affluence would lead to increased opportunities – opportunities for honest and dishonest practices. More cars, more stealing from cars, more money, more transfers of money by all the means of transfer. If a society facilitates the transfer of goods by legitimate means, it seems that, simultaneously, the facilities for illegitimate transfer will also increase. If more money is distributed according to the old rules, the differential distance between rich and poor will remain the same in terms of its perception by the poor, and their behaviour, according to Toby's theoretical basis, would vary according to their perception of the change in their needs.

It is difficult to find a good index of the increasing affluence in Western societies which has not shown a continuous increase over the years. Crime too, has continued to increase, but the similar trends over time in this general form are of no value for purposes of inference. A specific type of crime, relating to a specific variation in the 'opportunity' to commit that particular crime, may afford more convincing evidence. It is, of course, difficult to find a category of crime which is sociologically and economically specific. It may be agreed, however, that as a measure of our increasing affluence, the increase in the ownership of motor-cars is a fair index. If there are more cars, then there is more opportunity for those who may wish to do so, to steal from cars. *Table 1* and *Figure 2* show the number of indictable offences known to the police in respect of larceny from stationary vehicles and the number of motor vehicles registered in the years 1938 to 1961 (Criminal Statistics, England and Wales). It will be seen that the two sets of data follow each other extremely closely. The balance between legitimate opportunities (owning cars) and illegitimate opportunities for stealing from cars seems directly related to the frequency of illegitimate opportunities taken by members of the population. If more opportunities within the community mean more illegitimate opportunities taken by members of the community, it might seem reasonable to argue support from these data for Cloward and Ohlin's theory, although the connection is not a direct one. Two different factors are involved – Cloward and Ohlin invoke the concept of balance of opportunities within the *individual's* frame of reference,

FIGURE 2

The relationship between opportunities to commit crime and the incidence of crime (England and Wales)

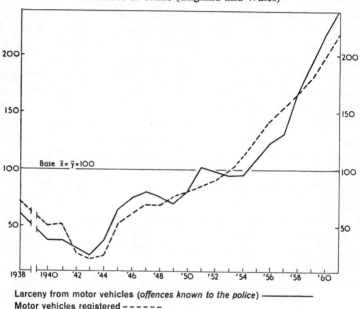

Larceny from motor vehicles (*offences known to the police*) ─────
Motor vehicles registered ─ ─ ─ ─ ─

not necessarily in aggregate for the social system. Further, the balance between legitimate and illegitimate opportunities may be changed in two ways:

(a) by defining a smaller proportion of the total opportunities as illegitimate (cutting-point change);
(b) by changing the distribution of opportunities among different classes of person within the culture (social change).

The constant ratio between legitimate and illegitimate opportunities taken, as illustrated by the trend in larceny from motor vehicles, may be a true constant, or it may be a constant derived from similar changes in compensating directions. As the 'haves' get more legitimately, there may be a tendency to define the theft of a small item by a 'have-not' as less criminal. The constants may derive from the observers and not from the situation; there may be a general factor of attitude towards deviance which could be incorporated into a general theory.

TABLE 1

The number of (a) Private motor vehicles registered; (b) cases of larceny from motor vehicles (crimes known to the police); (c) cases of larceny from shops and stalls (crimes known to the police)

Year	Motor vehicles ('000)	Larceny from motor vehicles	Larceny from shops and stalls
1938	1,944	25,281	15,273
1940	1,423	16,849	23,976
1941	1,503	15,672	19,845
1942	858	12,180	16,722
1943	718	11,084	15,131
1944	755	14,509	14,412
1945	1,487	26,520	12,946
1946	1,770	32,546	14,622
1947	1,943	33,984	18,723
1948	1,961	32,665	24,490
1949	2,131	30,297	22,054
1950	2,258	33,156	23,013
1951	2,380	43,127	24,652
1952	2,508	41,125	24,128
1953	2,762	39,739	21,736
1954	3,100	39,398	21,941
1955	3,526	43,304	23,308
1956	3,888	50,782	25,756
1957	4,187	54,937	29,690
1958	4,549	68,466	34,194
1959	4,966	79,899	35,123
1960	5,526	92,704	41,535
1961	5,979	112,671	48,466

A General Theory of Deviance

In the discussion of the definition of crime the concept of a continuous distribution was invoked. The distribution proposed as a probable model was the normal distribution (Gaussian curve) in the theory of probability. The point of a general theory of normality was indicated at that stage of the discussion, but not developed. It is necessary now to pursue the argument somewhat further, in terms of both the content and the range of the theory. Crime was indicated by actions at one end of the distribution, while particularly socially approved actions were suggested to lie at the other extreme of the curve. The point of cut-off from normality was the main issue, rather than the distribution itself. It is now proposed to try to make the argument completely general over a range of types of activity and to discuss modifications of the model that seem necessary to fit different cultures and sub-cultures.

Although it is desired to make the model proposed a completely general basis for the theory, it may first be illustrated by specific examples.

If I own a car there will be a number of events which arise out of this ownership, involving the car and myself, most of which I will regard as 'normal' because they are things which I have been led to expect to arise from car-ownership. But some events will not be expected and will be regarded as 'abnormal'. If an event is perceived by me as 'normal', no matter what the nature of the event, I will do nothing unusual about it. If I am in the habit of doing things which most people perceive to be *unusual*, with respect to events which they regard as *normal*, I shall myself be defined as *abnormal*. What are perceived as 'normal' events are expected to evoke 'normal' reactions in 'normal' people. Implicit in the concept of normality is the concept of prediction, that is, an expected type of response is one which can be predicted from the subjective summation of the experience of the observers.

Of all the events which may occur, some may be unexpectedly 'good' or functional, and others unexpectedly 'bad' or dysfunctional. It is not necessary at this time to define the dimension good → bad except as a dimension perceived by individuals in their own ways. Any very rare event, perceived as either 'good' or 'bad', say with a probability of occurrence of less than one in five thousand (or, for example, say $3 \cdot 5\sigma$ in terms of the normal curve) is most likely to be perceived as a rare event. Such an event is almost certain to be remarked upon, indeed it may well be described as 'remarkable'. Such events will usually call for some action – an action which is also somewhat unusual. Depending upon the way in which the event is perceived, and perhaps upon some personality factors also, the person experiencing a rare event may write to a newspaper, hold a party, say some special prayers, demand revenge, or the like. If the event is perceived by other members of society also as being a rare event, such behaviour will be accepted as 'normal' if it is perceived as matching the situation. The phrase 'I wouldn't do a thing like that!' gives the basis for the definition of behaviour and the reference of the 'normality' in terms of the summed experience of the observer.

All people have some concept of what they mean by expected and rare events. Ever since the dawn of civilization man has devised games of chance and has become conditioned to the *concept* of randomness, although it is only quite recently that a calculus to handle the concept has been worked out. Although no one has any prior knowledge of normality, almost instinctively we recognize 'abnormality'. We have, of course, nothing but our experience against which to assess the usual or the unusual, and we use this basis for the differential classification. *It is as though the human mind had a storage system linked to some classificatory and integrating device which was used for purposes of subjective prediction and regulation of behaviour in accordance with levels of expectation.* This storage system provides the basis for individual subjective concepts of probability.

The rare event, like the solar eclipse, was for primitive man an event so extraordinary that he was not able to accommodate it within his concept of normal events. The solar eclipse is equally rare today, but we are able to predict its occurrence, and we have found explanations for it. Rare events in nature which we cannot predict still continue to cause havoc and fear; the volcano may become active, floods may coincide with high seas, and many other events are seen as so unlikely or unusual that we do not take them into account in planning our work or pleasure. The unusual becomes headlines – but how unusual must an event be to come to be perceived as a rare event by the majority of people? There must be some tendency towards a constant measure or the newspapers would not know what to print! A serious crime becomes headlines, the building of a large bridge becomes headlines, what some important person has said is newsworthy. Is there not some constant underlying these different subjects which provides a single measure of their 'newsworthy' character – their unusualness? Is there any constant which will hold for different periods of time? A serious crime in 1963 may or may not have been newsworthy or regarded as at all serious had it taken place in 1600, but some crimes taking place in 1600 were doubtless unusual and newsworthy. It is probable that some bridges were being built in 1600, and that some of these were so large as to be newsworthy, but a bridge of the same size would not attract any attention today. It would appear that there is a calculus of 'extra-ordinary' events, because there is a calculus of 'ordinary' events.

The calculus of probabilities enables chance and rare events to be assessed in terms of their likelihood of occurrence. Whether the exact calculus of probability is the same or approximates to the subjective probability which people use in the determination of their behaviour or not, there will be sufficient agreement between 'true' and 'subjective' probabilities to enable the use of the standard measure (σ) as a reasonably descriptive term.

If we hold a dimension, say, good $\rightarrow$ bad, or large $\rightarrow$ small, or other perceived dimension, we will refer experience to it. It would seem reasonable to express the deviance from individual norms of experience in terms of the standard measure (σ) so that an event which was probable only once in every four hundred trials would be described as $2\cdot8\sigma$ deviant from the mean of the individual's experience. In general, the degree of unusualness of an event may be assessed by the value (x) in the term $x\sigma$. It seems probable that a bridge which was $x\sigma$ deviant from the experience of bridges in 1600 would be newsworthy in 1600 in the same way as a bridge which is $x\sigma$ deviant from the experience of bridges today would be newsworthy. To our eyes today the *unusualness* of an event is related to our sum of experience; similarly, the unusualness perceived by persons in the 1600s was related to their experience. That is to say, the value x in the term $x\sigma$ is probably the same today as in 1600 – the degree of unusualness in any event which would give rise to comment in 1600 was, relative to its surrounding events, just as abnormal as an event today, relative to its surrounding events, which is perceived to be deviant. The constant relationship is not in the nature of the event, but, like beauty, in the eye of the beholder! It seems reasonable to suppose that a crime which was $x\sigma$ deviant in 1600 (and thus 'surprising and unusual' to people at that time) was just as *unusual* then as the crimes which make headlines today. It is not the events, but the storage and classificatory system within the human mind which is the basis for the subjective concept of normality and probability.

How surprised a person must be to be surprised, that is, whether a person requires a 4σ or 5σ deviant event before he classifies it as unusual, will depend on the tolerance of deviation in the perceived direction, and may relate to a general factor of 'tolerance' of deviation from 'normality'. Such individual differences in the significant value of x in $x\sigma$ should not be confused with differences in the experience people have of unusual events. If a person is habitually experiencing events which to ordinary people are unusual, his classification will differ from that of ordinary people, but his required value of σ relative to his own experience may not differ from that of others.

It is necessary to keep clearly in mind the difference between the cultural definitions of deviance and the definitions of individuals. The definitions encoded in the legal system or enforced in other ways by the society will tend to be the common elements in the classifications of deviance resulting from the combined experience of members of the culture. Members of the culture will influence the definitions of the culture and in turn be influenced by the encoded definitions of the society within which they reside. The individual refers to his experience – the culture – for his basis of classification, and he carries on to others his classification system and hence the culture also.

Information Modifies Definitions of Deviance

The experience which forms the basis for classification of usual and unusual events is obtained in different ways and its content will differ. Experience is coded and stored as information, this the mind retrieves from the store as and when required. In the retrieval process the information may become distorted owing to its interaction with other information stored at earlier periods. Some discussion of the ways in which information influences classifications of deviance is necessary in presenting the general theory.

It would appear that information may be classified for the current purpose according to three types of consideration:

(a) content
(b) amount
(c) channel

By 'channel' is meant the different means of receiving information, particularly the difference between directly and indirectly received information. Some information may be regarded as trivial because of its content, or it may have no impact because the amount was small or the channel through which the information was received regarded as unreliable. What is regarded as trivial will relate to the perception of the culture in which the observer lives as much as to the degree of unusualness.

As an example of the trivial, but perhaps also unusual, the following might suffice. If I am unaccustomed to eating without wearing a jacket, I will perceive a person so eating as acting 'abnormally'. According to my interpretation of the action in relation to the culture and my status within the culture I may take a different seat at the restaurant, go to a different restaurant, or demand that the person be arrested! In general the dimension of 'unusualness' and the dimension of triviality will be negatively correlated. It is difficult to think of something that would be defined by every person as a trivial deviation from normality but that, at the same time, is an extremely rarely observed deviation. If an event or an act committed by any person is *sufficiently* rare, the rare nature of the event would normally be taken to imply lack of triviality. If I have never seen a thing in my life before, and it is very different from anything else I have ever seen, I am not likely to regard the matter as trivial unless I have other information to confirm the triviality.

A shopkeeper who notes that 2 per cent of his annual turnover seems to disappear in unaccountable ways may perceive this as normal, although he may know that it is due to shoplifting and staff pilfering. Depending upon his experience of variation about the 2 per cent, he may define 3 per cent loss as abnormal and take action which could result in an increase in the number of reported crimes, and perhaps also of arrested criminals.

It will be obvious that the hypothetical shopkeeper would adjust his behaviour and his definitions if he had further information regarding his expected losses. If, for example, he knew that the majority of stores in his particular chain experienced, say, only 1 per cent unaccountable loss, he would begin to consider ways and means of reducing his losses (2 per cent) to around the average or adjusted perception of 'normal' figures for his company. If he had other information enabling him to point to other 'abnormalities' in his district or type of trade, it might be possible that the two abnormalities would be perceived to cancel out to a total situation representing 'normality'.

As another example of the influence of information on the perception of normality, consider the following experience of the author. Rather late one Saturday evening he was returning to his home from central London. He joined a bus queue, which seemed to him to consist of some six or seven tough and probably delinquent gang members. He inferred this from the way they stood, and particularly from the manner of their dress. They had not spoken. His knowledge of the delinquent sub-culture did not relieve him of certain feelings of anxiety, or at least of a defensive attitude towards the members of the group. However, immediately they spoke he was able completely to modify his perception of 'abnormality' or deviance of the group – they spoke in French. From his knowledge of the habitual dress of French youth on holiday in England, he was able to fit this apparently 'deviant' behaviour and dress symbolism into a 'normal' or expected context. It would seem, therefore, that we may claim that what is defined as deviant is determined by our subjective experience of 'non-deviant' or 'normal', but that our experience and the resulting classifications can be changed by certain types of information. It would appear that information acts upon our expectations through our storage system and modifies the classifications which provide the basis for our prediction of behaviour.

The amount of information may influence the base against which events are considered with regard to their unusualness. The more odd experiences I may have, the less odd they will seem to be. The quantity of information available to an individual may increase his tolerance because it may increase the range of his experience of all forms of behaviour, or it may decrease his tolerance because his experience has been limited to more of the same kinds of observation. The shopkeeper may, for example, be tolerant of a loss of 2 per cent if he has information that only two or three other stores in his chain have a lower rate, but he may be less tolerant if he has information only from those with the lower rates; in the latter case his information is not only less but also biased. Increase in tolerance of events which would otherwise be defined as deviant is not a direct function of increased knowledge.

In recent years technological advance has mainly resulted in speedier communications between places in different parts of the world; highways, railways, and air travel have increased the range of communications both between nationalities and cultures and between different sub-cultures within the same nation. The shopkeeper of the

2 per cent loss store can no longer be unaware of the loss rate of other stores. The behaviour of people living in groups in what were once far-away mountains is now observable by tourists, administrators, and social agencies. In times gone by, deviant groups were able to establish their own cultures with reference only to their own sets of norms. Except perhaps for the intrusion of an occasional itinerant anthropologist they were left without contact with the norms of other societies. There have been numerous cultures where the total definitions of normality were out of accord with existing Western values. It was not until the increase in transportation and the increased speed of movement brought these communities into contact with other communities having different concepts of normality that their deviance was defined. The definition of 'deviance' was, of course, provided by the more powerful forces.

Types of Information

Let us refer again to the analogy of bridges. In total, the experience of bridges possessed by the population in 1600 would be much smaller than the experience of bridges possessed by the population today. The base of experience to which any new bridge could be referred for comparison by persons living in 1600 would be a sample of a much smaller (n) than would be the case now. The increase in speed of transport has increased the sample of bridges available to the population. The individual who travels widely will personally travel over and *directly* experience a large number of bridges in addition to those he may read about in the press. But the increase in travel may not be expected to increase his direct experience of crime. This is an example of a general point. The experience people have of *things* has tended to increase rapidly – things have to be extremely unusual to occasion surprise today. But the base of experience of *people* available by which we may be able to assess *people* may have diminished. In the village community were included all kinds of people, but the modern housing development tends to be limited in both class structure and age. There are communities where hardly an elderly person can be seen on the streets, and there are zones where children do not play in the public places. In the small local communities the farmer and the labourer and even the slave in feudal times were in direct contact with each other. Today more selective living is possible. The middle and upper classes do not necessarily *have* to know how the working classes live. There is no need even to give them their orders directly. Intermediary communications systems have been established so that the direct contact which was essential in earlier times is not now required.

The telephone makes it possible to talk to people without personally seeing them; the fact that even the lowest social classes can now be expected to read means that they may be sent letters and forms to complete. The administration may ask them whether they have a bathroom or not without seeing (and smelling) for itself. The insane, the criminal, and the deviant can now be isolated from society so that the normal members of the culture do not gain any experience of the non-normal. The unpleasant smell of the bathroomless homes contaminates a different sector of the town from that where the authorities concerned are likely to live. Even a world authority in criminology may not necessarily ever meet a criminal in order to become informed or to keep up to date.

In earlier times the young and the old were continuously in touch with each other; youth was aware of the problems of age, and age was aware of the problems of youth. The village was aware of the problems of mental deficiency – each village had its village idiot who was part of the total culture. Everybody knew 'Jack' who stood at the corner of the cross-roads and drooled. The newcomer to the village might feel threatened by Jack's behaviour, but immediately he spoke with a member of the village culture he would be assured, 'Oh! Jack's all right, he's just a little weak in the head – he was dropped on it when a baby.' Thus, apart from indirect experience derived from newspapers and other mass media, our modern culture has led to the isolation (and alienation) of deviant groups. The nature of the information obtained from direct experience and that obtained from mass media differs in both quality and type. The sample of experience obtained in the village contains different information, covers a wider range, and is of a different order from information indirectly obtained in the urban environment.

In urban societies the isolation of deviants has become institutionalized. Even the direct experience of one social class by visits for 'charitable purposes' has been reduced so that the paid social worker, quietly and decently, away from the normal citizen, is charged with the pacification of Jack, and the society has lost its direct information about and feeling for the problems of mental deficiency. The wealthy have moved from the downtown areas and have lost their direct experience of the problems of the idle youth, and so on. This is not merely a replacement of face-to-face communication and the information derived from such situations by other means, but a quantitative and qualitative change in the nature of the information. Clues may be picked up in face-to-face communication covering many dimensions and the information related to the situations which occur in a wide variety of ways. In a real sense members of the urban culture have suffered a *loss of information*, even though Jack may now be better cared for than previously. If it were possible for the urban culture to receive the *same type and quantity* of information regarding deviants as is obtained in the village, it might be possible for the urban cultures to accept a greater range of deviance. But, as will be noted later, the difference between rural and urban communication systems (face-to-face as compared with mass media and the like) necessarily involves also a difference in the type and the quantity of information received.

No value judgements are made here: we merely wish to bring out the point that information is a factor to be considered in explanations of definitions of deviance, and of societies' reactions to it. Value systems come into this discussion when we consider the mechanisms which people have constructed to insulate themselves from information – the ways in which societies' defects and shortcomings may be hidden because the deviants can be isolated and information regarding them rejected and distorted.

If the information individuals within a social system receive about the workings and expectations of the system is biased, they will be robbed of reinforcement of their definitions of normality. The effect of propaganda has been well documented in this regard. The individual's store of information, which serves as the reference for individual definitions of normal and abnormal behaviour, is today easily derived from the mass media. The larger units of society do not provide a set of information sufficiently varied for the individual to rely upon his own direct experience except within some limited range of activities. The average middle-class citizen living in the urban environment may be supposed to have information from his own experience, plus the information he derives from newspapers that is defined by their editors as 'newsworthy'. The concept of newsworthiness was, as noted earlier, related to the concept of unusualness and to terms involving $x\sigma$. The model used to describe deviant behaviour may perhaps be used to describe the differences between the nature of 'news' and the nature of information derived directly by experience, as shown in *Figure 3*. The region of overlap, where the individual has both direct experience of events and the experience of reading the news presentation of the same event, provides a check on the validity of the press comment and a base-line for the integration of the two types of information into a coherent 'experience' information set

FIGURE 3

A middle-class information set

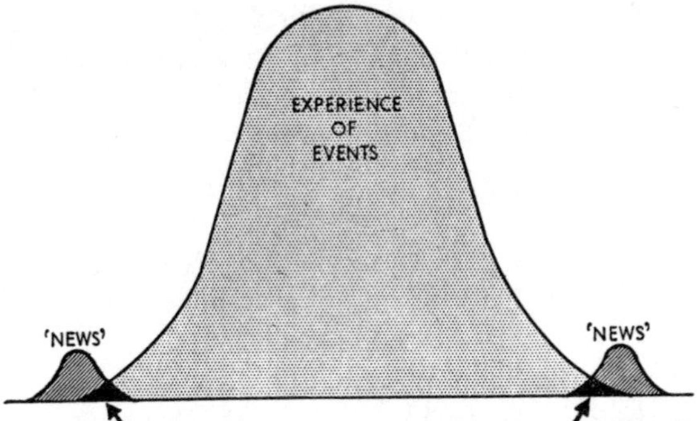

EXPERIENCE
OF
EVENTS

'NEWS'   'NEWS'

NEWS ITEMS OF WHICH INDIVIDUAL HAS DIRECT PERSONAL EXPERIENCE

against which further events may be matched. Where there is no common ground between the two types of information intake, there may be a tendency to sum them simply together, ignoring the difference.

Systems, Individuals, and Deviance

In the discussion so far we have carefully separated the concepts of deviance held by individuals and the concepts of deviance organized into a social system. In some cases such a distinction is unnecessary, since the individual takes his store of information from the society of which he has experience and relates his definitions of deviance to this store. There is a sense, however, in which the definitions of deviance adopted by a 'system' may be regarded somewhat differently from the individual classifications of members of that system. In much the same way as an individual, in order to feel secure with other people, needs to be able to predict their behaviour with reasonable precision and feels threatened by deviance (that is, abnormal behaviour), systems can operate only with material that is sufficiently homogeneous, or where the system is organized specifically to deal with heterogeneity. Merton's analysis of bureaucracy (Merton 1957) makes this point quite strongly. As he says, 'The bureaucratic struc-

65

ture exerts a constant pressure upon the official to be "methodological, prudent, disciplined". If the bureaucracy is to operate successfully it must attain a high degree of reliability of behaviour and an unusual degree of conformity with prescribed patterns of action.' Thus the bureaucratic definition of deviance may differ from the sum of the individual definitions of deviance of members of the bureaucracy. Within the village community the individual definitions are hardly distinguishable from the total definition; but even here there is a difference. In the village community, as a community, there is a greater tolerance of deviance than in the urban areas, but the deviance permitted to any one individual is greatly restricted (see *Figure 4*). The

FIGURE 4

Individual and social structure tolerance of different types of social organization

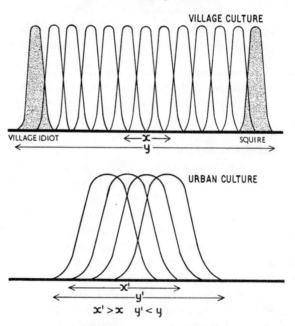

roles of each member of the village community (*x* in figure) are specified in considerable detail. There is conduct appropriate to the blacksmith and the village banker and the village idiot, but the black-smith may not behave like the banker even in his spare time, and even although he may be an extremely intelligent person; if for any reason he deviates from his defined role such behaviour will be interpreted by the village, and he will be helped, if help is perceived to be needed, or controlled, if social pressures seem to be required to re-establish the *status quo*. In the village each member has information regarding the expected roles of all other members of the community and the boundary conditions for work and leisure are narrowly defined by the culture. Each narrowly defined role is perceived to have a specific place in the culture; indeed, the tolerance of deviance from the role set for the individual may relate to the tolerance of a wide variety of roles (y) within the culture. While each piece of the mosaic stays the same shape it is easy to see how it fits into the whole, but if the blacksmith 'changes his shape', that is, fails to stay within the narrow limits of his perceived role, then the structure is seen to be threatened.

The differences between the village culture and the urban culture in terms of the ways in which deviance is controlled may be interpreted in the light of the different types of information available to members of the different environments. There is some behaviour which, because the village has *more* information, is more tolerated in the village; the village has many sets of information about Jack and can use these different sets to predict, explain, and control his behaviour within acceptable limits, where the limits are also perceived in terms of different sets of information. On the other hand, information regarding deviants in the urban culture is limited in its dimensions. In some cases this will result in less tolerance because information helping to explain and predict behaviour is missing where such prediction and explanation would assist control within the community, but there are also cases where the absence of information enables greater freedom for deviants because the urban culture defines certain types of information of interest in the village (and included in the wider information set) as irrelevant to its social control systems. It does not matter what the urban church organist does during the week to earn his living so long as he plays well on Sunday. The urban culture does not trouble itself too much with how its members dress so long as the dress is appropriate to the occasion, and the 'occasion' is frequently unknown to most observers. A native costume, a top hat and tails, khaki shorts and shirt, and many other varieties of clothing can be seen on the London streets at almost any time. For all the observers know, the wearing of whatever it is may be appropriate to the occasion, whatever it might be – the information set is restricted and the individual freedoms are increased. The village would know such dress was inappropriate to any possible role some people might play.

Dentler & Erickson (1959) studied deviance and social controls in small work groups in Quaker work camps. These groups were in face-to-face communication. The level of communication was very much higher than that to be expected in the village culture. Dentler's findings confirm the hypothesis suggested in the general theory of deviance. Small groups have specific roles for each member, whereas large groups tend towards anonymity. Dentler proposes three hypotheses (presumably restricting his inference to small face-to-face groups) thus:

1. Deviant behaviour tends to be induced, permitted, and sustained by a given group.
2. Deviant behaviour functions to help maintain group equilibrium.
3. Groups will resist any trend towards alienation of a member whose behaviour is deviant.

But the perception of deviance must differ in small groups from the perception of deviance in large groups. The information about deviance that is available to members of a small group will tend to cover a wide range of dimensions, whereas the deviant in the large group can be dealt with only in terms of the stereotype. The rural culture consists of groups of individuals whose roles are known, although perhaps not in so much detail as those of a Quaker work camp group. But the urban culture deals with groups of functionaries or roles without specific identification of the individuals in the roles. The individual in the village culture may be named Smith and identified with and perceived also as Smith in his role as blacksmith, and in this role he does very useful work for the village people. The village cannot perceive another individual as the blacksmith without difficulty. If Smith died, his son might take over, but if the forge was sold to a stranger, the stranger ('foreigner') would find it difficult to attract business and the confidence of the villagers. In the urban culture anybody may be Smith and anybody may be the blacksmith. In the village culture the *individual* seems essential to the functioning of the organization, as, indeed, Dentler makes very clear in his analysis of the work groups. He notes that the individuals who were perceived as deviant in his groups caused great efforts to be expended on the part of other members of the work group to retain them within the system, although they could leave if they wished. In the urban culture, individuals are expendable if they are replaceable in terms of their *roles*. In the urban culture it is not Mr Smith the blacksmith who is dealt with but a 'pool of labour', which may or may not include somebody (anybody) possessing the necessary skills – somebody with the essential skills is needed, but not Mr Smith. Perhaps one of the reasons why there is a wide tolerance of *individual* variance in urban cultures is because the role is perceived as more important than the personality. Similarly, the urban culture tends to reject *roles* that do not fit into the system, irrespective of the persons or personalities with which the roles tend not to be specifically identified. If 'Jack', the village idiot, is 'put away' in the urban culture, it is a person perceived not as 'Jack', but as somebody who is 'mad'. If the village puts away Jack, it is the person Jack who is put away. This does not mean that there is any more sentimentality in the village; indeed, the reverse may be the case. The village has more information about Jack. In the village the information about Jack is a matrix of n-dimensions – maybe he drools, but he is also known to be harmless, and his father was a good workman, and so on.

Criminologists, social workers, psychiatrists, and other specialists in human problems are often criticized as being 'soft' with 'criminals'. It is possible that this behaviour on the part of the specialists may be explained by the fact that they have a greater quantity of information than have members of the lay public. The lay public are prepared to deal with criminals and other perceived roles in terms of the current stereotype, whereas the social worker and criminologist have larger information sets. But the size of the information set is not the determinant. Information about something else, whatever something else is, is not information about 'it', whatever 'it' may be. Indeed, information on what is perceived as being along a different dimension is equated to zero in the perceived dimension. The information possessed by the village about Jack is *perceived as relevant* to the dimension of his place in the social structure of the village, and this perception of the relevance of the information may itself relate to the fact that the tolerance of deviation about the individual's norms in the village culture is *restricted*. A similar explanation would seem to fit the results obtained by Christie in his study of Quisling prison camp officers to which we have already referred. His concentration camp guards did not lack information about their prisoners, but it was perceived as *irrelevant* to the ways in which they were dealt with. This is to say, the information available was perceived as orthogonal to the dimensions of action.

Each member of a village receives training in the sociology of the village by observation and informal 'training on the job'. A form of apprenticeship in group management and parish politics is given to all. The training may be in a primitive form of government, but there is a system of passing on information regarding the role expectations of all within the social system. It is an individualized sociology at the level of anecdote and folklore, but *information about the system is fed into the system*. And perhaps even more important is the fact that that information covers the whole system, and this information is perceived as relevant. Moreover, the dimension of responsibility is not rejected in the village and other small group systems.

Some social systems are organized in such a way that they can allow varying degrees of deviance, or, in other words, heterogeneity or individual idiosyncrasies in the persons who are part of the system. On the other hand, there are systems which, by reason of their structure or social ethic, cannot operate efficiently where there is heterogeneity and individuals tend to behave in unpredictable ways. The unpredictability of the individual members of the society is regulated and controlled by rigorously enforced codes of behaviour. By such enforcement the individual becomes more predictable in terms of the system. The Communist Party in the U.S.S.R. spent many years trying to form the population into a homogeneous culture so that it would fit the particular ideology and machinery of their government. It is interesting to note that there is some evidence that this process is now being modified or reversed, and the U.S.S.R. is now able to tolerate a certain amount of heterogeneity, or in terms of their doctrine, deviance. Indeed, the definition of deviance and the way it has changed from the Stalin era to date are interesting and instructive phenomena to study.

It is also notable that some countries are able to operate an efficient social and legal system despite different languages and heterogeneity in the ethnic background of their population. By contrast with the tendency for some systems to increase the tolerance of heterogeneity and hence to define as 'deviance' aspects of behaviour which lie further out on the sigma scale, the governments of some other countries are finding it increasingly difficult to deal with heterogeneity in the cultures over which they have administrative responsibility.

Many different types of method have been used in attempts to divert the different kinds of nonconformist to conformist attitudes and behaviour.

The concept of deviance is, of course related to the concept of normality and is another way of expressing the concept of boundary conditions. Unacceptable deviance is variation about the central tendency (norm) which is perceived as abnormal. The perceived distance of the deviance from the central tendency will usually relate to the nature of the sanctions applied and the pressures exerted upon the individual to force him 'back into line'. The organization of boundary conditions is expressed in the legal codes – laws relating to individual behaviour but developed for the security and continuity of the social system.

Sinners, Saints, and the System

All societies tend to reject deviants. Both saints and criminals have been excluded from the cultures into which they were born, and the majority of saints have suffered exactly similar fates to the deviant sinners. Many saints were, in fact, *defined* specifically by their current society as criminals. Their society recognized deviance, but not the direction of the deviance. Different societies can tolerate different degrees and types of deviance, partly because of their machinery of government and partly because of the philosophy of their people – the way in which the people perceive their social systems and deviation within them. Some societies specifically try to stamp out nonconformity even at levels of deviance which are not threatening to its administrative structure. But intolerance of deviance is particularly noticeable when the leaders of the power structure feel insecure in their office.

Polygamous and matriarchal cultures had their own laws and standards of deviance. If these cultures had been more powerful there is every possibility that monogamy would have been defined as 'abnormal' even today, and our present Western civilizations' values would have been determined in quite a different way. It is difficult for societies to organize only when polygamous and monogamous cultures come into direct contact with each other. Similarly, as we have noted, a nomadic culture, whose members live on what they find on the lands over which they roam, cannot exist in a society where all land is partitioned out according to some definition of ownership. Thus 'systems' have tolerances as well as individuals; and, just as individual tolerance varies, so the tolerance of systems may vary in terms of the perception of deviance.

The difference between systems, populations, and individuals is often a difficult one to sustain in any conceptual model. Even Darwin apparently had this difficulty. As Gruber (1960) remarks, 'although in general his meaning is clear . . . Darwin is sometimes guilty of clouding the issue with respect to just what his mechanism does. In his language he sometimes confuses the individual with the population of which it is a part.' In the present discussion the distinction between the tolerance of systems and the tolerance of individuals within the system is most important, because the two types of tolerance may not increase or decrease together, nor may they be of similar types, as has been noted in the case of the village and urban cultures. Moreover, the effectiveness of communication and size of group would seem to influence the particular function of deviance both for the individual within the group and for the group itself. There are also different dimensions to which tolerance and deviance may be referred with respect both to individuals and to systems. A system may tolerate certain forms of individual deviance which individuals within the system may not wish to tolerate. Indeed, a system may find it unnecessary or even undesirable to restrict deviance if the individual self-disciplines are adequate for its purposes, or if sub-systems and informal sanctions provide the necessary degree of control or predictability.

In dictatorships it has been noted that the 'power structure' has often operated to provide the public with an excess of permissible deviance in one dimension and to restrict its definition of deviance in another. In the U.S.S.R. at one time, for example, considerable sexual freedoms were permitted, divorce could be obtained very simply, and the rights of national minorities were respected, but other freedoms were greatly restricted. Thus modification of the *system's* definition of deviance may be used *by the system* to retain its power.

In other social systems other uses of the definition of deviance appear which may function, consciously or unconsciously, as a means of protection for the system. Not many years ago a disastrous school fire resulted in the death of over one hundred children. The school happened to be a Roman Catholic School in a community which was about fifty per cent Roman Catholic, and where powerful political issues were associated with religious education. It is not surprising that the news commentators, without evidence of any kind, suggested that the cause of the fire might be arson. How convenient if the problem could be simplified to one villain or madman! There would then be no need to question the fire precautions, the state of the building, or many other politically inconvenient matters! There is no suggestion that the commentators were acting from any conscious desire to exculpate society or any member of the power structure. Over many years, socialization and experience of operating with organizations may well have provided sufficient conditioning for explanations of this kind to seem the most reasonable. In fact, after an inquiry, arson was ruled out, but the immediate public outcry had been tempered by time and by the early unsupported 'beliefs' that arson was the cause.

Everything was much simpler in the days when society merely punished offenders, when there was thought to be a direct relationship between cause and effect, and when devils could be blamed for things that did not fit into a straightforward and approved system. Perhaps the approach to criminal deviance has been ineffectual because criminal deviance has been separated from consideration of other forms of deviance; because it has been possible to simplify the crime problem by saying, 'He did it – deal with him!' instead of considering the more difficult task of examining our social systems and the multiplicity of the control mechanism and information sets. It should be clear by now that 'dealing with him' has not solved, and is most unlikely to solve, the crime problem.

But what is meant by 'dealing with the system'? Surely systems are composed of individuals, and, therefore, modifications of individuals are essential? If one takes the view that crime is identical with sin it is likely that one will restrict one's thinking to remedial measures affecting only the individual. It will be obvious, however, that when we are dealing with problems of social controls which do not involve the underlying concept of sin, we are able to consider modifications of the *system as such*. In the case of economic behaviour, society no longer relies upon the punishment of people who do not show the virtue of thrift. Rather we use macroscopic control systems, such as the budget and forms of taxation and rates of interest. These changes in the *system* are usually sufficient to persuade members of society to behave in the ways society desires. (There have been examples of enforced savings in wartime.) Perhaps the best examples of operation upon systems in order to influence individual human behaviour are to be found in applied economics.

A no-claims bonus is granted by motor insurance companies to encourage a form of behaviour that society desires, and of course there are prosecutions for careless or dangerous driving. If a society suffers a large number of credit frauds or cheque forgeries it might be able to make two types of decision – to maintain a large number of offenders in prison and to amend its credit laws. The various macroscopic systems of national insurance and the like which provide protection for certain vulnerable groups in society (e.g. children and the aged) represent operations on the systems as systems. Procedures which segregate different types or grades of child for different types of education represent systems, and there are many other such systems which could be expected to have an impact upon the individuals concerned to achieve some desired end. It would certainly appear that in criminological research a disproportionate amount of attention has been given to consideration of the offender as an individual and too little to the system with which his behaviour represents an interaction.

Between the system and the offender is the victim. The role of the system is generally perceived as being on the side of the victim against the offender. But both the offender and the victim are members of the 'system' – the culture which makes the laws which define them both. In advanced societies the 'system' does play a role in defence of victims, but there are instances where the victim and the offender may be better both seen as victims of the social order. The relationship between the victim, the offender, and the system is not a simple one which can be reduced to two dimensions with the system and the victim forming one unity.

The Role of the Victim

At least two parties are involved in criminal acts – the offender and the victim. Individual treatment procedures tend to consider only the offender, whereas the total series of incidents which precede a crime involve at least two situations, and a modification on the part of the crime-generating function could result in a different outcome.

It is not suggested that the offender (as an individual) should not receive some treatment or other form of attention, rather it is suggested that it may be a poor strategy to concentrate all or even most of the attention on the offender as though he were the only or main factor in the situation which resulted in the criminal act. It is often a good strategy to consider attacking on two fronts, particularly if these two fronts can be linked together in a common objective. Let any (non-criminal) reader try to imagine himself in the position of being required to commit a crime – say one of the most common crimes like larceny or breaking and entering – within the next twelve hours. Few readers would select the victim completely at random, unskilled at victim-selection though they might be. There will be something approaching rationality in the selection of the victim.

Criminals may not be rational, but there may be some proportion of the criminal world which behaves with some respect to rational considerations in some modified form. None the less, criminals are, by definition, distinguishable from normal citizens, and it would also appear that victims do not represent a totally unbiased cross-section of the population. It does not seem reasonable to postulate that no matter what the risk, the majority of offenders would continue to offend in exactly the same way; thus, changes in the victim role would seem to have an influence upon the role of the offender.

It has been shown that the number of crimes is related to the number of opportunities to commit them (see p. 54). When there were fewer cars available there were fewer thefts from cars. But is it not possible to reduce the opportunity to commit offences without reducing the number of opportunities (e.g. cars)? If a proportion of criminals behave in a rational way, and it seems that a proportion do operate with some sort of plan, it may be suggested that a rational criminal will follow the pattern of behaviour which nations use in warfare. The probability of gain is weighed against the probability of loss. If the risk is considered to be small and the probability of gain large, some people may be inhibited by moral considerations from committing illegal acts, but if not, crime may be attempted. Anything which changes the size of the probable gain, that is, *reduces the illegitimate opportunity structure* for the would-be offender, will change the balance between legitimate and illegitimate opportunity, and may change the outcome so that no crime is committed.

If goods are obtained by methods which are fully sanctioned by the society (legitimate means), no risk attends their acquisition, but as the means become more doubtful, the risk factor progressively increases according to the method of acquisition used. It would appear that the dimension of risk is orthogonal to the dimension of opportunity, but that rational behaviour is determined by 'pay-off', which is a function of the two factors.

Pay-off is not determined, even in business transactions, by the value of the goods acquired or the profit margin alone, but is a function of the value and the risk factor. Rates of interest available are also a function of risk. One side of this pay-off matrix is operated upon by the normal processes of crime control. The increase in the likelihood of being caught and in the size of the penalty if caught is expected, in classical penological thinking, to change the potential offender's assessment of pay-off, and hence inhibit his criminal actions.

The two functions of opportunity and risk are operationally independent until they are resolved into utilities in the mind of the would-be criminal. But, although criminal behaviour may be predictable, it may not be economic rational behaviour. That is to say, the criminal may not play his game according to utilities in terms of expected values. But neither do nations in warfare or diplomacy. The expected value of any chance operation is given by the probability times the prize. That is to say, if the prize is valued at $1,000 and the chance of winning is one in ten, the expected value to the gambler is $100 for each trial. People seem to operate as though the values they attribute to any game differed from the expectation, and differed according to the size of the prize or whether the chances were in terms of winning or losing. Kahn (1963), in a broadcast lecture, asked his audience to imagine that they were premiers of some imaginary country and that they were faced with a choice of three strategies: the first (A) if chosen would result with absolute certainty in the loss of $3,000 exactly; under policy B there was supposed to be one chance in ten of a loss of $300,000 giving an expected value of the loss of $30,000; but under policy C it was supposed that a loss of $300,000,000 could occur with a probability of one chance in a hundred – expected loss $300,000. Any rational person would choose policy A before policy B, and policy B over policy C, but, said Professor Kahn, 'If you were working on these sort of diplomatic exchanges where prestige gets committed, where there are all kinds of public humiliation, you are apt to argue that under policy C there is ninety-nine chances in a hundred that you will get away with it.'

It seems that very few people know how to deal with low-probability events, they tend to assume that the probability is zero.

Another example is afforded by the reaction of many persons to the British winter. Every few years a very severe winter occurs, disrupting transport, causing loss of life and heavy damage to property. It would, of course, be possible to assess by actuarial methods the cost of provision of equipment to deal with these rare events, even events as disrupting as the winters of 1947/8 and 1962/3. Yet, as the newspapers remark, while the public suffers 'nobody does anything about it'. But the newspapers do not complain in these terms during the following summer. The probability of occurrences of the kind, once past, are subjectively assessed differently from at other times. Immediately afterwards, the probability of another event seems likely, but as time passes the value assigned to the probability diminishes.

It is interesting to consider the reciprocal of this type of thinking in the attraction of football pools for the majority of the population of Britain. Investment, as it is called, in such pools has only a very small probability of winning a very large sum of money, yet the very small chance of a large gain attracts millions of persons to a most profitable industry for those who run it.[1]

No chairman of a business company could satisfy his shareholders by an explanation of his company's investment policy in the same economic terms as those used by football-pools investors. But this does not mean that we must regard the behaviour of football-pools investors as unpredictable or, given certain modifications in the variables, irrational. The subjective evaluation of the 'pay-off' is different for the shareholders of a company and the pools investors. A different set of utilities characterizes the different behaviours. May it not be that a different set of utilities characterizes many criminal acts? The remote chance of winning a large prize, plus the thrill of participation in a risky activity, considerations of prestige, and the involvement in the criminal culture doubtless influence criminal behaviour in a manner too strikingly similar to the field of international diplomacy! The actual odds for and against a certain policy may differ from the perceived odds, but action may not be in accord with the expected values of even perceived odds.

The defences of the individual potential victim may be correctly or incorrectly assessed by the criminal, as well as the defences of the society on behalf of the victim. But there are cases where the victim does not do all that is possible to prevent his becoming a victim, and even cases where the crime is precipitated by the victim. There are also cases where society may not do all that is possible to protect the victim, and, as has been noted in the case of the Soviet Union, the power

[1] It is possible to argue that football-pools betting is a rational activity for the working class. The average worker's chance of a clean break with his past and present status is absolutely zero without betting, but only nearly zero if he does bet.

structure may make use of definitions of deviance (crime) in one dimension as a protection against deviance in another. The defects of a society may be hidden either by tolerance of deviance or by attacks upon deviance. The type of deviance observed within any society is not independent of the type of society. Both the victim and the offender are members of the social order, and both are influenced by it.

It is not only dictatorship systems which make use of definitions of deviance to provide some defensive system for the power structure, and as a means of assistance or maintenance for the existing institutions of the system.

Individuals as Scapegoats for Systems

In any open or international setting the U.S.S.R. is reluctant to admit the existence of crime. Since the system is implicated in crimes against property, offenders against property must be defined as reactionaries or 'traitors' – obviously they cannot be good Communists!

But there are many ways in which other forms of society can deal with deviance which may represent a threat to the existing order. One way is to regard crime as individual sin. Sin can be punished without any involvement of the social system since it involves only the individual and an ethical code which is regarded as fixed. None the less, the majority of crimes, being crimes against property, must involve the social structure in some way or other because the social structure determines the rules for the ownership of property. When it becomes unreasonable to impute 'sin' so that the offender is dealt with without challenge to the existing order, the individual may be regarded as sick, since the concept of individual sickness is also capable of discussion independently of the social order.

This is the major difficulty of the U.S.S.R. Having abolished the idea of individual sin, the system is not able to explain individual deviance in that way. Sickness may be admitted, and the enemies of the society can be implicated, but not the social system itself.

Any form of individualization of the problem of crime seems unlikely, therefore, to provide an efficient theoretical framework for social action. *Individuals* cannot be dealt with outside the *society*, the *victim* cannot be forgotten – the three sectors must be considered.

It does not matter whether the call is for more priests, more psychiatrists, or more social workers – any form of individualization can be used to absolve defects in the social system and make it unnecessary to consider changes in the economic patterns of the institutions as at present perceived within the culture. Either type of explanation (sin or sickness) can suffice to protect the social system from criticism, except the criticism that it is dealing with the offender (sinner) with inadequate forms of punishment or providing insufficient help to assist him to get 'adjusted' to the system. Maladjusted children may be discussed, but not maladjusted educational systems or maladjusted employment practices. But the increase in crime which follows increases in consuming pressures cannot be well explained only in terms of either individual sin or individual maladjustment.

The general theory of deviance can be used to explain the factors of this situation. If a society wishes to see its members as conforming, consuming organization men, it may be necessary to create pressures to consume throughout the whole of the society, irrespective of the means available to some members of that society to achieve the goals which are advocated. If the means to obtain the goals legitimately are not well distributed throughout the social system, and the *whole system* is subjected to *similar pressures* (and this follows from the nature of mass media), it cannot be supposed that the pressures will operate differentially. Thus some members of the society may be influenced in the desired manner by the social pressures, but be unable to comply by approved means. They then have a choice: to try to achieve the goals by illegitimate means or to insulate themselves from the pressures to consume and conform. It is possible that some select one method and others the alternative.

The method selected may relate to the balance between legitimate and illegitimate means to attain the goals set by the general society which apply within the locality in which the 'non-achievers' live. If they prove unsuccessful in both legitimate and illegitimate means, they may seek to escape from the whole system. As Cloward and Ohlin (1961) suggest, it may be the 'two times losers' – those who do not succeed either in criminal or in legitimate worlds – who turn to drugs as a means of escape from reality. But this may be too easy an explanation. There are variables which need to be taken into account both in the individuals who become victim or offender and in the social system which includes them both. It is necessary to consider this interaction much more closely before a reasonable solution can be proposed.

Consider some facts reported regarding the economic system. It has been said that controllers of certain supermarkets use the shoplifting rates for different stores in their chains as an index of the efficiency and attractiveness of the displays of their shop-managers. If the rate is *too low* the goods must be unattractively displayed. This seems to be a valid inference to make from changes and variations in the shoplifting rate; it is certainly more valid than many other inferences.[1]

It would, of course, if this practice is widespread, be more consistent with ethics and business facts if minor shoplifting and petty pilfering were to be dealt with along the same lines as evasion of customs duty or taxes. There is, however, no need to consider all the complex relationships between legal structures and political systems. The general theory of deviance could, but will not here, be extended to cover other dimensions, such as the sociology of law.

Without doubt, individual sin and the protection of normal individuals from those individuals who desire to behave in unacceptable ways do not explain the methods of crime control at all completely. In addition to the protection of individuals, social systems build into their legal and extra-legal controls methods to reduce behaviour which might challenge the social system. Not only in dictatorship systems is nonconformity (within those dimensions regarded as appropriate) not tolerated, but in Western democracies also the rejection of nonconformity and nonconformists is to be noted in the tendency to inculcate, through social administration and social work as well as informally, middle-class value systems into all strata of society. Indeed, as Whyte (1956) has pointed out, the encoded systems of controls are frequently less demanding than the uncoded social controls through means of group pressures. If the social system tends to define deviant behaviour by means of the same process as the individual, that is to say, behaviour which is perceived to be $x\sigma$ deviant is defined as 'crime', and if the value of x does not change with time, the rates which describe deviant behaviour would be expected to show a constant proportion of the population defined as 'criminal'.

It will be recalled, however, that as the number of cars increased the number of thefts from cars also increased; similarly, according to the general theory of deviance, if the number of financial transactions

[1] There is no suggestion in the preceding arguments that individual sin is irrelevant, rather the argument is that the concept of original and individual sin does not explain a large proportion of the social phenomena observed in the present-day society. Nor does the argument maintain that the concept of sickness which may give rise to behaviour disorders is irrelevant, but again, this explanation does not itself describe the major proportion of incidents defined as 'crimes'. The theory put forward here is a general theory of deviance, and a theory of the middle range (Reckless, 1961).

increased, there would be expected a similar increase in the illegitimate transfer of money. In these circumstances would a society tend to define more and more persons as criminal and to apply sanctions more widely, or would there be a tendency for the value of x in $x\sigma$ to adjust to the higher level of both legitimate and illegitimate transfers of money or goods? Over the last thirty years the number of offences has increased, but the number of opportunities to commit offences has also increased. Both the number of deviant acts and the base of experience to which the experience of deviant acts may be referred have increased together. Thus if $x\sigma$ is a constant the actions of society based on this constant should show a steady figure. Moreover, because the experience to which the unusual events are referred may be expected to differ from culture to culture and from country to country, it would be expected that the proportion of persons defined as offenders by a society would vary less *within* societies than *between* societies. Within societies it would be expected that, given a stable social structure, the *proportion* of acquisitions of goods which are defined as illegitimate would tend towards a constant.

It will be expected, in terms of the general theory of deviance, that even if behaviour within a society 'improves' the $x\sigma$ values will remain much the same, so that there will be a tendency for that society to apply more stringent definitions of unacceptable behaviour. The *system* is conceived as having some self-regulating device of a similar kind to that described for the *individual* case as a classificatory and integrating system within the mind against which experience is checked and which affords the basis for individual prediction. There would appear to be some evidence that societies do tend to show attitudes towards deviants which accord with the expectation. If crimes of violence are considered, it would seem that, as human life has come to be more valued, there has been a tendency to define more actions as requiring the application of sanctions of society. It has been reported by anthropologists that, in the working-class north of England communities, the husband would regularly use some physical violence towards the wife, particularly if drunk on the weekly pay-day. According to observers, violence has *decreased* very considerably, but such a decrease does not show in the general criminal statistics of violence against the person. It would appear that as the 'store' of experience of events has changed, the $x\sigma$ values regarded as deviant have remained the same.

It is difficult to obtain any exact measures of violence, but the non-indictable crimes of violence reported in England and Wales have tended to decrease over the years, whereas the indictable crimes of violence have tended to increase sharply. This can hardly mean that when a person hits another today he tends to hit harder than in previous years! It seems more reasonable to suppose that the increase in indictable offences is due in the main to a more serious view being taken of incidents which previously would have been treated as non-indictable. The picture provided by the figures can be no more than suggestive because it would be expected that the same trend would bring into the non-indictable range some actions which would not previously have been reported at all. Doubtless crime changes, but so also does society's view of it, and the view taken is likely to depend upon the general store of information and the concept of deviance ($x\sigma$) rather than upon absolute values.

It is not expected that the cutting-point between legitimate and illegitimate means for the acquisition of property, and the cutting-point between acceptable and unacceptable violence will be adjusted in such a way that the amount of recorded crime remains a constant, nor will the proportion of persons removed from a society remain absolutely proportional to the population, but it would appear that the *definitions of crime will change to accommodate proportions of events ($x\sigma$ values) rather than proportions change to accommodate constant definitions.*

What is defined as 'crime' may be expected to change from time to time on legal-linguistic grounds alone, without direct relation to the actions and counter-actions of a society. In order to investigate somewhat further the claim that the definition of deviance (in standard measure) tends towards a constant with respect to the total experience of a culture, it might, perhaps, be represented that the best measure of the attitudes of a society towards deviants may be the way in which the *society behaves.* In other words, we should look not to the number of events which, at a certain period of time within a particular culture, are defined as 'crimes', but to the number of persons defined by that society as behaving in such a way that they can no longer be tolerated at liberty within that culture. The society removes such persons from contact with its social and administrative systems – with 'normal' members of the particular culture. By this definition we could discuss the number of persons placed in prisons or otherwise committed to certain institutions or 'otherwise disposed of'.

As Christie (1963) reports, it is not a simple matter to obtain figures for the incarcerated population of certain countries. In the United States, for example, there are Federal prisons, state prisons, and local jails, as well as some state youth institutions which in some states would be classified as prisons. It may not provide a good basis to regard the whole of the United States as one country; there are very considerable differences between the North and the South and even contiguous states can present wide differences of legal system and culture. Christie's best estimates, ensuring what comparability was possible, for 1960 were:

United States about 200 per 100,000 population
Finland   153
Denmark   73
Sweden   63
England and Wales   59
Norway   44

The figure for England and Wales includes the population of borstals as well as prisons, but does not include the population of approved schools, and provides a basis similar to that used for the other countries noted. Scotland is well known to show a different pattern of sentencing of offenders from that in England and Wales. The incarceration rate for Scotland in 1962, derived from the report of the Scottish Office, was 61 per hundred thousand population.

It is immediately apparent that there are extremely large differences in the incarceration rate between countries having apparently otherwise similar cultural patterns and penal codes. The variation in the rates appears to be very much larger between countries at the same time than over time but within country. For example, it would be necessary to go back to before 1852 to find an incarceration rate for England and Wales which reached half of the current figure for the United States, and even the current rate for Denmark does not differ much from that for England and Wales at the turn of the century. Christie has noted that the proportion of the population incarcerated in penal and similar institutions in the three countries, Denmark, Sweden, and Norway, has remained fairly constant for at least the last fifty years. But even between these countries, the rate differs quite considerably. Perhaps Finland presents the most interest, since until recently it showed an incarceration rate not very different from those of the other three countries (around fifty) but there was a discrete break in 1918 concomitant with political changes, and the rate moved suddenly to around figures three times those shown before.

Figures for England and Wales are available on a similar basis for over a hundred years, and, although there have been changes with time, time does not seem to be so important a factor in explaining the proportion of persons removed from the society as differences between the societies. Data covering certain years during the last century for England and Wales are given in *Table 2* below.

TABLE 2

Incarceration rates per 100,000 population (England and Wales)

Year	Average population in prison, etc.	Population of country	Rate per 100,000 population	
1852	17,500	18,000,000	94	
1889	21,250	26,000,000	81	
1920	11,000	37,596,000	29·3	
1925	10,509	38,935,000	27·0	
1930	11,346	39,801,000	28·5	about 30
1935	11,306	40,645,000	27·8	
1940	9,377	41,862,000	22·4	
1945	14,708	42,636,000	34·5	
1950	20,474	44,020,000	46·5	about 47
1955	21,134	44,441,000	47·6	
1960	27,099	45,755,000	59·2	
1961	29,025	46,166,000	62·9	about 65
1962	31,063	46,669,000	66·6	

Perhaps the trend of most interest in the above figures is the remarkable stability for the period of twenty years following the 1914–1918 war, compared with the change in rate following the 1939–1945 war. Compare, for example, the rate for 1925 to 1935 – a decade following closely the end of the first world war – with the decade 1950–1960. In the first period there was no change in the rate (27·0 for 1925 and

84

27·8 for 1935), but during the decade following the second world war it was characterized by a very sharp increase, which has continued until 1962; indeed, the present incarceration rate is nearly twice that at the end of the war and nearly three times the rate at the commencement of the war.

It is not possible to explain the variations in the incarceration rates in terms only of the changes in the pattern or amount of crime over time within countries, nor does it seem reasonable to suggest that differences between countries are explained wholly or mainly by differences in their criminal population. Indeed, it is difficult to explain the variations in the rates except in terms of the general theory of deviance. Different social systems and different social administrative machineries are, it seems, by reason of their structure, able to accommodate a greater or lesser degree of nonconformity. The types of tolerance of nonconformity may operate in similar ways to that which determines the differences between village and urban culture. In the village *information about the system is fed into the system,* and it is likely that this information influences the perceptions of members of the system with regard to the nature of the system. Informational feedback loops may form part of the basis of experience to which the concept of deviance is itself related.

It seems probable that the population incarcerated, and perhaps even crime rates, are influenced by factors of a 'deviation amplification' nature – like the relationship between prices and confidence. There would seem to be similar deviation amplifying systems operating both within cultures (countries), revealing their effects in the changes of rates as they vary over time, or over some periods of time and not over others, and providing some explanation of the large differences between apparently similar cultures (countries). If this hypothesis is correct, it provides a new emphasis for cross-cultural studies and leads to suggestions regarding the validity of research methods.

It has been suggested by some writers that there is a relationship between the degrees of individual and system tolerance of deviance which is some function of the size of the social system or organization. Size, however, is usually found to be negatively correlated with information flow, and it would seem to be a more sophisticated view that the apparent correlation between size and tolerance is a spurious one due to the correlation between information flow and size. In other words, the main variable is not size, but the nature and quantity

85

of information within the system. Certain information might reduce tolerance of deviance; other information might tend to increase it. In the case of the village, it is obvious that each individual member has more information about both the structure of the system and individual members within it, than, say the urban dweller. Size cannot explain the differences between the different countries' incarceration rates given above. Norway has a small population and low incarceration rates, Finland also has a small population but high incarceration rates, and although England and Wales are small in area, the population is large and the incarceration rate low. It would seem that rather than size being the factor, there is an informational feedback loop which changes the experience set with which members of the system operate and which influences the definition of deviance.

Information Loops and Definitions of Deviance

It may be argued that the variations in incarceration rates, although tending to show greater differences between countries than within them over time, are a reflection of the crime rate. Variations over time in the proportion defined as criminal may be explained in terms of the general change in social development such that variations within a country tend to vanish by reason of adjustment of definitions, but it may be claimed that variations between countries are not described by the same law. May it not be that there is, in fact, more crime in the United States of America than in Great Britain or Scandinavia? But even if there is more crime in some countries than others, does this provide an explanation? Rather should not a theory help to explain why countries with similar systems of government and similar ethnic stock show such widely different crime rates or incarceration rates, or both? If a cross-section of the population of the United States were removed to any of the countries with lower crime or incarceration rates, would they define the crime and incarceration rate as within the United States or adopt the values of the country to which they were transferred? Crime variations may explain to some extent incarceration rates, but what explains the differences in crime rates?

International comparisons of criminal statistics are quite impossible at the present stage of their development. Legal categories differ and the types of behaviour subsumed under similar categories also differ. A few examples can, however, be selected. In the United States of America drug addiction is a very serious problem; indeed, large proportions of those imprisoned are incarcerated for drug addiction or peddling. In Great Britain and the Scandinavian countries there is no drug addiction problem. In the United States drug addiction is treated as a most serious crime and convicted offenders are sentenced to very long terms of imprisonment, whereas in Great Britain the drug addict is dealt with as a sick person and treated with sympathy, if not with tolerance. But drug addiction used to be a serious matter in England.

It is possible that some societies, for some reason, find it necessary to treat deviance with extreme intolerance, and others are able to accommodate greater degrees of deviance, and, *as a result of such tolerance, experience less serious deviance.* It seems that it is possible for a society to operate in such a way that its social-sanctions systems become devalued. If such a feedback mechanism is in operation, the system within which it is applied tends towards instability. If a small initial stimulus generates a response, part of which response becomes a further stimulus, a highly critical and powerful servo-mechanism results. Such a feedback mechanism is at least implicit in the theoretical work of Kitsuse and Dietrick (1959). Re-examination of Sutherland's theory of differential association led Kitsuse and Dietrick to modify it in the following way (see p. 39):

(i) The individual learns the values of the delinquent subculture through his participation in gangs which embody that subculture.
(ii) The motivations of individuals for participation in gangs are varied.
(iii) The malicious, non-utilitarian, and negativistic behaviour which is learned through participation in the subculture is met by formal negative sanctions, rejection, and limitation of access to prestigeful status within the middle-class system.
(iv) Thus, participation in the delinquent subculture creates similar problems for all its participants.
(v) The participants' response to the barriers raised to exclude them from status in the middle-class system . . . is a hostile rejection of the standards of "respectable" society and an emphasis upon status within the delinquent gang.
(vi) The hostile rejection response reinforces the malicious, non-utilitarian, and negativistic norms of the subculture.'

The links in this circular chain may be described as a 'positive feedback loop'. While such a loop continues the situation will continue to get further and further out of control. The point of entry into such a system which may result in modification of the loop does not have any significance in terms of the outcome. It may be easier to enter at one point rather than another, but ideally the modification required is to change the loop into a negative feedback so that the system tends towards a desirable stability. It will be noted that, like Cloward and Ohlin, Kitsuse and Dietrick limit their model to gang behaviour, though such restrictions seem to be unnecessary if their theory is extended to a general theory of deviance.

Progressions, Good and Bad

According to the general theory of deviance, the definitions of deviant behaviour relate to the information and cultural experiences of the individuals making the definitions; there is no meaning to the term $x\sigma$ except as it relates to the total information set. It was remarked that both communities of saints and communities of criminals would define certain behaviour as lying outside the limits of tolerance of that particular culture. If the definitions of deviance lead to the removal from the experience of 'normal' people of certain deviant persons, the future definitions of deviance will not include the experience relating to those so removed. Moreover, if the action against deviants is such that they are not retained within the general system of values and controls, the new group created by the definition, as well as the residual group, will tend to construct new values and controls. Not only will the parent population cease to include within its experience the information relevant to the deviant, but the deviants may cease to have information regarding normal behaviour. This mechanism relates to the loop proposed by Kitsuse and Dietrick.

In terms of the earlier model based on the calculus of probabilities, the situation does not remain static. The sector which is cut off by the definition does not remain attached to the general distribution. The transition from one distribution to different distributions may be related to the theories of 'reference groups', and in terms of the present model is as illustrated in *Figure 5*.

Let us first consider deviations at the left-hand cut-off point which have been associated in these illustrations with the 'sinful' or 'criminal' end of the scales. It will be possible to show similar mechanisms which operate at the right-hand cut-off point, and to generalize the theory at a later stage.

The modification of the information available within the truncated sections of the distributions will generate forces which will force the two distributions apart. The norms of the distributions cut off will

FIGURE 5

Evolution of sub-cultural and deviant social systems

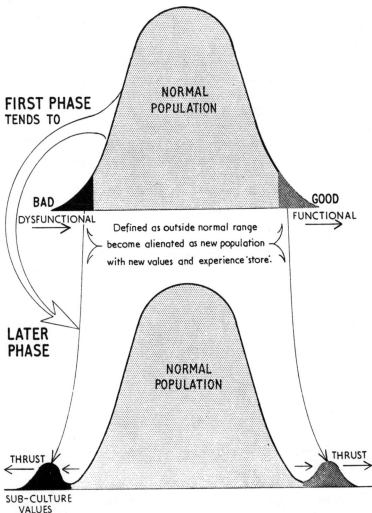

no longer be the same as the norms of the distributions from which identification has been severed (i.e. the parent distributions). That is to say, instead of a centripetal force towards the general (parent) norm of the culture, the norms of the truncated parts of the distribution will reveal characteristics of a centrifugal force. This is, of course, another way of expressing the effect of the 'positive feedback loop'.

Using Kitsuse and Dietrick's style of presentation as in the preceding section, the following feedback system may be proposed:

Less tolerance leads to →
        more acts being defined as crimes
        leads to →
        more action against criminals
        leads to →
        more alienation of deviants
        leads to →
        more crime by deviant groups
        leads to →
        less tolerance of deviants by conforming groups
               and round again ↑

The General Model

It is now possible to take the general postulates put forward individually in the preceding pages and to attempt to relate them together into a complex theory. The following postulates have been stated:

1. People tend to behave with respect to situations and things as they perceive them to be.
2. Distinctions between what is legitimate and what is illegitimate are made culturally.
3. Legitimate and illegitimate opportunities can be distinguished, and the *balance* between the two types of opportunity presents an important variable.
4. If the balance between legitimate and illegitimate opportunities remains constant, the amount of crime will tend to vary according to the total number of opportunities. Hence it follows that the disturbance of the balance will modify the crime rate, if the rate is considered in relation to the opportunity structure.
5. Since perceptions influence behaviour, the definitions (perceptions) of the culture have an influence upon the members of the culture and the sub-cultures as perceived and defined by the culture itself.

6. Human decision-making skill (information processing) is influenced not only by the nature of the information, but by the 'channel' through which it is received.

7. Information which is perceived as irrelevant (orthogonal) to the dimension of action is treated as no information.

8. Systems in which information regarding the functioning of the system is fed back into the system present different characteristics from systems where such feedback information is lacking or is minimal.

9. People do not play 'expected values', thus actual odds do not explain behaviour; even perceived expected values may not provide a sufficient basis for prediction of behaviour since small probabilities are not treated in terms of pay-off maximization.

10. Norms are set for the culture, but different sections of a culture will experience greater or lesser difficulties in achieving success within the norms.

The above set of postulates cannot be related together in any simple unidirectional cause → effect model. The model proposed may be described as a deviation-amplifying system. The type of model proposed is well stated by Magoroh Maruyama (1962). As he says, 'The law of causality may now be revised to state A SMALL INITIAL DEVIATION WHICH IS WITHIN THE RANGE OF HIGH PROBABIL-ITY MAY DEVELOP INTO A DEVIATION OF A VERY LOW PROBA-BILITY or (more precisely) into a deviation which is very improbable within the framework of probabilistic unidirectional causality.' Models based on deviation-amplifying systems have been found to be necessary to explain economic behaviour, and it is not surprising, nor does it represent a high degree of originality, to propose similar models for other forms of satisfaction-seeking human behaviour.

The implications of the deviation-amplifying system are far-reaching; as Maruyama says, 'these models are not in keeping with the sacred law of causality in the classical philosophy (which) stated that similar conditions produce similar effects'. It is now possible to demonstrate that in some cases similar conditions may result in dissimilar products.

Applying the general dynamic model and the postulates stated above to the particular problem of crime, the following system may be proposed:

(a) Certain types of information, in relation to certain systems, lead to more acts being defined as deviant (the x in $x\sigma$ is given a reduced value).

(b) The individuals involved in the acts so defined are 'cut off' from the values of the parent system by the very process of definition.

(c) The defining act provides an information set for the individuals concerned and they begin to perceive themselves as deviant. (Perhaps the main way in which any person gets to know what sort of person he is is through feedback from other persons.)

(d) The action taken by society and the resulting self-perception of the individuals defined as deviant, lead to the isolation and alienation of the specified individuals.

(e) This provides the first part of a deviation-amplifying system. The definition of society leads to the development of the self-perception as 'deviant' on the part of the 'outliers' (outlaws), and it is hardly to be expected that people who are excluded by a system will continue to regard themselves as part of it.

(f) The deviant groups will tend to develop their own values which may run counter to the values of the parent system, the system which defined them as 'outliers'.

(g) The increased deviance demonstrated by the deviant groups (resulting from the deviation-amplifying effect of the self-perception, which in turn may have derived from the defining acts of society) results in more forceful action by the conforming groups against the nonconformists.

(h) Thus information about the behaviour of the nonconformists (i.e. as (f) above) received by the conforming groups leads to more acts being defined as deviant, or to more stringent action against the 'outliers';

and thus the whole system (a)–(g) can itself continue round and round again in an amplifying circuit.

This type of model need not be regarded as too surprising. A similar situation explains the relationship between confidence and prices on the Stock Market. If this type of model is a fair representation of the social system in relation to deviant behaviour, some interesting predictions can be made from the theory. In particular, if a model of this kind applies, it is not necessary to show that the individual parts have a large effect on any detail of the system; the important feature of this type of model is that it represents an unstable system. Small initial differences, perhaps even due to chance variations in the network, can build up into quite large forces. A number of mutual causal processes can be identified in other fields of science where the initial stimulus was extremely small, and possibly randomly generated, but where the final results were of very considerable importance.

It is possible to examine this model in relation to some differences in criminal behaviour which have not been satisfactorily explained by the simple unidirectional cause → effect model. The majority of students of the problem of drug addiction have expressed interest in the fact that Britain has no real problem in this area whereas it represents a very considerable problem in the United States and in some other countries.

Many observers from the United States have studied the system of drug addiction and narcotics control in England. Although different observers from America were in England at the same time and discussed with the same people, their views differ regarding what was observed. Some writers have reported that they could find no differences between the British and the United States systems of control, others have found what they believe to be major differences. It would appear that the perception of systems of control differs between observers who are, in fact, observing the same thing and taking similar evidence. Some have claimed that the different systems of control in the two countries could explain the difference in the incidence of addiction, others have claimed that since there are no differences, or none of any significance, the different patterns of addiction cannot be due to any differences in the systems of control. It may be that these conflicting views by experts are capable of resolution through the theory proposed. Perhaps the following summary statements indicate a satisfactory model for this problem:

(a) the perception ('image') of the use of drugs in England differs from that in the United States;

(b) the perception of the addict differs;

(c) the perception of the police differs;

(d) small differences in the control system, or even in the perception of the control system, could generate large differences in the perception of addiction, which could amplify the effects of the official controls;

(e) less action is defined as 'crime' in Britain, and as a result, or in addition, fewer people are defined as 'criminal', whatever the objective differences may be;

(f) the *balance* between legitimate and illegitimate means for obtaining drugs in the two countries differs;

(g) the 'information set' (or folklore – it does not have to be true!) regarding the official control system and the function of drugs, both culturally and in the sub-cultures of the two countries, differs;

(h) a different perception of a situation will give rise to behaviour which differs, since behaviour tends to be consistent with perception.

If this model is a sound one, it would be possible for the situation in England to change rapidly and radically owing only to minor changes in the balance of factors. Which factors are critical in an unstable (feedback) situation of this kind is not a particularly meaningful question – any change in the situation may change the outcome throughout the whole field. It is possible, or even probable, that any attempt to tighten up the British regulations with a view to making a minor problem even less of a problem may be a disturbance of the generating system of perceptions which could produce a more serious problem.

If complex models of this kind do in fact explain types of human behaviour which are disapproved of by society, social action to remedy a perceived 'evil' (dysfunctional behaviour) could take place at many points, but any action is likely to misfire and to result in the opposite effect to that which the action is desired to achieve.

If people are excluded by the system they are not likely to feel themselves to be part of it. This is the same argument as is made in theories of alienation and anomie. It would appear that the sanctions applied by a society to its sub-cultures may appear to them to be so extreme that they are alienated from the general values system of that society. The rejection of an $x\sigma$ deviant, if the value x is not large, may act as an information set modifying his own tolerance ($x\sigma$) through his experience of the culture (that is his 'store'). If a society truncates its normal distribution at low values of standard deviations it will tend to reduce the cohesiveness of its own social order. Lack of tolerance for behaviour which is not completely *intolerable* may defeat its own ends, not only through the devaluation of sanctions, but by inducing a self-definition of deviance, where such a definition is not justified in terms of the social dysfunction of the behaviour.

This is a similar mechanism to that discussed by Merton in the quite different connection of the operation of bureaucracies. Merton (1957) points out that the rules of procedure within bureaucracies may come to be applied too rigidly, or interpreted too narrowly. 'A margin of safety such as engineers use in bridge construction is applied – with the result that the officers of the bureaucracy become frustrated and the objectives of the organization distorted.'

Some Supporting Evidence for Feedback Models

Mannheim and Wilkins (1955) showed that treatment in 'open' borstal institutions appeared to be more successful in reducing recidivism than treatment in 'closed ' institutions, after making allowance for the fact that the better risk categories were allocated to 'open' conditions. However, in interpreting these findings it was noted that 'there was at first a tendency to think that "treatment" meant the systematic treatment organized differently in the two classes of institution, and that this explained at least the main effect. But there are many features of treatment that are not directly organized – the effect of interpersonal relationships, masters and boys, and particularly boys with boys' (Wilkins, 1955). Wilkins has also shown that so far as it was possible to compare the age groups of offenders who might be committed to either borstal or approved school training, the 16-year-old borstal boys succeeded in 48 per cent of the cases compared with 63 per cent for approved-school boys. Interpreting this result, Wilkins remarked, 'in approved school training the 16 year old boys would associate with boys on average having a better prognosis than themselves while in borstal institutions they would be associating with cases generally having a worse prognosis . . . the "normative process"[1] affords a possible explanation'. In terms of the diagrams using the normal distribution, this would mean that the further away from the general norm of the culture the individual was defined as being, the further he was likely to move away from that norm. A later analysis within the approved-school system provided even more specific evidence. Standardizing the different risk categories allocated to different approved schools by means of a regression equation, it was found that the school which received average risks had a success rate exactly at the average, whereas a school which received worse-than-average cases showed a success rate worse than

---

[1] A term used in earlier writings to mean much the same as that now described as 'deviation amplifying' to conform with that of other writers.

would be predicted in terms of the 'type of material' in the system, and conversely, at a school where there was better-than-average material, the result was better than could be explained in terms of the input material alone. A similar effect was noted by Croft and Grygier (1956). Using sociometric analysis, they found in most classes in a school which they studied, that delinquent boys were rejected by others (had more enemies), that truants were isolated (had few friends), and that the boys rated by the teachers as behaving badly were disliked by other boys. In other words, in most classes they found that the choices on their sociometric scales tended to follow the values of the teachers. But in the class reserved for 'backward' children the situation was different. Conforming behaviour was unrelated to sociometric status. Both truants and delinquents were relatively more popular in the backward classes.

Moreno and Jennings had earlier reported that the most popular individuals in prisons tended to have had an outstanding record of antisocial activities. Similar results were noted by Clemmer (1940). It would appear that, in general, a group which has been defined to be, *or defines itself to be*, cut off from the general distribution will develop its own norms which will in turn reveal some centrifugal force away from the norms of the parent distribution.[1]

Jackson Toby[2] has also provided some data which support this thesis. Re-examining the Cambridge-Somerville experiment, where potential delinquents were identified in the schools and given a form of preventive treatment, he reports that, although over the whole sample of cases there was no evidence that the treatment had any good effects, this could be due to the fact that merely the identification of middle-class children as 'potential delinquents' – marking them out for treatment – could have resulted in their being more likely to have a criminal record than if they had been left alone. Among the working-class children, however, it seems that the treatment may have had a positive effect. Thus the effect of *identifying* a group as 'potentially delinquent' was such as both to offset the effects of preventive measures and to have an additional negative effect. Or, in terms of the general theory of deviance, the children 'identified' were provided with an information set which modified their views of

---

[1] In an unpublished manuscript, T. D. Grygier (1963) refers to this phenomenon as 'social progression', pointing out that there is no assumption of values in the concept of progression – it may be the Rake's Progress.

[2] Personal communication.

themselves and provided a frame of alienation from the values which they, as middle-class children, might otherwise have internalized.

There is little evidence from research literature regarding the general concept of deviance, except deviance which is regarded as dysfunctional. Nevertheless, it would appear that the problems of the aged, that problems of education and health, find an echo in the analysis of deviance in terms of $x\sigma$ values. Educational policy, for example, makes use of the concept of deviance in terms of the normal distribution through the media of educational testing. This has been the case for many years. The 'educationally sub-normal' are defined specifically in terms of $x\sigma$ deviance on standard tests which use as their base of comparison the general population of scores for the factors considered relevant. The numbers or proportions of children selected for grammar schools, the selection for university places, and other educational policy decisions are based on the concept of the normal distribution, and the cutting-points are intentionally fixed in terms of values of $x\sigma$. How does this practice fit with the general theory proposed here? Clearly, it gives it some support, but the theory put forward here is a serious challenge to the ways in which the concepts of normality and 'brightness' are translated into educational policy. If the definition of unacceptable behaviour tends to produce a self-concept which in turn tends to separate the defined deviant group from the general values of the culture, may not a similar centrifugal effect result from the classifications in terms of educational deviance? There is indeed detailed evidence that this particular phenomenon does occur.

Vernon (1955) studied the effects of classifying children in English schools and placing them in 'streams'. He found that children allocated to the 'A' (upper) streams emerged from the educational process with considerable increases in the measured level of intelligence. But those allocated to and educated in 'B' streams emerged showing a drop in intelligence scores. He also showed that this process had continuing effects, and that a person with both secondary and university education had an average test score 12 points above the person who was *equally* scored at 15 years of age, but who had not had the stimulus of further education since that time. Vernon's result may be compared directly with those of the reconvictions of boys committed to approved schools and allocated to different types of school, where the different types of school were described in terms of the other boys committed to them.

97

Some General Observations in Relation to the Theory

Research studies over a number of years have thrown up a number of facts regarding the incidence of crime and delinquency which seem to be beyond reasonable doubt. Certain ethnic minority groups, for example, show considerable differences in the incidence of known criminal activity. Some, like the Jews, are far less involved than others; whereas Puerto Ricans and Negroes tend to be over-represented in criminal statistics of countries where they are minority groups. Of course, ethnic and socio-economic factors are associated, but not all the differences between ethnic groups can be explained in socio-economic terms. This is especially so for the Jews. In most countries Jewish children show delinquency rates about half that of the national averages, but in Holland there is no difference. In Holland the Jewish people have been completely integrated into the culture, but in Great Britain and in the United States where a separate Jewish culture exists, studies consistently show a lower rate of juvenile delinquency than the national mean.

Rural criminality has been noted to be much lower than urban; and serious crime, apart from murder, seems to be essentially an urban, young male, lower socio-economic group phenomenon.

The majority of crimes in Western democracies consist of offences against property.

In the rural community, as has been noted, *individuals* are not tolerant of individual deviance, while the *system* itself can accommodate a wide range of behaviour. An individual who is discontented with his role which, in the village, is rigidly defined, must, if he wishes to change it, move to the urban society. The removal to urban society is not only an economic necessity, but, and this is perhaps more important, it is a social necessity. The rural community with its lower delinquency rates is a self-selected culture; a culture of those who are less driven by the desire to become conforming, consuming achievers. While they remain in the village they are within a social system which has a very effective information network. The support and correction will tend to be immediate upon any deviation owing to the ready flow of information and the general knowledge of the individual norms. The Jewish community, even in the urban setting, is of the form of the village; it is supportive of deviance, and has a good informational network. The common elements explaining, at least in part, the rural and Jewish delinquency rates seem to be information and integration.

Similarly, involved in problems of Negro and Puerto Rican excess of delinquency is the matter of information and integration. Information is particularly relevant in the ways in which it interacts with the perception of deviance within both the community and the sub-communities and individuals. The areas where Negroes live are not communities; they are constellations of people for whom the social and informational systems of the village have been broken down and have not been replaced by another system. The lower-class Negro does not tend to identify himself with the Negro who has made his way ahead in the total society.[1] The American Negro technologist who goes back to his ethnic group in Africa is referred to as a 'Black European'. Nationalism had not developed in those countries from which the slaves were removed, and there is no national culture underlying their ethnic background. The victims of crimes committed by Negroes are as likely to be other Negroes as members of other races. There is thus no culture, no information set of controls such as protect the villager and the Jew. The Negro in the U.S.A. is thrice rejected – by being coloured, by being working-class, and by being an under-achiever in the educational system.

The pressure to consume and the impact of affluent societies on the relationship between legitimate and illegitimate means have been discussed in terms of the theory of deviance. The male in urban societies is doubtless subjected to more pressures to consume than the rural male or the urban female. The relationship between school failure and near failure and delinquency has been consistently noted in the literature. Are these factors not related to each other? A society which is trying to demonstrate its superiority over other social systems is a discontented society. Indeed, discontent leads to achievement. But discontent leads also to intolerance. (Discontent is perhaps another way of noting lack of tolerance with existing situations.) Intolerance leads to rejection of the under-achievers. The under-achievers at school, like the deviants on other dimensions, are marked out in terms of a value $x\sigma$, and form an image of themselves which does not fit the 'normal' definitions of the society. From that situation they are soon forced into the feedback network.

The Negroes, the lower class, the educationally sub-normal, the under-achievers are all alike pressured to consume and to conform to the same standards by the same mass media, and are subjected to the

[1] After this manuscript was written there was a sudden change in the social consciousness of Negroes in the U.S.A., evidenced by (generally) passive resistance and non-violent campaigns for their civil rights and influencing all social levels.

same conditions as those who can achieve or who have strong cultural value systems and informational networks which insulate them from the definitions of the total society, or who find the total society in accord with their values.

Even experience in school may have a positive effect on the behaviour and happiness of children of the middle and upper classes but a negative effect on children whose background differs (Wilkins, 1948). The nature of the system may well interact differently with different types of individual. The lower classes may find some defence against middle-class value systems as they experience them in schools by defining themselves into a different sub-population, thus insulating themselves from value systems which they cannot, or believe they cannot, excel in. Certainly there is plenty of evidence from sample surveys that children of the lower class are far more likely to reflect upon their school experiences as 'unhappy' when questioned in their late teens, even although they have attended the same schools, been subjected to the same discipline and teaching methods as the middle-class children who regard their experiences as 'happy'. It is difficult to accept that these differences repose entirely in the children; they seem rather to be in the *interaction* between the experiences of the child in his lower-class environment and the experiences he has in school.

Implications for Action

If the theory of deviance provides a reasonable model and explanation of observed phenomena, it has implications for social action in many fields.

In the area of education, some authorities have noted problems in applying the theory of normality in the definition of persons who are able to benefit by higher education. The static model provided by the cut-off of sections of the normal curve has been noted by Floud (1962). She states, 'There is no iron law of the national intellect imposing an upper limit upon the educational potential of the population. The gap between the outstanding and the average achievement ($x\sigma$) may not narrow but the educational threshold of mediocrity is for ever rising and the distribution of the population as between different educational levels shifts. These movements reflect social change and social policy, and create problems of economics and engineering in the field of education; to conceive them in any other terms is misleading.' Or to refer again to our dynamic model over time, let it be assumed that in 1600 the same tests (or better tests normed in the same ways as current educational tests) had been used to determine educational placings and had been given to a cross-section of children. Suppose that the educational policy of the 17th century had been determined on the basis of these results in the same way as the policy for the latter part of the 20th century is being determined. What percentage of the population would it then have been deemed worth while to try to teach to read? Even if the same philosophy had been applied to children less than one hundred years ago, one wonders how many children would today be receiving more than a few years of school. '*But what the few could do a century or less ago, the many can now do*' (Floud, 1962). What the few can do today, it seems reasonable to suppose, the many will be able to do in the future, if we do not restrict them through intolerance of deviations from our concepts of the norms that are required for levels of learning.

The definition of deviance is relative to the 'store' of information. It is not an absolute value. There is no level of 'general intelligence' or other factor which is absolute, any more than there is any absolute measure of deviance on the dimension of crime. The same reasoning seems to be equally applicable to educational concepts of deviance at the high or low intelligence ends of the scales. If we fix our policy in terms of our present-day concepts we will move forward extremely slowly, if at all.

If the universities will not tolerate intelligence levels beyond a certain $x\sigma$ value, only the few will be able to do what the many might otherwise be enabled to do. The *absolute* value which was equivalent to the *relative* value $x\sigma$ some years ago is a lower *absolute* value than that associated with the *relative* value $x\sigma$ today. The idea of a pool of talent which may be found by bringing into the higher educational system those who for, say, financial reasons are now excluded may seem to be reasonable, but it is not far from the idea of a 'pool of ability' or 'reserves of talent' to the idea that 'pools' can be drained, and the reserves exhausted, and from there it is not very far to the 'scraping of the barrel'. A report in the *Washington Post*[1] records that Professor W. Albert Noyse, Jr., professor of chemistry at the University of Rochester, U.S.A., said, 'given twice as many fellowships at the university . . . we could not fill them today, we are already scraping the bottom of the barrel'. Where is the bottom of what

[1] Local Ed. (24 Jan 1963).

101

barrel? It would seem that this reasoning is confounding absolute and relative types of measurement.[1]

It would appear that in health, education, crime, and all forms of social action we can refer to dimensions and to deviation from them. The mathematical models seem to hold up quite well under sociological analysis.

The problems of the aged are so similar to those of the young that it is unnecessary to elaborate. How old is 'old'? Ask any child of five or six and you will get quite different replies from those of a youth of 16 – the $x\sigma$ concept holds in the definition of deviance of age which is defined as 'old'. Ask any sample of individuals when they think 'middle age' begins and ends and their replies will correlate in an interesting way with their own ages. The problems of the aged are not problems of crime, and do not appear so dysfunctional to society, yet the aged are similarly alienated from the culture, except perhaps in the villages and certain other communities. It seems highly probable that societies which integrate aged persons into their culture have few problems with juvenile delinquency. Chinese minorities are well known for both their care of their aged and their low delinquency rates. It seems that societies which reject deviants reject them in terms of a number of dimensions. If they can integrate deviants of one form, they tend to be able to integrate deviants of another form. If they can integrate the aged, they can also integrate the young; if they can cope with the mentally sub-normal, they can cope with the talented; if the information systems include information which modifies the behaviour with regard to one type of deviance, information with respect to other types of deviance also exists within the system.

It seems that, no matter whether the theoretical framework proposed in this chapter is true or partially true or whether it is only plausible, the type of model put forward should be examined before action is contemplated which may, for very good reasons and with very good intentions, produce undesirable results. Social action should not be undertaken lightly. It is possible to mortgage the future to the good intentions of the present.

If the model holds, then it seems that optimal social action might proceed along something like the following lines:

(a) develop and maintain a social structure such that at all times

[1] In one sense there are no 'absolute' measurements, but rather degrees of relativeness in measurement.

all levels of persons are able to select *legitimate means* to obtain objectives which are defined as *legitimate ends;*

(b) ensure that its social sanctions do not become devalued by excessive use or misuse (in much the same way as money can become devalued);

(c) define as deviant the *minimum* number of actions regarded as dysfunctional, and hence also minimize the number of persons who are defined as *deviants;*

(d) ensure that information is available both with regard to the controls of the social system and as a means of control. For example, it will be necessary for those in authority to know, by careful investigation, the nature of the perceptions (image) of the social system which are characteristic of different sectors of it.

At the other extreme, it would seem desirable to define the maximum number of persons whose 'deviant behaviour' is perceived to be unusually functional, but, again, the devaluation of incentive will need careful attention – in the same way as the devaluation of sanctions or deterrents.

Control of deviants can, it seems, be achieved by a society if the deviants are retained within the general value systems of the culture. If deviants could be integrated into the society before their deviance reached a level where it is impossible to deal with it without a definition as 'outlier' ($x\sigma$ greater than a critical level) there would be fewer dysfunctional acts. What levels of deviance can be dealt with in such a manner may depend upon the system of organization and informational networks of the society, and the proportion that will have to be truncated (and the $x\sigma$ values associated with this proportion) will be an important factor for research. The centripetal and centrifugal forces will, perhaps, be related to some human variables analogous to the physical concept of mass. Ways and means for transforming a deviation-amplifying system into a self-regulatory system (from positive feedback loop to negative feedback loop) may be worth exploration.

It is clear that we must get away from the static models and evolve some dynamic theories which take into account the ever-changing society in which we live.

As the first step towards advance, we must seek to build social systems which can tolerate deviance. If we do not, we are committing ourselves, at best, to the production of a new mediocrity.

REFERENCES

CHRISTIE, NILS (1963). Paper read to Research Symposium at National Institute of Mental Health Washington, D.C.

CLEMMER, D. (1940). *The Prison Community.* Boston: Christopher.

CLOWARD, R. S. & OHLIN, L. E. (1961). Illegitimate Means and Delinquent Subcultures. *Delinquency and Opportunity.* Glencoe, Ill.: The Free Press.

CROFT, I. J. & GRYGIER, T. G. (1956). Social Relationships of Truants and Juvenile Delinquents. *Hum. Relat.*, vol. 9, pp. 439–66.

DENTLER, R. A. & ERICKSON, K. T. (1959). The Function of Deviance in Groups. *Social Problems*, vol. 7, pp. 98–107.

DENTLER, R. A. & MONROE, L. J. (1960). Social Correlates of Early Adolescent Theft. *Amer. Sociol. Rev.*, p. 733.

FLOUD, J. (1962). Quality and Quantity in Higher Education. Paper read to Royal Statistical Society Conference at Cambridge, England.

GRUBER, J. W. (1960). *A Conscience in Conflict.* Columbia, N.Y.

KITSUSE, J. I. & DIETRICK, D. C. (1959). Delinquent Boys: a Critique. *Amer. Sociol. Rev.*, vol. 24, no. 2.

MANNHEIM, H. & WILKINS, L. T. (1955). *Prediction Methods in relation to Borstal Training.* London: H.M.S.O.

MARTIN, J. P. (1962). *Offenders as Employees.* London: Heinemann.

MARUYAMA, M. (1962). Mimeo paper circulated by Research Department of the Department of Corrections, Sacramento, California.

MERTON, R. K. (1957). *Social Theory and Social Structure.* Glencoe, Ill.: The Free Press.

RECKLESS, W. C. (1961). A New Theory of Delinquency and Crime. *Federal Probation*, December 1861.

REISS, A. J. & RHODES, A. L. (1960). The Distribution of Juvenile Delinquency in the Social Structure. *Amer. Soc. Rev.*, p. 720.

SHORT, J. F. & NYE, F. I. (1957). Reported Behaviour as a Criterion of Deviant Behaviour. *Social Problems*, vol. 5, no. 3.

TOBY, J. (1961). *Social Problems in America.* New York: Wiley.

VERNON, P. E. (1955). *Studies in Education No. 7.* London University, Institute of Education, and Evans Bros, pp. 89, 215.

WHYTE, W. H. (1956). *The Organization Man.* New York: Simon & Schuster; London: Cape, 1957.

WILKINS, L. T. (1948). *Adolescents in Britain.* London: H.M.S.O.

WILKINS, L. T. (1955). Classification and Contamination. A Home Office Research Unit Research Memorandum, Mimeo, London.

CHAPTER 5

Models or Muddles?

TOWARDS A STRATEGY FOR SOCIAL WORK AND RESEARCH

General nature of scientific method – Strategy and management – An analogue: war and peace strategies: (a) the role of intelligence; (b) assessment of intelligence reports – Allies and enemies – The language of military operations – The war on crime: (a) psychological warfare; (b) the concept of deterrence; (c) defensive strategies; (d) panzer research strategy; (e) the mass attack; (f) raiding operations – Morale: personnel policy in research and action – Individual, community, and system modification strategies – The unity of society

---

General Nature of Scientific Method

The claim has been made that the methods of science are essentially the same, irrespective of the subject-matter of the field of operation. The effectiveness of operational research applied to wartime problems has been noted and it was suggested that the same methods as were used for purposes of destruction could be just as effectively used for purposes of social construction. Can these claims be substantiated? Can the techniques, not only of operational research, but of operational policy and theory, provide any guidance to the solution of problems of social action in peace?

It is, of course, possible to talk about the 'war on want' and to express other social problems in similar picturesque language, but can the metaphor be turned into a model or analogue in any of the details? Is the concept of a strategy for social research and action one which can be developed from war systems? There are many difficulties in any translation of any methods and systems from one field of application to another. Analogues and models may not be sustained completely, but the reference of a known set of concepts to another area affords, at least, a method of exposition which often has much to commend it. For this latter reason alone it may be profitable to examine the techniques and terms of warfare and seek any meaning they might have for action against the social ills or 'enemies of society'. In research, the enemy is ignorance and inefficiency.

Webster's Dictionary defines STRATEGY solely in terms of warfare as 'the science of military movements' and 'use of artifice and sometimes deceit'. Although the concept of psychological warfare has some counterpart in social action, deceit does not seem to be any part of the concept of strategy which will be advocated here, nor will ways of deceiving the 'enemy' whoever or whatever the 'enemy' be discussed. Perhaps a more appropriate definition of strategy, as the term is used in this chapter, is 'the disposal of forces into favourable positions so as to maximize the likelihood of obtaining objectives'.

One major distinction between peacetime and wartime problems will be immediately obvious. The objectives to be attained, or the factors to be maximized or minimized as a result of social action, are seldom expressed in terms so precise and agreed as are the objectives of society in warfare. None the less, in social action the problems of choice of operations to be attempted, the disposition of scarce resources of materials and manpower, and problems of morale constitute important issues.

To some extent it is possible to sustain the analogy of an 'enemy frontier' – the frontier of our ignorance. Other analogies such as the 'hostile forces of nature' have been used as a basis for certain logical models in investigations of human behaviour.

Strategy and Management

Research strategy is not the same as research management, nor is a strategy for social action the same as a social agency management policy. Management problems, problems of staff relations, questions of information flow and discipline are important, but they do not fall within the concept of a strategy any more than military personnel policy is strategy. The strategy determined for military purposes will have an impact upon personnel management, but it is not part of personnel management. Very little study has been devoted to research management or to management of social agencies. Doubtless management of staffs employed in a 'creative environment' requires different techniques from management in other fields of endeavour. Until more investigations have been made in this area our knowledge remains at a most unsatisfactory level. There are a few novels, a number of anecdotes, but nothing beyond intuition to provide guidance. This is a most unsatisfactory state of affairs. Morale seems generally to be lower in research teams than in other groups of workers. It may be that some measure of frustration is a necessary concomitant of a 'creative environment', and that scientists and others concerned with change are dissatisfied types of people! But feelings of frustration can quickly degenerate into serious morale problems. There is perhaps an optimum point somewhere between frustration and stimulation, but no real evidence as to its location.[1]

The productivity of a research group is a different matter from the strategy used in the deployment of the group. The former is a matter for research management, while the latter is the concern of the general policy makers of the organization. Strategy may be considered only in terms of abstract concepts because there are no empirical data, and data cannot be sought until the nature of the problem has been identified. Problems of management can be identified, and it is possible to obtain empirical data.

Perhaps the nearest approach to a research strategy has been worked out in certain industrial and commercial establishments. In such establishments there is usually a well-stated general policy so that the concept of a strategy may be related directly to the disposition of forces into favourable positions so as to maximize the likelihood of obtaining the objective. Perhaps research in commercial establishments can state objectives quite clearly and classify them as long and short term. In social policy research, however, the goals are not frequently stated in very specific terms, and there is little consensus among those who are engaged in the different fields of social action. In industrial and commercial concerns there is usually no problem of consensus on major issues of policy – generally the firm will regard the making of a profit as a major objective. Profit, since it refers to

---

[1] Within the week that this chapter was written two incidents helped to underline for the author the relationship between frustration and creativity. A new theory of mathematical sets was developed by J. Gerver (aged 14) while listening to his mathematics lecturer. The lecture, it seems, proved rather dull, and Gerver turned his attention to problems more to his liking and produced his solution before the lecture terminated. The second instance came to notice because an unknown car-driver stopped and offered a lift. The driver proved to be a patent agent about to visit a client who had invented 'Typits' (a system for adding separate symbols to any ordinary typewriter so that mathematical and other unusual symbols could be produced). The inventor had had a routine task of inserting the symbols in drawings and typed documents and turned his mind towards making this work unnecessary. If the former person had had a good lecturer, and if the latter had been interested in his job (for which he was doubtless too intelligent and a 'bad' placement from the viewpoint of any employment agency!), neither the mathematical theorem nor the means for adding to normal typewriters characters for typing mathematical symbols would have been developed at this time.

money, is measurable. The absence of consensus in matters of social action raises serious problems in applying the concept of strategy.

An Analogue – War and Peace Strategies

(a) The Role of Intelligence

It is possible to consider warfare operations as being of two basic types; although the division has become somewhat blurred with recent emphasis upon the concept of a 'cold war'. War ('hot war') is discontinuous, but certain operations related to war or its possibility are continuous. Every country attempts to identify all its potential enemies and to obtain continuously 'intelligence' (information) regarding many aspects of their economy, war potential, and intent. A balance is struck between the amount of money, manpower, and other resources which are deployed in obtaining intelligence and those which are concerned with fighting or training for fighting. The relationship between 'information', decisions, and objectives in a rational process has already been noted. The idea of a strategy indicates the need to consider a balance between information and action. No military machine which spent all its time and energy in the collection of intelligence could win a war, but, on the other hand, lack of good intelligence could result in the war being lost.

If we are considering the strategy of research, again the concept of intelligence is valid. The direction of research requires intelligence, and it may be necessary to spend some proportion of any available resources not on research itself, but on research intended to facilitate the efficient direction of research. Research is no substitute for action, and action is no substitute for research. But if there is to be research to provide guidance for action, why not also research to provide guidance for the direction of research? Is it logical to stop at the first level of abstraction? Misdirected research may be just as wasteful as misdirected action. But the progression, research for action, research for research, may seem to lead to a potential infinite regress. This is not the last time that the problem of the potential infinite regression will be faced; it arises in consideration of problems of aims and objectives and the selection of criteria, and especially in the concept of 'causation'. (If a is the 'cause' of b, then what is the cause of $a \ldots$? and so on.) Such systems are a feature of our world – we must not say, 'Ah! Infinite regress!' and then assume that, having identified the 'circularity', we must stop there. Almost all scientific advance has looked like leading to an infinite regression at some stage before the advance was made.

The social scientist's behaviour is itself human behaviour, and the techniques which are used to study behaviour in others can be used to study the behaviour of the social scientist. In particular, it would seem meaningful that the social scientist should spend a proportion of his time investigating his own techniques with a view to obtaining scientific information to guide him towards an optimum strategy for research. The idea of a 'science of science' is more than a circular concept, it is a central feature of the idea of a research strategy. A spiral may appear to be no more than circular if observed in terms of one dimension. And, as remarked earlier, it is necessary now to consider other models than the single directional model of cause → effect (see p. 91).

It is now generally agreed that it is not optimal to stop at the first level and to put all our faith and money into what we believe to be the right kinds of action. Social action, it is now claimed, should be evaluated; and this means research. The argument for moving to at least one stage further removed is not so generally agreed. At present we do not know the value of different levels of abstraction in terms of any measure of 'pay-off'. But the fact that we can state our ignorance would seem to be a challenge, and a valid challenge, to research. It may be thought that the higher the level of abstraction, or the less subjectively certain it seems that a pay-off will be secured, the fewer resources should be employed. But this was not the philosophy which it is generally believed established the physical sciences in their strong positions. There is, however, the problem of how much of the total resources should be devoted to different stages of action or intelligence-seeking activities. Taking no decision does not solve the problem. The problem of apportioning resources does not, of course, begin at the level of 'research into research', but at the level of the relationship between research and action. Some proportion of the funds available for social action are now usually marked down for research and evaluation. These proportions vary widely. In California, well known for advanced research in the field of the treatment of offenders, 2 per cent of the total state vote for the Department of Corrections is spent on evaluation and research. Is this too large or too small? At this time this percentage represents perhaps the largest that any state or country in the world is allocating from the total cost of penal systems to research. In these circumstances it is, perhaps, not surprising that only a few persons are prepared to consider the stage next removed from direct action and to propose the allocation of some percentage of the percentage available for research to matters connected with the problems of a science of science.[1]

It seems reasonable to continue the analogue of the relationship of intelligence to strategy in military operations somewhat further. It may be suggested that there are different areas of information involved in military intelligence which have some similarities with social action. Military intelligence units will be interested to obtain information regarding:

(a) the nature of the enemy terrain
(b) the type of forces and their armour
(c) the probable nature of their deployment
(d) the morale of troops
(e) the likely technical developments which may change the nature of the course of warfare if it is begun
(f) the support of civil installations and institutions.

Information regarding these and other factors is related to:

(i) structure and types of own and friendly forces
(ii) probable effects of different methods of attack
(iii) evaluation of operations.

In the terms we have used heretofore, the first set of items may be regarded as 'the nature of the problem', while the second group relates to the resources available for action and research. But it may be useful now to adopt the terms of the strategy of warfare. It will be clear that the resources of social action may attack social problems at many points, or resources may be concentrated, techniques akin to raids may be used, or advance may be sought by weight of numbers and armour on a selected sector. Which method of attack is employed should have regard to the intelligence reports. Intelligence, besides being sought specifically by personnel trained for that purpose, is obtained also by the troops in the field. No operation is carried out

---

[1] Perhaps the future will look somewhat different. More and more human action is becoming automated, and human qualities are not going to be so much in demand at the direct levels of activity. Perhaps more and more human endeavour will be spent on research and at levels of abstraction one stage removed from the direct processes. After the next few technical revolutions it seems probable that we shall be discussing, not the balance between direct action costs and research and evaluation costs, but the balance between research costs and the costs of research into research!

without its providing some information which the Intelligence Corps will not wish to have and sift through.

(b) Assessment of Intelligence Reports

It is doubtful whether the forces of social action have any means for assessing and utilizing information which could stand comparison with the ways in which military intelligence is processed. At present each social research unit (or even individual worker) tends to carry out whatever assessment there is made. There is no satisfactory clearing-house for information and no organized system for its appraisal. While successful raids (or other operations) are reported in the appropriate journals, the failures (those who do not come back!) are seldom reported. But in the development of intelligence for the basis of a meaningful strategy, failures are at least as significant as successes. Many social scientists, perhaps like many generals, tend to try to see a measure of success in operations which are essentially failures. The failure of a well-designed experiment to substantiate a well-phrased hypothesis should not be regarded as a 'failure'. On the other hand, a study which supports a loosely stated hypothesis, or whose research design is weak, is certainly a failure. In research there is no concern with failure or success, but only with the quantity and quality of the information.

It is true that librarians do an almost religious job of storing information; it is placed on record, but without evaluation, and much of it is not worth its rental of space.

Each operational unit tends to use its own special language, and translators are very few. In warfare, the questioning of returning forces is regarded as a highly skilled speciality. Would social action (and perhaps social research) not gain much if an analogous speciality could be created to assess and consolidate relevant information? Such an organization could not confine its attention to information retrieval, no matter how efficient such a retrieval process might be. Storage and retrieval systems do not represent evaluation and consolidation of information.

Economy and efficiency seem to imply that the maximum use should always be made of information already available. Where information of a suitable kind is not available, the cost of obtaining it should be considered most carefully. Good information in warfare is one of the best safeguards against unnecessary loss of lives and material – in fact, it may be said that good information saves men and money. In this light it may seem odd that the majority of social workers are not cost-conscious. It is always claimed that resources to combat social ills are scarce, and, if this is agreed, it would seem to follow that the economic use of resources should be regarded as an important issue for study. But systematic cost analysis in social action and social research is seldom rigorously applied. Cost analysis could provide much raw material to guide future action.

The value of theoretical frameworks has already been discussed (see Chapter 3). Every theory, if it is a scientific theory, has implications for action – for testing the practical consequences of the theory. Proposed action must be related to theory as any plan of battle must take into account intelligence reports. Every proposed social action which refers to the 'needs' of clients or communities implies a theoretical background. In modern society, almost everything which is done on behalf of that society will have some cost to that society. It seems reasonable, therefore, that the cost should be assessed against the pay-off and related to the general intelligence of the situation.

There is one other factor in the evaluation of intelligence where the military analogue may be challenging. If certain items in a military intelligence report are mutually inconsistent, or if comparisons of different intelligence reports reveal inconsistencies, it is usually deemed desirable to straighten these out before action takes place. Inconsistencies may reveal limitations in the sets of information which should be filled in by carrying out some further intelligence 'raids' before any major attack is launched.

Allies and Enemies

In warfare, strategy is very necessary to make it possible to discriminate allies, neutrals, and enemies! It may not be too absurd to suggest that the development of a strategy for social science and social action is inhibited today because the analogous distinctions are not recognized. The point has already been made that social administration and social research cannot be independent of each other. In achieving desirable social change they are allies. Immediately we consider moving towards a strategy for social research and action, it becomes apparent that not only are these two interests dependent upon each other, but within the sphere of 'science' itself there cannot be independence between disciplines. The results of current physical research and developments in the field of mechanical and electrical engineering and, indeed, almost all 'non-human' sciences and technologies will have an important impact upon our society and individual members of it in the future.

Some of the problems which now concern social administration and social research may find their solution, not in social science, but in developments in the physical sciences. But it is also probable that developments in the physical sciences will raise more problems for the social administrator, and hence the social scientist may regard these as his concern. As early as 1955, *Fortune* magazine published an article in which the major point made was that, about 1950, developments in the physical sciences changed in form. Prior to 1950, when a system was improved in some way, whether these were improvements in transportation, communication, or data-processing, the social unit was made *larger*; much the same things were done, only in a bigger way. 'Then suddenly we ran out of space, and from then on, whenever technology improved transport, communications or other things, it was as though we were crowding people closer together.' Whether this suggestion, that there was a complete change in the *nature* of the impact of other sciences upon social problems, is correct or not, the fact remains that in recent years, 'every ten years has seen about two technical revolutions. And this is new in the history of the world.' Thus the social scientist may well be spending time trying to solve problems which may exist today, but which will exist either in an entirely different form, or not at all, in the foreseeable future, unless there can be built up a close liaison between the disciplines. Unfortunately, there are few signs of such development taking place: most physical scientists seem even to resent the term 'scientist' being used by those who are attempting to apply the scientific method to assist with the solution of social problems.

The organization of our institutes of higher learning and research is hierarchical within disciplines. How little communication there is across the disciplines it is difficult for those outside such institutions to imagine. Each discipline is protected by its own 'language'. Although others may overhear conversations in the senior common room, from the point of view of communication they might well not be within earshot. The situation can be like that described by Goffman (1961) in relation to the special language of medicine. He notes, 'when the examining physician is accompanied by colleagues and subordinates, as when making rounds . . . he will have participants available for technical conversation about the case. So effective is this way of suppressing the social presence of the patient that his fate can

113

be openly discussed around his bed without the discussants having to feel undue concern; a technical vocabulary presumably unknown to the patient helps in this regard.'

Each discipline or profession attempts to isolate or insulate itself from others by means of its own special language. But while the disciplines are able to communicate vertically, that is within their own structure, the problems of society often run horizontally across the different disciplines – in just the direction in which communication is particularly difficult. No army uses codes against friendly forces! Communication barriers (codes?) may represent one of the major obstacles to a meaningful strategy of research and social action.

The future does not come unheralded. There are pointers for tomorrow's problems available today – perhaps in the code language of some other disciplines. Some developments spend a long time in the 'pipeline', and many projects now on the drawing-boards of other sciences have a high probability of practical realization in the future. Ways must be found for the implications of 'what is in the pipeline' of physical research to be considered in terms of its potential impact on other disciplines, and especially the ways in which the future developments of technology will relate to social problems of today and tomorrow. Tomorrow's labour force has already been born. Demographers can, of course, make estimates of future populations and forecast a number of separate factors such as age and sex distributions. But although the forecasts of demographers have made an impact upon the social sciences (perhaps demography is a social science?), similar communication does not exist between other sciences and social science, although these other sciences may have an even greater impact than population changes upon the shape of the social problems of the future. Clearly, it is poor strategy to spend resources in attacking problems which will vanish of their own accord, or to deploy forces in such a way that we are unprepared for new developments. Dynamic models are necessary – models that will enable us to relate information derived in today's settings to useful application in changed situations. Social research cannot remain rigid while all around is dynamic. If a research is planned to deal with a current problem and will take five years to complete, will the situation in five years' time be served by the study? This question raises two considerations: (a) the nature of the research design, and (b) the extent to which it is possible to predict the future situation. Perhaps some other aspects of the methods of warfare strategy may help to throw light on these matters.

The Language of Military Operations

It may, eventually, become necessary to develop a special vocabulary for the concepts of strategy in social action, but the general terms used in military operations are widely understood and will suffice for the presentation of this case. Indeed, it seems remarkable that so many of the terms used to describe military operations may be applied to social action problems without supplementary explanation. For example, in the 'war on want' or 'war on crime' or in our attacks upon any social ill, it is necessary to know what sort of war we are expected to fight. Merely to know that we have to fight a *general war* in a general sort of way does not help. We need to know something about the terrain, the type of enemy forces, their equipment and disposition. Such information has an import for the type of our own forces, their number and training, and the type of armour we should provide. We can consider the problems of economy and efficiency in the use of units of different sizes and the balance between the types of service and ways for optimizing our use of specialists. It will also be obvious that different types of attack are possible, and that these should be selected in terms of our knowledge of the enemy and our own resources so as not to waste manpower or materials. We may consider the questions of when a 'cold war' might become a 'hot war'. In the 'hot war' we may decide upon one or more of the following methods of attack:

(a) defensive ('trouble-shooting')
(b) raiding by specialist forces or combined operations
(c) panzer strategies[1]
(d) mass attacks by specialist or combined forces.

At least these terms suggest analogies which are worthy of examination, and at the worst, they will serve as mnemonic aids. The meaning of most of these terms applied to social problems will be self-evident. In passing, it may be remarked that the theories of strategy and the application of high-speed computer simulation and other routines which have been developed for studies of problems of actual warfare might be adjusted to provide powerful tools of analysis in application

[1] See p. 122 for explanation.

to social problems. But the taking-over of models from one discipline by another is not a simple matter, and until social scientists and others concerned with human problems can state their objectives and the factors involved with the precision of the military strategist, modification and application of available techniques will not be possible. But to continue the use of the language of strategy.

A defensive strategy may be optimal when forces are small. Even random strategies may be optimum strategies at times, but a random strategy is not a muddle-through strategy, it is a specific model which is consciously adopted when it is likely to achieve the optimizing of the pay-off desired. Defensive strategies are sometimes akin to trouble-shooting – a form of research activity well known in industrial organizations. In some industries special teams termed 'trouble-shooters' are regularly employed. Short-term research projects and trouble-shooting social action programmes are usually thought up quickly to deal with problems as they arise. The impromptu nature of the planning of most of these types of activity is not an essential feature of this form of strategy. In social-work terms, such operations are often picturesquely referred to as 'putting out fires'; for example, investigations of prison riots, racial disturbances, and action to deal with 'hot' situations generally, would fall within this category, and perhaps be termed 'defensive strategies'. But such strategies should not happen by default, nor should staff employed mainly on other work be suddenly diverted to deal with such situations. A defensive strategy is a legitimate strategy and can be planned as such. In warfare, from enemy aircraft shot down in defensive operations much intelligence can be gained about the enemy which may be as useful as any obtained by other far more costly means.

If more forces are available, or a defensive strategy is not the only possible strategy, attention may be turned to raiding tactics. These may, of course, be small combined operations or specialist raids. The distinction between a raiding strategy and a panzer strategy is that, in a raid, the forces return to base, whereas it is hoped that a panzer attack will hold ground and then be reinforced, and the separate probes of panzer forces are dispatched with a view to their linking together in further advanced positions. Raids are one-shot operations not usually related in any overall plan to other raids, but providing information regarding specific sectors. In raids, it is usually undesirable to disturb the enemy too much or too extensively – the objectives are highly specific and limited. Raids, in social research applications, may not differ very much from trouble-shooting or defensive strategies. A raid may precede a panzer attack, and a panzer attack may, if it holds ground, be converted into a mass attack. In a panzer strategy it is essential to have sufficient forces available to be able to back up any advantage obtained. Not to do so may lose ground and prove costly. The cost of mass attacks may be very large and the cost of failure even greater.

The Maginot Line strategy has no place in modern warfare, nor has its analogous social policy – the social system is dynamic and any Maginot Line will be rapidly turned by events.

Each of these possible strategies has certain basic requirements which must be met if they are to be effective. These requirements differ according to whether the analogy of warfare strategy is applied to social action or to social research, or to a combination of attack by both research and action elements. It may be that different aspects of the military analogue apply to different aspects of social action, and, in order to make the case for a strategy more explicit and definitive, the illustrative area of social research and action regarding delinquent and criminal behaviour may be used.

The War on Crime

(a) Psychological Warfare

The activities of social workers, institutional systems, and the like in the 'attack upon crime' or other forms of social deviance are well established. But is the attack on crime analogous to a 'hot' or a 'cold' war? In general, the model of the 'hot' war seems to be the main approach to the problem of crime; but is it not possible to use propaganda, information, and communication (psychological warfare) against crime? Is it not possible to operate on 'systems' as well as on individuals?

The distinction between the two classes of warfare is evident in medical problems. In addition to treatment for ill health by individual or mass medication or inoculation, the use of the mass media of communication will be noted. For example, since it has been suggested that smoking is associated with lung cancer, attempts have been made in some countries to discourage people, particularly young people, from smoking. It may be stretching the analogy a little too far, but perhaps one function of psychological warfare is to persuade the enemy not to attack. Such an analogy is quite close to the concept of prevention of disease or, in the field of criminology, of deterrence.

(b) The Concept of Deterrence

One of the central concepts in the cold war is that of deterrence. The concept of deterrence is also important in the action taken by social agencies to prevent crime. Perhaps the concept of deterrence in international affairs is no more hotly debated than the concept of deterrence in social policy of crime control. Let us consider the latter problem. Although the concept of deterrence features very considerably in any layman's consideration of the crime problem, research workers and social action personnel working in the field of delinquency have not given this factor much consideration in recent years. Few social scientists would advocate corporal punishment for offenders through the judicial process.

Advocates of corporal punishment and other severe forms of treatment for offenders against the law quite frequently claim that such punishments are more likely than humanitarian methods to prevent the particular offender from committing further offences through fear of the consequences. This, it is claimed, is intuitively obvious. The claim has, however, been tested by various research workers and, in all known cases, it has been found that those flogged or birched are either equally or more likely to recidivate than those otherwise dealt with. The more informed among the advocates of corporal punishment at the present time place their faith in the deterrent effect *upon others* – not upon those so punished. This claim is more difficult to test. It is, however, an interesting claim in the light of the military analogue, since it proposes that the direct attack may not be effective (the person punished may not show better results), whereas the 'psychological warfare' factor (what may happen if . . .) may be effective, and justifies the use of such methods.

The term 'deterrence' is a negativistic word – it has meaning only if it is considered as an inhibitor of a tendency already existing. It proposes in itself a pressure towards something (crime or deviance) which it is the purpose of the deterrent to offset. It does not seem logical to argue that deterrence has a meaning if there is no need to deter. The average housewife does not need to be deterred from poisoning her husband, but possibly does need a deterrent to shoplifting! Perhaps the average motorist does not need a deterrent to stealing cars, but the majority seem to be in need of a deterrent to speeding or parking in unsuitable places. It seems obvious that no one piece of information or action can be regarded as a deterrent in its own right and in all circumstances. There cannot, it seems, be a general deterrent, since the pressures to be offset are not invariant. If psychiatrists are correct in suggesting that some offenders commit crimes because they want to be punished, punishment cannot, for such persons, be a deterrent. Indeed, punishment would be an incentive, and only its withholding would be likely to be a deterrent. It is not, however, essential to accept the idea of punishment-seeking behaviour in order to demonstrate the intractability of the concept of deterrence in the control of human behaviour.

Before any factor may be considered a deterrent (that is to say, likely to be effective in psychological warfare against crime) it is essential to be able to predict its effect. Further, before it is possible to predict an effect upon a human being, it must be assumed that people behave in a consistent manner, even if their behaviour may, by other frames of reference, be defined as irrational. If the behaviour of criminals or would-be criminals is unpredictable, then no action may logically be regarded as a deterrent. Even if there are only a few cases in such a category, the argument must still hold, and once the argument of limitation of deterrence is accepted, the whole concept takes a different form.

It seems reasonably safe to assume that for most serious offences the offender does not know the true probability of being caught, nor does he know the likelihood attaching to particular penalties if he were caught. The doctrine of deterrence would state that, if he knew these facts, his behaviour would be inhibited by heavy punishment. But may he not be deterred only because he has beliefs about what might happen to him which are *incorrect*? May not some people over-estimate the risk and the likely penalty, or under-estimate the gains? It is certain that people's actions are determined by what they believe to be true rather than by what is in fact true. There may be little association between fact and belief. Thus it may be possible to change behaviour in desired directions, not only by changing situations, but by changing *beliefs* about situations. In any event, it seems unprofitable to change actual situations if they are likely to be perceived as unchanged.

Perhaps the concept of deterrence has a greater utility if it is considered as a negative incentive. Although little research has been carried out into deterrence, considerable work has been done on incentives, particularly in industry. It would seem that the research findings regarding incentives may hold true at the other end of the continuum. Wilkins (1950) has shown that what is an incentive to persons of high intelligence (or higher social class) is not likely to be a very strong one to persons of low intelligence (or lower social class). This may be true also of deterrence. It has been shown that some persons seek long-term incentives, whereas others prefer short-term; it may be that deterrents that are seen as remote may apply to some people and not to others. Thus some 'psychological warfare' might be applied by means of propaganda to bring the concept of deterrence (or incentive) nearer to those it is desired to influence. This concept is not new in social medicine. Those concerned with accident prevention have specifically attempted to bring the consequences of certain actions nearer to the consciousness of those concerned. It is surprising that this class of social control mechanism has been neglected in many areas of social deviance.

Perhaps enough has been said to indicate that the analogy of 'psychological warfare' has some relevance in terms of the 'war on crime' and perhaps other areas of social action. It would seem worthy of some exploration when plans are made in connection with delinquency control and prevention measures. It may be no more than a challenging thought, but, in international strategies today, if the 'psychological' or 'cold' war operations are successful there is no need to fight a 'hot' war. A 'hot' war represents the failure of the 'cold' war methods and strategies. Perhaps if society had more knowledge of the processes of information flow, and of the relationship between information and perceptual processes in relation to individual and group decisions, such processes would afford a 'cold war' strategy as a means of dealing with problems which are now dealt with by the more costly methods of direct action.

(c) Defensive Strategies (putting out fires)
Both research and social workers tend to dislike dealing with 'panic' situations – providing information or taking action to deal with unpredicted emergencies. It may be true that all too often emergency situations arise only because of poor intelligence or inefficiency, but trouble-shooting functions may be necessary in the best-run organizations. The more efficient the administration, the less should be the effort required for such situations, since efficiency implies a lower probability of being taken by surprise. None the less, trouble-shooting is an important function, and the levels of skill required are usually as high as those required for other types of operation. In bureaucracies, particularly in governmental agencies, a large proportion of

research and social work activity tends to fall into this category. Organizations are frequently introduced to the values of research in operational problems through the use of trouble-shooting research and action teams. The prison riots in the United States of America were, perhaps, one of the main factors in establishing research in the correctional field; it began with trouble-shooting investigations.

Perhaps the main objection to such methods is that this type of work usually has to be done quickly and badly. The answer was really required yesterday, but a poor sort of answer today is better than a good answer tomorrow. Questionnaires have to be drawn up within hours, or at most days, and put into the field without pre-trials, or the social worker finds himself forced to 'deal with the symptoms' because he has no time to investigate the nature of the ailment.

In governmental agencies there are special problems related to communication systems and the mass media which are often factors in trouble-shooting and defensive strategies. An official agency which is in the public eye may not be able to acknowledge the existence of a problem, even although fully aware of it, until some symptom has become manifest. It might be that public opinion is not prepared to accept the action necessary at the time it is really required. An incident is necessary to alert the public and to have its own impact upon public opinion. Research usually requires an open diplomacy. It is not possible to do much research in the social field, and no action is possible without information regarding such research and action becoming public knowledge. Such public knowledge of research activity in a particular sector could, at times, have undesirable feedback to the problem situation itself. Research activity could spark off a delicate situation by revealing that the administration was aware of its existence. The press has a lively interest in potential trouble spots, and often a good sense as to how these are likely to blow up to headline size! A news story headed, 'THE ADMINISTRATION ARE WORRIED ABOUT THE STATE OF . . . IN . . . THEY HAVE ORDERED THEIR RESEARCH STAFF TO . . .' could raise issues which a good administration might prefer to remain dormant, at least for a time. Social research generally represents some sort of social action. If the problem is highly abstracted and dealt with quietly in a laboratory setting, the abstraction of the problem may not represent a good model of the 'real-world' problem. None the less, the use of laboratory models does not seem to have been explored sufficiently as a means of building up a body of highly abstracted general information which may be useful in emergency situations. Again, the analogy from warfare strategy seems to hold – computer simulation of different aspects of warfare is now commonplace. Computer simulation does not raise diplomatic problems as do manoeuvres or test explosions or other forms of military research. Yet such simulation provides a store of information which would be valuable in any emergency situation.

If a defensive, trouble-shooting strategy is likely to be a part of any social research or social action operation, and it usually is, it should be planned as thoroughly as any other operation. To regard research staff engaged on long-term projects as a reserve force for emergency 'fire-fighting' activities is not a satisfactory solution and can only lead to wasteful inefficiency.

(d) Panzer Research Strategy

With the reserves of manpower and facilities for research as limited as they are at the present time, the panzer strategy model has strong claims to be the optimum. The panzer model is a strategy similar to that used by the German army in the 1939–45 war which was notably successful in turning the Maginot Line. Highly mobile tank and armoured forces, each reasonably self-contained and with considerable delegated powers of freedom of action, pushed deeply into enemy territory and operated 'behind the lines'. These forces, initially independent, would join together behind the 'front' – indeed the concept of a front line became almost meaningless.

A panzer research strategy would be one which involved a large number of 'probes', perhaps small and self-contained research teams or even individuals deployed at various points (problems). Each team or person would have a limited and specific objective, but there would be a general objective underlying and integrating the individual projects. The investment in any one project might be very small, at least until it had been shown that the particular 'probe' was meeting with success and promised to 'hold ground' and to make further headway. The reasons for the success of any individual project might differ. Success might be due to a well-chosen area for attack, selected on the basis of good intelligence and some sound theoretical work, or it may be that a particular research person or team was unusually creative. The commander of a particular panzer force might not know or bother very much about the location or progress of other commanders – he had his own broadly specified task and objective, but intelligence was passed to headquarters, and, of course, considerable intelligence was gained before the panzer forces were put into operation.

Research along the lines of the 'panzer model' has certain requirements. *Figure 6* illustrates a particular case (somewhat modified)

FIGURE 6

Research strategy – panzer style

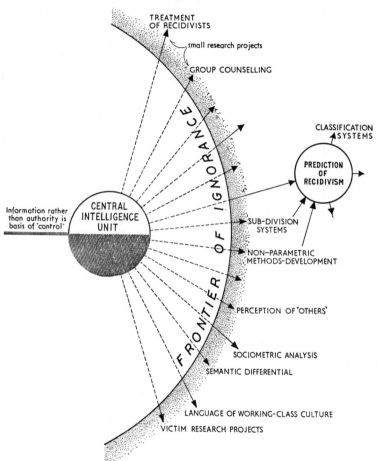

where a 'panzer model strategy' was more or less consciously applied. It will be noted that a central 'intelligence' or information unit is necessary so that each 'force' (research project team) can be kept

123

informed as necessary of the position of other forces. As with the panzer commanders, the individual research teams are permitted a large degree of autonomy. This is usually appreciated by research workers; indeed, it would be difficult to make optimum use of specialist personnel unless considerable freedom were permitted. The desire of every research worker to 'do something original' provides a self-control system that makes it unnecessary to have a central *control*, but only a central information unit; the information provides its own control through the motivation of the research personnel employed. It is only necessary to inform any prospective candidate for research funds that the area he proposes to attack is already being covered, or that something essentially similar is being carried out elsewhere, and he will quickly put forward a different proposal!

But the central intelligence unit cannot be a mere passive information-passing agency; it has to ensure that the same 'code' is being used to pass information to different 'forces'. Since the 'force' will be diversified in any criminological research activity – psychologists, sociologists, statisticians, lawyers, and many others being involved perhaps together or in different projects, the 'decoding' operation is one requiring a mixed disciplinary team at the centre.

There are, of course, dangers in adopting a 'panzer' model research strategy. In research it is often desirable to disturb the situation as little as possible. If the ongoing processes under examination are changed by reason of the research itself, there will be difficult problems in drawing valid inferences, and these are best avoided. Feedback may prejudice research or make more costly designs essential to measure the interaction effects which are generated through the impact of the project upon the situation. The more complex the effects to be isolated, the more expensive the project will be. Even the publication of interim results may lead to changes in the behaviour of those persons or processes under study. If such interaction is not noted and measured, inferences originally true may not hold when 'backing up' takes place. It may be very dangerous to fiddle with certain types of social problem. In medicine the drug-resistant strains are now carefully guarded against.

Interactions between stages of projects, between situations and research action, and the like ought always to be considered in the initial designs. Something should be known about the second step before the first is taken. It is usually possible to state the expected outcomes of research or action as a fundamental set and to attach an assessment of the probability of each. Ways of meeting the postulated different outcomes of the first set provide weighting factors in determining the desirability of the initial strategy. Such analysis might be verbalized thus, 'Suppose we obtain a significant result in favour of treatment *A* . . .' or, 'Suppose the result of this trial is inconclusive . . .' It should be possible to attach some estimated boundary conditions to statements of this kind, and then to think through 'what then . . .' questions. Where science cannot as yet proceed, intelligent human judgement has no substitute; but even subjective judgements can be guided by the rules of the scientific method.

If the answers to the 'what then . . .' types of question are noted, they may be more important to the research planning in deciding lines of action than answers to other questions which may be more obvious and more accurately framed. Failure to look one step ahead is a most common reason for very considerable waste of time, both of research staff and of the subjects who take part in the inquiries. The panzer model research strategy seems to make it somewhat easier to obtain answers to the 'what then . . .' questions than some other forms of strategy, and for this reason alone it has much to commend it.

(e) The Mass Attack

In recent years the 'mass research attack' upon specific targets has become fairly commonplace; it has characterized those areas where the public has felt particularly threatened. Research on cancer, coronary thrombosis, and juvenile delinquency are examples. In these areas public demand has generated large sums of money for research and action. Mass attacks may now produce a reasonable pay-off in the developed sciences, like the natural sciences and medicine, but strategies of this kind present many difficulties, which become almost insurmountable if the target for the attack cannot be located with any precision. Crime is not definable like cancer, and the methods proposed for action and research are of quite a different order. A few rounds of the game 'suppose . . . what then?' will reveal the nature of the difference between the different fields. Clearly, a mass attack by social action or social research cannot be made on all sectors of all problems at the same time. Even the limited field denoted by the concept of crime or delinquency involves a very large number of problem areas, many of which have not been explored. If some sectors are subjected to mass attack, others must be left uncovered. It may seem reasonable to suggest that attention should first be directed towards gaining information about the 'enemy territory' – that is, to defining in operational terms the precise nature of the problem area it is proposed to attack. Even if a mass attack is regarded as the desirable strategy, it should be directed at sectors of the problem which are most ripe for attack.

The logical basis for social action in the form of mass attacks is usually claimed to derive from the so-called theory of 'multiple causation'. Although, as appears from the discussion in Chapter 3, this theory has been shown to be inadequate, its influence on social action thinking is still considerable. The popular argument runs something like this. If crime is multi-causal (!) the only thing to do to prevent it is to saturate a particular trial area with all possible forms of social action. If only one or two provisions are made or if facilities are provided or other attempts made to remedy one or two related social ills ('causes'!), the 'target' population will avoid contact with the remedial measures and evade the new controls. If everything possible is done, something must be achieved. Attack in mass forms, and simultaneously, has been proposed upon the following areas perceived as 'causal factors' of criminal behaviour: attitudes towards school, reading ability, modification of attitudes towards authority such as the police, modification of authority roles, therapy to improve the self-image in deprived groups, instruction regarding food habits, training of character to reduce impulsive behaviour, provision of facilities for more leisure activities, provision of more opportunities for employment, provision of challenge and excitement as substitute for crime in providing 'kicks', modification of child-rearing procedures through guidance in clinics, and the like. In fact, more and more, and more intensively, everything which social workers and the social services have ever been able to attempt to provide. And all these aspects of reform, control, and advice are, it is proposed, to be vented upon a relatively small geographical area – a super-saturation mass attack!

Using the 'if . . . then' test of these proposals, we may ask (supposing that the mass attack were successful) whether there is any point in knowing that something that was done, or believed to have been done, had some effect, at some time, in some way, on some people? Do we not really need to know what had what effect and on whom, and, if possible, in what ways? Mass attacks in some fields of inquiry can answer these kinds of question, but it is doubtful if mass attacks, as at present planned, can gain even the vaguest estimates of these essential facts.

There is, of course, a further factor. The mass attack can be applied only to a geographically or otherwise limited, defined population or area. The current and proposed social action, mass attack schemes each and all attempt to raise the sights of persons living in the 'target areas' by operating upon individuals or family groups. The major approach is through the medium of social casework. Testing again by the 'if . . . then' test, let us assume that some of the people who received the treatment, or who were exposed to the new opportunities, were to improve their levels of achievement. It has been demonstrated that, in the past, the main concomitant of improvement in individual social orientation among such persons has always been their immediate desire to remove themselves from the environment which they then perceived to be undesirable to an area more in keeping with their new norms. Thus, if the projects are successful in improving the perceptions of the target population, and, particularly, if success attends the provision of opportunities in education, so that more skills are learned and a better attitude towards authority is developed, leisure pursuits become more sophisticated, and so on, the first expected result would be the removal from the district of just those people with whom the scheme had been most successful. Thus it seems probable that the target neighbourhood, as a neighbourhood, may deteriorate as a direct result of a successful social action mass attack programme! This is in accord with the general theory of deviance proposed earlier. But there are still other problems in the mass attack strategy, and further criticisms may be proferred.

The assumption underlying the mass attack is that the whole of a programme is greater than the sum of its individual parts. But may not the reverse be equally probable? Indeed there are empirical data to show that a combination of two treatments for offenders which are good treatments singly is capable of having worse results (higher recidivism rates) than either treatment separately. Some actions may be operating to cancel out, or even render negative, the results of other actions. The whole may be *less* than the sum of the parts, and certainly less than the sum of some of the parts. More of a good thing is not necessarily better!

Consider also the possibility that a particular measure may be successful in a particular area only because the positive changes in the target area are able to find the necessary conditions for fulfilment in some other areas not subject to the action. That is to say, for example, as a result of improvements in the employability of members of the target area, it may be that those in other areas at present employed but considered marginal by their employers will be replaced by the 'improved' individuals from the target area. Input and output mechanisms are not independent of each other.

The mere multiplication of individual projects is also unlikely to solve the total problem. If overall there are more persons seeking jobs than jobs available, the simplest way, and apparently a fair way, for employers to reduce the number of applicants to agree with the number of vacancies is to raise the stated levels of achievement required. Whether such levels of achievement are essential require-ments of the particular tasks may be an entirely different question.

(f) Raiding Operations

Raiding operations in warfare have various objectives, but one of the frequent purposes is to get information regarding enemy terrain and the disposition of forces. Raids are not expected to win a war, but they may make the enemy more cautious as to how he attacks. By analogy, raids in research may take the form of small-scale 'opera-tional research' designs – some social action is taken, linked with research in a specific sector and on a rather small scale. Raids are rather like panzer attacks on a small scale. Such tactics in social research have their main value in assisting the specification of the problem area (the nature of the terrain). The first problem in research is to state and define the problem! Matters relating to this activity will be explored in some detail in the next chapter, but a few notes may be appropriate here in relation to the imagery of strategy. In the war on crime, for example, it seems essential to know where the problem may be tackled most effectively with maximum chances of quick pay-off. The problem of serious crime, it may be thought trivial to remark, is more serious than that of minor crime. But if we do not know whether most serious crimes are committed by habitual offenders or whether first offenders or one-time recidivists account for the larger proportion of these events we are unlikely to be able to direct our efforts in a meaningful way. If we have no measures for assessing the seriousness of crime we are rather like an army without a technique for mapping enemy territory. But this is an almost fair assessment of the present state of ignorance.

It is true that where scientific methods are not yet available the best of human judgement must be used, but rather than making uninformed guesses it might be better to employ our best judgements in defining the probable types of terrain and then to utilize 'raids' to test these theories. Quite superficial investigation may indicate that the field of 'crime' is not one problem area but many. We may, for example, direct our attention to that sector which is identified as 'treatment' or to the sector of 'prevention'. It will be obvious that these two different territories have different structures. If we concern ourselves with the problems of treatment of offenders the boundary conditions of the problems are determined by the person to be given treatment. The individual offender will already be identified for us by the due processes of law and society. If, on the other hand, we are concerned with prevention problems these problems are not defined, nor are they definable in terms of individuals, but in terms of some cutting-point in a continuous classification of human behaviour (see p. 46). Further investigation, or even a little serious thought, will reveal that those persons admitted for treatment have varying degrees of involvement in criminal activity – some will be first offenders and others recidivists. Perhaps different strategies are indicated for these different types of problem? The integration of theory and prior research should provide guidance as to the nature of the terrain, and some indications may usually be obtained from the general social accounting data.

The nature of the terrain is, of course, not the only factor in determining an optimum strategy, we are concerned with the different types of offensive which it is possible for us to utilize. In terms of the problems of crime control and prevention, it seems desirable to inquire whether it would seem more profitable to limit our attack to:

(a) problems of prevention
(b) problems of treatment of recidivists
(c) problems of treatment of first offenders
or
(d) to try to attack on all fronts at once.

If, as has sometimes been believed, the majority of serious crimes are committed by recidivist offenders, it might be considered a good strategy to concentrate our limited forces on the problems of the treatment of recidivists (b). On the other hand, we may be impressed by arguments about the closing of the proverbial stable-door and feel inclined to concentrate our attention on prevention. It would seem to be a relatively simple matter *first* to use research to find out the relative size of the different problem areas – to ascertain something about the nature of the terrain. The choice of research and action tactics may be best facilitated by first employing some research methods. In this connection it may be well to remind ourselves that it is possible that one of the reasons why social research has so far achieved relatively little may be because it has too often attempted too much, that is, it has failed to identify and maintain solid boundary conditions around the problems with which it has been concerned.

Morale: Personnel Policy in Research and Action

Perhaps sufficient use has been made of the analogy afforded by the phrase 'war on crime'. Analogies do not often withstand heavy and detailed pressures, and this is no exception; none the less, the substance of the discussion does not depend only upon the strength of the analogy. It has been used mainly to raise challenging points for consideration rather than to suggest detailed ways and means of effecting any solution or determining the detailed plans of action. One last point, however, may be made using the model language, before noting where the analogy begins to break down.

It may be remarked that the morale of the forces used in any action depends upon the nature of the strategy employed and in turn influences the strategy. Morale in research teams is often at a very low ebb, and in many sectors of social action the mortality rate (labour turnover) is extremely high. Mortality rates and morale of troops in warfare are often related to factors in armament and training. It may be asked whether the forces of social research and action are not too frequently dispatched ill armed and not particularly well trained. Many do not seem to know how to make use of the different types of armament available, and not many of the weapons in current use have been subjected to rigorous tests of effectiveness. It seems also that highly specialized personnel are very frequently engaged on duties similar to those of service batmen for quite large proportions of their time. These factors, and perhaps others, must be related to morale.

Worst of all, hardly any of these matters have been subjected to any rigorous study. Those few studies which have been made have been limited to rather minor aspects of the research function.

Individual, Community, and System Modification Strategies

It may be an unfortunate feature of present-day research and action in the social sector that the analogy of warfare strategy should hold as well as it does. This very fact may indicate the undeveloped nature of the existing knowledge. Most social action planned to review social problems is directed towards individuals through forms of individual casework. But there are other methods, one of which fitted the analogy of 'psychological warfare', namely, the use of propaganda (or perhaps we should say information). It may be suggested that there are five levels of social action and related fields for social research:

(a) biological (individual)
(b) psychological (individual)
(c) sociological (groups)
(d) cultural (neighbourhoods, etc.)
(e) social structural (macroscopic control systems).

It is possible to carry out operations and research at each of these levels. Action taken at one level may interact with effects at a different level. The costs of operations at different levels may vary as well as the pay-off. Those operations which take the individual as the unit of action must necessarily select individuals with whom it is proposed to work. If a large proportion of the population is deviant, individual treatments would require a very large proportion of the 'non-deviant' population to be 'treaters'. It is obvious that if operations on systems can be effective they are likely to be much cheaper than other forms of operation. In the general theory of deviance a method for operating upon systems was suggested – the system might be modified to 'tolerate' (or accommodate) more deviance, particularly deviance perceived as dysfunctional. According to this theory a change in the *system* would have desirable repercussions at other levels down to the individual. Similarly, the same theory proposes that the identification of individuals may lead to their isolation, and perhaps their self-identification as deviant, so that even therapeutic treatments may have undesirable effects owing to the very fact of isolating the individual from the general social control system. But there are ways of operating on *systems*, particularly in respect of crime prevention measures.

The use of macroscopic control systems in the field of economic behaviour is well established. The use of the budget and rates of interest to modify individual economic behaviour is one example of a macroscopic control system. The provision of the no-claims bonus in motor insurance is another. Although the no-claims bonus may be prejudiced by a prosecution for careless driving, the two systems of control are operationally independent. The one is an incentive, the other a deterrent, but both are making use of the same basic *dimension*. There is no need for all controls to be negative mechanisms – not even in the control of crime. But examples of the use of macroscopic controls operating in the incentive, positive, or opportunity dimension are few; the majority of crime control systems operate on the dimension of risk. But perhaps better locks on car doors could reduce the need for more locks on prison doors! Or, to take another example, householders who spend both money and thought on making their houses more secure, and by this means reducing the opportunity structure for criminals, are doing a socially desirable thing, but at the moment there is no incentive for them to do so in any direct form; they pay the same insurance premiums as other householders who take few similar precautions or none. Or again, in the United States of America, a very large number of taxi-drivers are held up and robbed, yet in London such robberies are extremely rare. This may have something to do with the different types of criminal in the two countries (and, of course, the New York cab-driver is unique!), but may it not also have something to do with the different designs of taxi-cabs. The sliding glass partition in the London cab may be little more than a psychological barrier, but it may be just that and still be effective. There would seem to be many ways for making crime less economically attractive and ways for making it less psychologically and sociologically attractive that do not depend upon modifications of individual personality but operate upon *systems*.

It may be argued that such increase in risk or decrease in opportunity would not deter the habitual offender. This may be true, but it must be remembered that all criminals begin at some time as first offenders, and for them an increase in legitimate opportunities, a decrease in illegitimate opportunities, or a change in the risk factors may all play a part in the modification of the undesirable behaviour. For those offenders who are totally irrational there can be no case for this method of control, nor for many other current methods of control, since the concept of deterrence is meaningless also.

The Unity of Society

The analogy of war on crime should break down, because it is only when the enemies of society are perceived as outside that society that the concept of war as it has been used in this chapter has any significance. Maybe the criminal is a social misfit, but who is misfitting what? The criminal and the deviant are part of our society until we *define* them as outside it. Society is not a configuration of independent dichotomies – criminal v. law-abiding, good v. bad, truth v. falsity, black v. white, us v. them . . . The model of warfare strategy does not hold because society cannot be divided into 'friend' and 'foe'. Rather, the model of society as we can now perceive it is a matrix of n-dimensions, each of which is characterized by loop systems and interactions with other dimensions. Thus there is no 'them' and 'us' except as defined by the institutions of our society. These defining acts themselves produce informational loop systems in the total structure of society. The main way in which people get to know what sort of persons they are is through information received from other persons. The roles people play in society are conditioned by their experience, or, in terms of the information concept, by their information sets. Each person in each role functions both as a transmitter and as a receiver of information. Simply, if I am defined by society; if, that is, the information I receive from those around me conveys the message that I am perceived by them to be an artist, scientist, crook, or fanatic, this information (given that my information-receiving and decoding abilities are not specifically impaired) will influence my self-concept and the roles which I play. Information input influences information output. There is nothing new in this model – perhaps St Paul even proposed it when he remarked, 'Ye are all members one of another.' The value of the model now proposed is that the concept of information enables logical and mathematical analysis to be made, since information is measurable. Moreover, if this model is a reasonable one, it means that simple models of 'cause' and 'effect' will not be adequate to explain social phenomena. If the universe of discourse is n-dimensional, a single dimension (cause →effect) will not suffice. N-dimensional hypotheses are called for; or, in terms of warfare strategy, the nearest model to that which we now require is the 'panzer strategy' model – this at least is not inconsistent with the more complex problems which it is now possible to describe.

Perhaps it is a good thing that man – sociologically, psychologically, and biologically – is highly resistant to treatments of all kinds, and any attempts at effecting change are met with opposition. Any ends we may seek, any changes we may wish to make, will meet with resistance, and this resistance may be functional for society. The concept of 'advance' cannot be sustained in the complex n-dimensional structure of society, since there is no base-line which can be located in this hyper-space. But it may be functional that *change* should be sought, and particularly change in the directions which are perceived as 'forward'. If we believe in progress we must use all the technical assistance we can and not allow our thinking to be inhibited. By this means we may hope to make headway. But we can only hope, we cannot really know, that the ways we believe to be ahead are in fact forward of our present position. We shall not even be able to make probabilistic statements about our 'progress' unless we are prepared to check *continuously* our position according to some standards other than our own subjective judgement and personal impressions of progress. Since we subscribe to the democratic ethic, the best check on our position is afforded by the constant interchange of opinion and completely open availability to all of any facts that are known. All those concerned with the future of mankind and society are concerned with this informational set – this is the meaning of the concept of the 'open society'. If there is such a mechanism as social evolution, then the selective mechanism of that evolutionary process is communication.

As Lord Hailsham (1962) has said, 'A society must bear within itself the means of constant change, endlessly adjusting itself to the alterations of technology and education and other social changes as they endlessly occur, and automatically providing the basis for new advance. This is democracy. . . . If the evolutionary theory gives rise, as it surely should, to the doctrine of the "open society", surely we democrats are entitled to take heart from the nature of the logic and the dynamism of the technical revolution . . .'

Thus there is no 'front line'; or everything, everywhere, is front line! The situation is not static. Our models must relate to the infinite regress (or progress) of the nature of the world, and they should be derived through cooperation of all those concerned with the various aspects of change. The mechanism of society is an all-embracing network of systems and information, and if the machine is not working efficiently it is not meaningful to try to blame saboteurs! If society is in need of adjustment (and few will doubt this) the means must be found *within itself*. If such means or systems do not exist, they must be produced; and the means of their production is effective and uninhibited communication. The interdependence of social problems does not mean that the field is too complex for systematic scientific study, nor does it mean that a mass and muddled attack is to be made on all problems at once and at a superficial level. Rather, the fact of complex interdependence presents a challenge to research design and social action which cannot be avoided. Interdependence of factors in economics does not inhibit objective study. It does not follow because a problem cannot be specified by two variables – two cells in a matrix – that the problem is insoluble, or that rigorous methods must be replaced by feeling and intuition. The influence of any one cell (problem) over other cells (problem areas) will tend to fall off with distance in the same way as changes in the price of coal have different fields of economic influence from changes in the price of wheat. The interdependence of blocks of transactions can and has been studied. Econometricians have developed systems of 'input-output analysis' (matrices of interdependence of economic factors). Even the demonstration of the complexity of the problems does not mean that all simple direct methods have to be abandoned, but they have to be selected with greater care than has been exercised in general in the past. Even in economics the zero-order correlation $(a \rightarrow b)$ has some utility, but it is not confused with the concept of cause $\rightarrow$ effect. It is meaningless to study the 'causes of crime' but not useless to study problems of deviant behaviour. The larger field of reference does not indicate a need for less rigorous methods nor for 'broader-based studies' so much as a need carefully to set the boundary conditions of problems and sub-problems. The need is to be not more superficial but more systematic in the design of social research, and more 'hard-headed' in terms of social action.

In the next chapter some attempts will be made to move from considerations of a general philosophical nature to some more specific problems and to indicate some methods likely to be of value in the study of social issues in the immediate future which are consistent with the general theory of deviance and the concept of interdependence of social situations.

REFERENCES

FORTUNE MAGAZINE (1955). As quoted in Radio Broadcast talk, source unidentified.

GOFFMAN, E. (1961). *Asylums*. New York: Doubleday.

HAILSHAM, LORD [HOGG, Q.] (1962). In lecture to the Faculty of Harvard University, November 1962.

WILKINS, L. T. (1950). Incentives and the Young Worker. *Internat. J. Opinion & Attitude Res.*, vol. 4, no. 3.

CHAPTER 6

What Problems? What Priority?

GENERAL SOCIAL ACCOUNTING AND PRIORITY FOR ACTION

Problems of priority – Support for social action and research – The initial stimulus – First steps in problem-solving – First questions – An example of initial questions and some answers – How large is the problem? – Problems of general statistics – Process analysis: an example – Crime and morals, and other semi-attached concepts – Two measures are better than one – Assessment of statistical data – Relevance of mass statistical data – Classification and categorization – A classification of types of crime – Crime and indictable offences – An approach to a crime index: (a) time factors; (b) spatial factors – Static and dynamic indices – Selection of fields

More is known about ways of dealing with individual and specific problems than about the interdependence of problems or about the best ways of selecting those problems which should receive priority. Priority in research is determined, in the main, by other than research considerations. The demand for social action is pressing on all sectors – help prisoners – reduce poverty – help the elderly – stop child neglect – find a cure for the common cold – find a cure for cancer – reduce unemployment – stop industrial unrest – find out about this – find out about that – stop official interference – find out – stop asking questions – do something – cut public spending ... !

Problems of Priority

Many of these demands spring from direct personal positions, but many do not. Few people are worried about juvenile delinquency because their own children are delinquent, but because of information obtained indirectly. How good is this basis of indirect information which results in the general clamour for action? Are the problems real problems? When people read figures about 'crime', do they think of 'morals'; when people read about the number of persons passing examinations, do they equate this with some personal interpretation of the concept of education; how closely are the concepts which give rise to the demands for action related to the data which may be perceived as related to the concepts?

The many and varied social agencies can each put forward convincing cases for their action in the past and their proposed action to remedy or alleviate the sundry social ills which they perceive as their current concerns. But are the real problems addressed? Are the priorities right? What is meant by 'real' and 'right'? How can priorities be determined? Is there information to help in answering this question, or must we rely upon emotional appeals to provide the basis for selection of the problems?

Support for Social Action and Research

Some appeals for welfare activities receive public support, whereas others seem to fail to raise any substantial funds. Is charity the best way to determine the priority for social action and research? Gregory (1962) points out that 'in 1959 the National Institute for the Deaf had an income of £21,000, whereas the Royal National Institute for the Blind had £1,086,000, and in 1960–61 the National Spastics Society had £1,836,000. This, despite the fact that Helen Keller, who is both deaf and blind, says, "the problem of deafness is deeper and more complex, if not more important than that of blindness. Deafness is a much worse misfortune. For it means the loss of the most valuable stimulus – the sound of the human voice – that brings language, sets thoughts astir, and keeps us in the intellectual company of man". And Dr Johnson referred to deafness as the "most desperate of human calamities".'

It might be argued that the problem of ageing populations is more important than the problem of juvenile delinquency; that the six thousand persons, mainly elderly, who commit suicide each year in England and Wales provide an indication of a more serious problem than the rare murder, minor personal injuries, and loss of property due to juvenile offenders. But our democratic institutions have not pointed up the problems in this way, and this may be both ethically and scientifically correct. If any person thinks that an incorrect assessment has been made of the priorities he is perfectly at liberty to seek to publicize his ideas, and even to do some small-scale research with a view to influencing people to change the priorities. Such flexibility, related to efficient communication systems, is part of our general social ethic, within which administration, social action, and social research alike play their respective roles. But the democratic ethic relies upon information. If the information is not adequate or is missing, the ethic cannot be meaningfully interpreted. Perhaps we do not have sufficient of the right kind of information from which to make inferences that would lead to a satisfactory application of the general social ethic. Or perhaps the social ethic is not generally accepted, and some minorities are attempting to project their own value systems upon the general population. If the latter is the case, we do not have a democratic system but an autocratic system, benevolent though it may be. But even a benevolent (or other) autocracy needs information in order to be advised regarding the application of its values. Thus, if information is missing, it does not matter whether society is of one form or the other, either will be equally inefficient. Let us examine the problem of efficiency.

The initial stimulus for social action may be no more than the dramatic incident which affects a powerful personage; it may be the subjective summation of newspaper reports; or it may derive from the general social accounting statistics which provide data for the management of currently operating social institutions.

The Initial Stimulus

The gross general social-accounting statistics may be criticized on many grounds, but they doubtless provide the best indicators of the need for further information. But data which are valuable for pointing to the needs for further work are not adequate for other purposes. The initial stimulus for research may be unsubstantial – newspaper reports do not provide research information, but they do provide a communication system which is important in the total democratic social processes. Even the dramatic incident which afflicts some important personage in the power structure in any country may be a *legitimate* initial stimulus for research. The initial stimulus is like the scientific hypothesis – indeed, the scientific hypothesis may also be a valid initial stimulus. Hypotheses should be cheap and plentiful and their mortality rate should be high. The important factor is that information which can regulate the system is fed into the system in an optimum manner. It does not matter whether the initial stimulus to social action is the wildest of wild-cat ideas, so long as its wildness is quickly noted and research and other effort are not deployed in a wasteful way. The democratic process is provided with its own control system, if it furnishes information continuously, and this information is processed in a rational manner leading to a self-regulatory system.

Research endeavour should not be 'pre-set'. Research should provide its own feedback networks to divert the effort towards the target as more information becomes available. The 'missile' which 'self-homes' onto its target provides a very good engineering model of the sort of system which it is the intention to advocate here. At which points what kinds of information are optimal, it is, unfortunately, at this stage, impossible to say. At present these are matters for the best subjective judgement of research and administration.

It must be supposed that, at the stage when a new research action or demonstration programme is proposed, the initial information which led to the suggestion of the development provided an adequate 'trigger'. But 'trigger' information should not be expected to serve other purposes. Once the imagination has been stirred, once the hypothesis has been formed, or, to use the missile analogy again, once the process has been triggered-off, efficient self-regulating systems should, it seems, begin to be developed. Moreover, the frequency with which adjustments are made to hold the project (-ile) on the true course towards the target may be expected to relate to how far it diverts; the more frequent the adjustments, the less the divergence. But the cost of providing frequent adjustments (feedback mechanisms) and building in redirectional information signals may exceed the cost of the loss of a number of projects which crash on take-off, or pursue 'ghost' targets. No social-action-research projects have yet been costed and described in such detail that any reasonable estimates can be made of the pay-off of different types of general deployment strategy for research and action staffs and resources. This argument again emphasizes the need for a science of science. But it is not possible to wait until an optimum policy can be developed.

Policies have to be developed as the operations proceed. This may seem somewhat illogical, since, if the problems which need action can be discriminated so very simply from those which do not, why should it not be equally obvious when that social action has changed the situation needing attention to one which no longer needs attention? If problems requiring *priority of attention* can be distinguished from others not having priority by the 'feel of the situation', why cannot the same 'feel of the situation' suffice for *assessing any changes* which may occur? There would appear to be no more logic in *assuming* that the problem of concern is obvious than in later *assuming* that changes in the nature of the problem were due to the social action initiated. If one assessment can be obtained through 'obvious experience of the situation' there seems to be no rational reason why a change in the initial situation cannot be similarly assessed. There is no point in demanding rigorous assessment of social action if the social action was unnecessary in the first place!

At the present time the ratio between research and action or demonstration personnel is established by decisions made at a level far beyond that where research decisions can reach. Free and frank meaningful communication between research, administration, and social action is an essential requirement if a science is to develop to deal with problems of this nature. This requirement does not yet seem to be met in most operational situations. Nor do we know enough about communication processes as such.

Taking the situation as it is, what factors seem to characterize a rational policy for research in the social action field?

First Steps in Problem-Solving

Before a major attack is launched on any social problem, it would seem desirable to investigate whether it really exists. Suppose the field of concern is defined as juvenile delinquency; then it might seem worth while to investigate first whether juvenile delinquency was, in fact, the real problem, or whether the problem perceived as 'juvenile delinquency' would be better expressed and more open to social action if it were defined somewhat differently. Current research policy does not usually lead to such a systematic investigation of the relevance of problems, and often such a function is not regarded as appropriate for research personnel – the problem should be taken as defined for them. Moreover, it will usually be the case that the stimulus which gave rise to the setting up of the demonstration-research-action proposals is information of a kind which would not withstand critical scientific analysis. Indeed this must be so. If all the necessary information were to be available, there would be little need to investigate the problem by research methods. The very concept of a problem involves the concept of ignorance, or lack of information. It may or may not be true that juvenile delinquency is one of the outstanding social problems of the present time. None the less, the general social indicators – the social-accounting statistics, press reports, and public opinion – would appear to suggest that it is a field in which some investigation and some action should take place. It would appear that juvenile delinquency is a problem which will not cure itself in the near future, indeed all indicators point to an increase. Whether this is likely to be true immediately poses a problem of measurement.

It is, of course, obvious for those who favour measurement that measurement is necessary at all levels of discussion, whether for assessments of changes or for assessments of priorities. Measurement of juvenile delinquency is a complex problem, but it seems reasonable to conclude that effort devoted to attempts to assess the problem is in accord with rational democratic processes. The public are worried about juvenile delinquency – or whatever it is that they perceive within this classification. If their views are distorted, they are likely to remain distorted until some work has been carried out; if their views are sustained, then also, action is necessary. It is true that social research and action devoted to this problem will divert resources from other fields of social research and social work. The most that research methodology can assure is that the diversion, if it seems unprofitable, can be re-routed quickly. *It is necessary to build conditions for change into research designs* if they are to be most economically related to the problems of the real world.

First Questions

It would appear that the questions which need answering at the early stages of research planning are best answered by more abstract questions than the problem itself may suggest. If the problem exists, will it exist in the same way and to the same extent in the foreseeable future? Is the intensity of the problem likely to increase or diminish? Particularly, is the real problem the problem as defined, or merely some obvious part of it? If it is only a part, with what parts should action proceed? To answer these questions pilot projects, concentrating on describing the *nature* of the problems, seem to be called for. It may, of course, be possible to make use of reported research of other investigators, but if such other work exists it should be brought into formal consideration of the proposed demonstration-action-research proposals under review.

It is not possible to compare two or more different social problems and to assess their merits for social-research investment, unless each single problem area is assessed in similar terms; comparison assumes similar terms. Whenever comparisons are made, the terms in which they are made are taken as equal, although this may frequently not be made explicit. The implicit similarity of terms can often be a useful concept for the basis for research methodology. Is the problem as such something which it is required that something should be done to modify, or is it only the side-effects of the problem that are disturbing? Is it the actual cases or their side-effects that need attention, and is the only way of dealing with the side-effects to deal with the basic problem itself? Is real action necessary, or will a placebo suffice, or even be more efficient, to achieve the objective? How much of the problem of crime and juvenile delinquency is a serious problem, and how much is a side-effect of publicity? If the public are continuously told that 'crime is going up' it is likely that they will become anxious in terms of *what they perceive as crime*; but what they perceive as crime may be quite different from what crime in fact represents. The mere information set – 'crime is going up' – might lead to the public being more suspicious of actions and persons that do not justify anxiety, and such suspicion could lead to further alienation of people who are merely 'different' in a harmless way, and turn into a self-fulfilling prophecy.

An Example of Initial Questions and Some Answers

It would seem to be a simple matter to say how much crime there was during a particular period in a particular jurisdiction or, at least, it should be possible to say how many crimes were committed. Many people have asked such questions and have usually been given some answers. In most Western democratic countries, at the appropriate season of the year, the newspapers record in their headlines that 'crime has gone up', or, much more rarely, 'crime has decreased' during the year. It would be very interesting to find out exactly what the average reader understands by such news items. It may be assumed that the average layman, reading of a 'serious increase in crime', rests a little less easily at night, and looks upon persons who are not behaving in the manner he would predict with more suspicion. In many cases it would seem that the concept generated is as though a summation sign (Σ) had been placed in front of the headlines covering stories of crime that had been read in the same paper during the year. Few will realize that the general statistical data giving rise to the general concept of the 'crime rate' and to the news headlines involve technical definitions which may not be similar to those underlying the layman's views of crime (see Chapter 4).

The 'crime rate' in different countries is derived from different types of sources. In England and Wales the figures usually quoted as 'crime rates' or more frequently as 'crimes known to the police' are 'indictable offences known to the police'. In other countries the 'crime rate' may relate to 'arrests' or to persons dealt with at different stages in the various courts or other bodies concerned with the disposal of offenders. It will be obvious that figures relating to arrests or to disposals of persons do not relate to 'crimes'.

It has been suggested by some authorities that the nearer the figures are to the origin of the act defined as a crime, the more reliable are they likely to be as measures of crime. Hence it is the figures for 'crimes known to the police' which are usually believed to give the best picture of the crime situation. But let us examine the matter a little more closely.

Figures relating to crime and criminals are static representations of a situation which is essentially dynamic. The situation is changing continuously, right from the moment that the offender first conceives of the criminal act and his 'normal' actions come to be modified towards this end, through to the time when he is past all the judicial processes and has been placed in a correctional establishment or handed over to some other treatment authority considered to be appropriate. In theory it should be possible to insert a 'counting mechanism' at almost any point in this time-series of events and to produce data. But it is clear that the nature of the data collected will differ and need different interpretations according to the point at which the counting mechanism was inserted into the continuum. The situation is even more complex than this.

How Large is the Problem?

Many criminologists have referred to the 'dark figure' of crime. The general definition of this term relates to the difference between the figures for 'crimes known to the police' and the number of 'crimes cleared up'. This gap is, of course, a dark figure – but at least it is possible to record some figure. Whether the recording of an apparently specific figure is anything more than misleading will depend on many other factors, but its value will always be doubtful. It will be clear that 'crimes known to the police' do not become known to them by some direct process of 'knowing'. No published figures seem to be available indicating the means by which the police do in fact get to 'know' about 'crimes'. It may be supposed that the great majority of 'crimes known to the police' are known to them because they were reported by some lay person, normally the victim who desired police action on his behalf. But the reports of the victims are 'complaints', not necessarily 'crimes'. A person might well report a suspicious loss of, say, a wallet on a suburban train. But how certain must he be that he had his pocket picked before it should be noted as a 'crime' rather than a 'loss'? How many reports of losses are, in fact, 'crimes', and, conversely, how many reports of 'crimes' are losses, is something we shall never really know. Perhaps the marginal cases are small in proportion to the total number of complaints which are honestly believed by the reporters to be crimes. Before an incident can become a 'crime known to the police' it must be defined by a layman, normally the victim, as 'something-that-the-police-ought-to-do-something-about'. In terms of the theory of normality, the incident is perceived to lie at a given value of $x\sigma$ from the usual experiences of the reporter. Whether this something-that-the-police-ought-to-do-something-about is a crime or not is a technical issue about which the layman will almost certainly be uninformed. Similarly there are 'crimes' which the victims do *not* define as something-that-the-police-ought-to-do-something-about, and hence the police do not get to know about them.

Martin (1962), basing his remarks on a sample survey of employers, notes, 'It would be easy for the great majority of employees to enrich themselves at their employer's expense. . . . It is well known that the taking of these opportunities on a large scale is likely to be regarded as morally wrong, and to be detected by auditing and other methods of control. The man who works on a really large scale and is caught knows full well that his acts are criminal, and that he is risking imprisonment. Equally it is well known that in many jobs employees are, by custom of the trade or tradition of the firm, allowed either to take materials etc. for themselves, or to use the firm's resources for their own benefit. These are things not detectable by audit largely because the expense of recording detailed information would exceed the cost and services consumed in this way.' Martin quotes one employer who does not seem atypical, 'The building industry always accepts that no man ever pays for nails, screws, or firewood, but if he took something bigger it would be different'. The value of the stolen goods seems to be the general determining factor, although the type of industry is also important. Another employer also quoted by Martin, said, 'Something worth £1 would be pilfering, something worth £25 would be a more serious theft, but we could not say exactly where the line of demarcation would come between the two.' (Note, in his definition of pilfering, Martin made it clear that this was *not* something-that-the-police-ought-to-do-something-about.) There would appear to be clear distinctions made by most members of the lay public between what is morally wrong and what is 'crime'. Yet, for offences against property, the legal definition of 'crime' is often more strict than the general concept of even minor morally deviant acts.

It may be taken as common practice, except perhaps in banks and financial houses, for a certain level of theft to be regarded as a normal hazard of business, and to write off a proportion of the turnover to unaccountable losses as an 'on-cost' rather than to take measures to reduce the incidence of minor thefts. Indeed, in almost all business enterprises it is extremely difficult and often impossible to separate honest inefficiency from efficient dishonesty, and in most Western societies, inefficiency is not (yet!) defined as a crime, nor even as something-that-the-police-should-do-something-about.

All incidents which do in fact become known to the police because someone has defined them as requiring police action pass through a kind of filtering system. The police must be reasonably certain that the incident complained of actually took place, and that, if it took place, it would be regarded as an 'indictable offence' should an offender subsequently be apprehended. In England and Wales, and in most other countries, it is only the incidents which are regarded as 'indictable offences' which are recorded as 'crimes known to the police'; indeed, the phrase 'crimes known to the police' is not the appropriate technical term – it should be 'indictable offences known to the police'. The cutting-point between indictable and non-indictable offences bears some relationship to what the average layman would regard as the distinction between serious and trivial offences, but this is not a very close relationship. As Lodge (1953), discussing criminal statistics before the Royal Statistical Society, notes, 'only large changes or persistent trends can be relied on with any degree of safety to have a cause which is worth while to investigate. There should be borne in mind the possibility of factors such as improved police methods, greater readiness of the public to report the offence, a court decision affecting the name given to an offence, or other such changes.'

The situation in the case of figures relating to crime may not be very different from the situation regarding figures relating to many other social indices which are used from time to time in the evaluation of social policy. As Huff (1955) points out in his humorous textbook, *How to Lie with Statistics*, 'averages and relationships, trends and graphs are not always what they seem. There may be more than meets the eye, or there may be a great deal less.' Huff records that the official figures for encephalitis in the Central Valley of California in 1952 showed triple the figures for the worst previous year. 'Many alarmed residents,' he says, 'shipped their children away, but when the reckoning was in, there had been no increase in deaths from sleeping sickness. What had happened was that the State and Federal health people had come in great numbers to tackle a long standing problem, and as a result of their efforts a great many low grade cases were recorded that in other years would have been overlooked, possibly not even recognised.' Thus the situation regarding health measurement and the situation regarding the measurement of crime have similar problems and difficulties.

Problems of General Statistics

It is often claimed that statistics are misleading, or that figures can be found to support any argument. It is true that figures can be misleading, but more often the figures are correct enough, it is their use which is misleading. The statistical data which are open to criticism, in that they do not measure 'health' or 'crime' or other important social factors, are normally derived from the administrative processes of provisioning of institutions, cost accounting, staff budgeting, and related matters. For the purposes for which the initial data are collected, they are doubtless adequate. The trouble occurs when these data are made to serve other functions. Some problems also arise because, while these data are usually termed statistics, statisticians have concerned themselves less and less with problems in this field and have become more and more interested in experimental designs and in the techniques of sampling and problems of inference. There are few areas where thorough studies of user requirements of statistical data have been made. There has been a tendency to make the best use possible of available data, and this has often resulted in the use of what Huff calls the 'semi-attached' figure; a device which he commends to those who have a desire to 'lie with the apparent support of statistics'.

Of course, statistics can be erroneous, and there are different types of error which may occur and which it is important to distinguish.

146

Statistics may, at times, claim to represent situations which they do not adequately describe because of *arithmetical* errors, but this type of error is seldom of any real significance. There are many more types of error or bias which will be noted later in this chapter. There is no reason why, say, the number of persons disposed of by particular courts in a jurisdiction area should not represent accurately the number of persons so dealt with. Clearly, however, the number of persons does not represent the number of crimes, nor is it representative of the number of criminals. Although there cannot be a 'criminal' without a 'crime', there can be crimes without criminals. Some persons may have passed through the court machinery on more than one occasion during the period. The figures for 'disposals' do not refer to 'persons' in the usually accepted meaning of the term, although the tables may be headed with the term 'persons disposed of'. The number of juvenile delinquents in a particular area is not measured by the number of juveniles found guilty in any one year by an appropriately constituted authority. Persons and person/ passages are different concepts. If, for example, a juvenile delinquent is defined as a person under eighteen years of age who has at some time previously been found guilty of an indictable offence, the proportion of the population in an area having had this experience may well be between five and ten times the annual court figures. But this is an inference based on the number of persons who appear in court for the first time compared with those who have appeared previously.

Lord Kelvin is often credited with remarking, 'When you can measure what you are speaking about and express it in numbers you know something about it, but when you cannot measure it, when you cannot express it in numbers, your knowledge is of a meagre and unsatisfactory kind.' The problem of *validity* – how closely do the figures relate to the 'thing we are talking about' must be separated from the problem of *reliability* – how accurate are the figures themselves. The numbers of persons in hospitals, in mental or penal institutions on any particular day can, doubtless, be accurately counted, although there may be some difficulties in defining 'hospital' or 'institution', but this accuracy does not help if we wish to talk about the numbers of persons sick, mentally ill, or criminal. These figures represent such levels and types of sickness or crime as, *in relation to the social structure of the time* and its interrelation with other personality factors, have resulted in institutionalization.

147

Process Analysis: An Example

When persons are dealt with by some administrative process resulting in a specific movement, there is no reason to suspect the accuracy of the figures in terms of what they claim to be, if the machinery for collecting the data is efficient. When, however, the factor being measured is a continuum, like health, mental state, or crime, much will depend on the cutting-point of the underlying distribution. Cutting-points cannot be defined so precisely that different individuals who may be responsible for the initial classification into categories may not perceive the same situations in different ways; neither does a constant definition ensure that the same situations are not perceived differently at different times. Words change their meanings by use.

Interest in the concepts of crime, ill health, mental state, and similar continua does not usually centre on the abstract concept and its cutting-points; these subjects are interesting and important because they affect people. It would seem that the ways in which people are affected provide a better basis for statistical data than definitions relating to abstract concepts. The process of deterioration from health to ill health, or from law-abiding behaviour to criminal activity, is a dynamic process involving various stages. The victim of an offence may report it to the police, the person who is in failing health may seek medical advice, the crime may or may not be detected, the person may or may not be arrested, the police may or may not decide to prosecute, and so on. At all these points decisions are made *regarding* people, *by* people in authority, *resulting* in an action which is describable and which takes into account preceding known facts. Most of these points refer to decisions resulting in the diversion of the individual subject (criminal, suspect, sick person) from one track of the process to another within whatever system is concerned. These points of decision may thus be looked upon as 'gates', and these 'gates' may be given some sort of counting mechanism. In any consideration of statistical data relating to human, or even other, dynamic systems, it is convenient to trace these points by means of an analysis of the process. An abbreviated example relating to the concept of crime and criminal behaviour is given as *Figure 7*. It will be apparent that different statistical data which are often loosely said to relate to the concept of 'crime' in fact relate to figures from counting mechanisms on different 'gates' in the system. If information is available regarding the number of 'gate-passages'

148

FIGURE 7

An abbreviated flow chart showing 'gates'

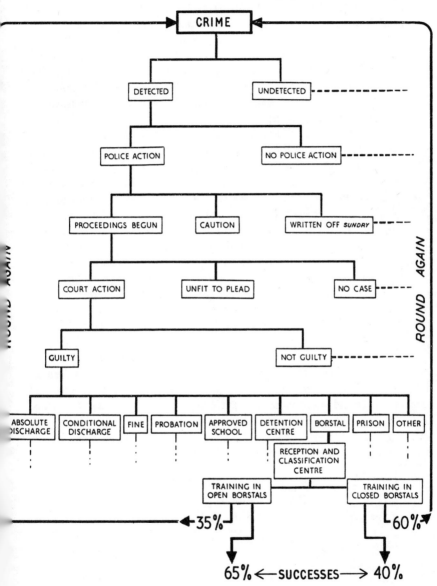

through any gate within an appropriate system, useful information is available about *the system*. The relationship between the statistical data obtained from the 'gate' counting mechanisms (i.e. where individuals are diverted from one track to another) and the abstract concepts is not easy to determine. None the less, it might be considered that where the main purpose of the data is to facilitate decisions about people, data relating to decisions about people should be the more relevant. The 'gate' system and the 'decisions' systems are directly related, and it will be necessary to return to the concept of decision processes again later.

Statistical data obtained from counting mechanisms placed on 'gates' relate to decisions, and there is no reason why such data should not always be *reliable*. There is no reason why the figures should not record the process accurately. In this connection it is interesting to note that the Criminal Justice Act, 1948, section 77 (i)(b) for England and Wales, gave the Secretary of State the authority to incur expenditure 'in the conduct of research into the causes of delinquency and the treatment of offenders and matters connected therewith'. The wording of this section of the Act is interesting. It separates the concept of the 'causes of crime' from the 'treatment of offenders'. The problem of the 'causes of crime' is a very large, perhaps unlimited problem. The treatment of offenders, although complex, has at least the limitation that an offender has been identified by some 'due process' (i.e. a gate has been involved). The distinction between research that is limited to persons and that which is concerned with broad and general concepts is important. Data relating to persons and their movements through the decision networks of systems can be accurately determined; it is a matter only of technical efficiency. For what purposes it is *valid* to use these decision-gate counts depends upon the purpose for which they are used. Perhaps one example may be given of misuse by means of the semi-attached figure.

Crime and Morals, and Other Semi-Attached Concepts

It is often argued that the figures showing an increase in crime indicate a fall in the moral standards of the country. Alternatively, it is often claimed that the main 'cause' of the crime wave is a drop in the moral values of a society. If this type of argument is not circular (i.e. crime is *defined* as the best indicator of moral values) it might be equally true if it were to be inverted! That is to say, any increase in reported crime is an indication that our moral values have improved! The reasoning may be something like the following: It is known that 'crimes known to the police' do not include a large proportion of all crimes committed. In particular there are many thousands of incidents of shop-lifting and larceny, which are certainly 'crimes', but which are not defined by the victim as something-that-the-police-ought-to-do-something-about, and hence do not appear in the crimes-known figures. If the number of such incidents remains constant, but the victims come to require a higher standard of conduct, the number of reported incidents may be expected to increase. In general, it is possible to argue that if our moral standards improve – that is to say, we become more conforming and require more legally correct behaviour, the democratic definition of crime will change. In terms of the model used earlier, the line · — · in *Figure 1* (p. 46) will move to the right, nearer to the legal definitions, and will include very many more persons and incidents, because the majority of definitions and criminal incidents are cut off by the democratic definition as it appears at present. The type of curve and its location in the defined space need not change, but the improvement in moral values may mean that more incidents will be defined as 'criminal', that is, as something-that-the-police-should-do-something-about. If, then, we are talking about moral issues, the best we can decide is that crime figures have no meaning. The crime rate may increase or decrease independently of the moral standards of a country.

This is a very similar issue to that discussed by Huff in regard to encephalitis in California. It is probable that the 'health' of California was 'better' when more cases were recorded than previously. In the problem of administrative decisions and research concerning health, the figures often used relate to mortality. How can death be a measure of health? There are very few problems where the semi-attached figure of mortality may be used to provide valid guidance for problems of health. The nature and distribution of diseases which people suffer from and about which they seek the advice of their general practitioner in medicine are quite different from the distribution of causes of death. It is true that the general practitioner should be able to distinguish the serious from the non-serious illness, but he will seldom treat the former.

Two Measures are Better than One

Where individual figures can be misleading, it is often possible to use some configuration of more than one set of data to derive figures which give a more meaningful measure. So far as the problem of measuring crime is concerned, the preceding discussion indicates a method which may assist in some types of problem. If we may postulate a continuous distribution of events from which the 'gate' systems cut off varying proportions, some assessment of the working of the 'gate' system, taken into account with the numbers passing through the various gates, may give a reasonably good index. Specifically, if public opinion is changing, so that the democratic definition of a crime or of an event which-the-police-ought-to-do-something-about is varying, it should be possible to get assessments of the direction and nature of the variation in 'democratic definitions' by means of population sample surveys. Changes in public attitudes towards the police, or changes in the attitudes of the police towards the public, may be related to the ways in which different or similar events are perceived. If similar events are perceived differently it is unlikely that definitions will be applied in exactly the same ways, even although the wording of the definitions may not be changed. It would seem to be possible to relate:

(a) changes in *reporting* behaviour
(b) changes in *reported* behaviour

on the part of both the police and the public, and this relationship could, it seems, provide a better measure than either singly of what is usually understood to be 'crime'. Each incident would need to be traced from the 'complaint' (democratic definition) through the official (legal) definition to the end outcome. Each filtering process would need to have an independent estimate made of its effects, before its results could be related to the concept of 'crime'. The first filter would doubtless relate to events perceived by the public as not worth notifying to the police, the second filter to events which are notified, but which do not fit the legal classifications. In a similar way, in the field of public health, studies by means of sample surveys covering complaints of sickness serve a different and complementary purpose to studies of mortality, hospitalization, or medical treatment.

Assessment of Statistical Data

Perhaps the main general problem encountered in social-accounting statistics relating to human behaviour, and particularly deviant human behaviour, is the essentially static picture presented by such data. Although time-series of data are frequently produced, the definitions

152

which serve as the basis for the categorization are verbal, and even if these definitions remain unchanged, the ways in which the words are interpreted at different times, or are perceived by those responsible in the initial stages for data collection, may change. What is regarded as crime today may not be regarded as crime tomorrow, what is regarded as a reasonable level of expected health today may be regarded as below par at some time in the future; the level of literacy which is required of a citizen to function effectively in the society of today may well be inadequate in the society of tomorrow.

The measurements with which we are concerned in descriptions of human behaviour cannot be recorded in terms of ratio scales like weight and height or distance. The main types of datum with which the social administrator and social research worker are alike concerned may be considered mainly to fall into the following three groups:

CLASSIFICATIONS. Data collected under this heading are presented as frequency counts. The numbers of persons married or single, the numbers of children who truant from school, the numbers of offenders guilty of different types of offence and received into penal establishments, and the like, fall into this category.

ORDINAL SCALES. These relate to categories of data which may be placed in some specific 'order'. Persons may be ranked in order of height rather than have their height measured; crime might be ranked in order of 'seriousness'; teachers might place students in order of 'merit'.

INTERVAL SCALES. In this category fall the majority of standardized intelligence tests. Such scales present some special difficulties owing to the process of establishing 'norms' (see Chapter 8).

The power of these different types of measurement varies and the techniques used in the analyses of the different kinds of datum must also be appropriate to the type. The different types must always be distinguished. There is no reason why any type of datum should not provide some valuable information. How much value depends both on the type of measurement and on the ways in which it is obtained. Very accurate data may have a quite negative value if they are used inappropriately, whereas poor estimates which are appropriate may greatly assist with the task. Frequently some quite inaccurate data today are worth more in terms of the decisions which have to be made than perfectly accurate data later. A census, even if completely accurately taken, published a year from the event may not reflect the current situation as well as a sample inquiry of more recent date. Data, counts, or measurements as such have no value. Value can be imputed only in terms of utility.

Since the collection and analysis of statistical data are highly specialized functions, those who have not had years of experience may be reluctant to trust even figures which are reliable and useful, and the danger of making use of figures which are not sound may be considerable. It is possible to set forth some pointers which may serve as a check-list for testing the reliability and validity of data collected by either sample or census. Whether the information relates directly to the problem at issue, or whether it is merely semi-attached to it, is a matter of extreme importance which only the user can decide. Without doubt, the appropriateness of the information for the purpose is the first question to be settled. If data are inappropriate it does not matter how accurate or inaccurate they might be.

Many clues as to the reliability of the data collected by any agency may be obtained from a study of the manner of the reporting. There are certain standards of conduct and honesty of reporting which, if not satisfied, throw some doubt upon other aspects of the data. Standards vary from agency to agency, depending upon the type of work to which they are most accustomed. No firm requirements can be laid down without knowledge of the exact nature of the data and the organizations concerned, but the following questions will, in general, have obvious answers.[1]

    (a) Does the report include:
        (i) full details of the agency?
        (ii) date and period of the data collection?
        (iii) details of the method of data collection?
        (iv) area or region covered?
        (v) details of method of sampling?
        (v) full copy of original documents – list of questions used, notes for investigators, etc.?
    (b) Are tables presented so that the actual numbers (as well as percentages or the like) of observations can be noted?
    (c) Are subjective findings distinguished from the more objective?
    (d) Are 'no response', 'no reply', 'not at home', and other important categories separated?

[1] See more detailed check-list in Chapter 9.

No complete check-list of items which it might be useful to consider in evaluating the efficiency or honesty of a data-collecting agency or system can be drawn up. Not all the items given above are required to be satisfactorily met in all cases before reasonable reliance can be placed on the figures. Sometimes even the most reliable of agencies produce data with extremely large errors; censuses can be far less accurate than samples covering only a small fraction of the total population. The size of a census operation can quite often mean that teams of workers are drawn together for short periods of time, and the supervision ratios will tend to be low.

Under the headline MISSING MILLION TRACED, *The Times* of 8 March 1949 records that when the new National Health Insurance Scheme was put into operation in Great Britain, the 'working population' increased three million over the previous figures, and 'included in this figure is the "missing million" – a section of the population which the statisticians have for years been unable to trace but which has now mysteriously reappeared'. Since the total working population was twenty-three million, the missing-million error represents an error of almost 5 per cent, or far greater than the standard error of a sample of only 2,000 persons of the total British population! Sampling errors, if the sample is efficiently prepared, are no longer any serious consideration; far greater errors can occur from other factors which are common to census and sample; indeed, some types of error may be more likely in a total census. Of course, a sample covering Great Britain will not provide figures which are accurate for a small town, but they can be adequate for any estimates required for the whole country. A sample based on any small town would provide data for that small town – sampling techniques can be tailored to the problem and have the merit of being cheaper.

It is surprising that the use of sampling techniques has not been fully realized in many administrations. It is extremely difficult for a non-technical person to realize that a very small proportion of the population can yield figures which are more reliable than a total count. This is one of the facts of mathematics which is not intuitively recognizable, even given a very high general intelligence. Nor is the mathematical fact that, in most cases, it is not the proportion of the population which is included in the sample which determines the sampling efficiency, but the absolute size of the sample. Nearly all questions addressed to sampling statisticians regarding the size of the sample required begin, 'What proportion . . . ?' It seems intuitively that a sampled proportion of, say, one in a hundred must be twice as good as, say, one in two hundred. The fact that when the sample is small in proportion to the total population, the proportion makes so little difference that it is ignored (the population from which the sample is drawn is taken to be infinity) seems totally unreasonable!

There are facets of statistical data evaluation where the specialist must be trusted, and there are other facets where the user interest is supreme. The best evaluation can be secured only when competent persons who can respect and trust each other are prepared to co-operate completely in the common task.

Unfortunately the purposes for which many mass statistical data are collected seem to have become lost in antiquity! In days gone by, the philosophy underlying much statistical data collection was that if people only knew what was happening they would know what to do about it; now we are not so sure that we know what we ought to do. A change in the needs that mass data are supposed to serve should mean a change in the nature of the information supplied. The collection of data in past times was closely associated with specific research investigations and with problems of management. Although the needs of management are still met, the linkage with research has become more remote with the development of sampling techniques. It is no longer necessary to study a whole town or to include information in a census inquiry to meet research needs, and the research workers have tended to lose interest in mass data. This has not been any loss to the research workers, but it has resulted in a loss to those who do not have access to research material and who tend to rely upon general statistics. Data obtained as the result of *ad hoc* research investigations should be considered in terms of their implications for modifications of the mass statistical returns. The purpose served by mass data should be continuously reviewed. If money is spent on data collection it should at least serve its purpose. Continuity of series is not meaningful if the series do not now throw light on current problems in the best possible way.

The connection between mass general statistical data and research results has been fairly closely maintained in the field of economics, but little of the work of social scientists concerned with human behaviour in its other aspects can be traced in the published statistical tables of many administrative departments in the majority of countries. Some have done well in this regard, but all could do better by encouraging more liaison between the research workers and the producers of mass data, and between the producers and the consumers of information.

Relevance of Mass Statistical Data

Perhaps the main question which should be asked about any statistical data is whether they represent the particular concept about which information is sought. The definitions and the application of the definitions must be studied, but it should also be noted that statistics add together items which differ in greater or lesser degrees in different ways. Some techniques are available for examining the systems of classification so that the data themselves decide the best summation.

Classification and Categorization

No problems would be solved if the full individual details of every case involving a social problem were to be collected and presented to social administrators. No decisions could be made if it were necessary to go into all the details. Classification and summary are essential. Statistical data provide such summaries, and these summaries, if they are appropriate, assist the decision-making processes. But all classifications have an inherent danger of obscuring the factors that are important. If like is added together with unlike, the total will not be meaningful. Techniques are available for assisting with problems of classification, and some notes on these, together with some examples, may serve to indicate the kinds of result that are possible with some of the more recent statistical techniques.

An example may be given from age-grouping of juvenile offenders. Crime rates vary over time and from age-group to age-group. In criminal statistics and in research designs generally, it is often necessary to combine age-groups of offenders, either because the numbers in single age years are too small for research purposes, or to save space in publications. Age-groupings are normally made up from single years of age in accordance with some theory or to accord with legal definitions. It is possible to use the data themselves to suggest age-groupings which are most homogeneous. Using data from the Criminal Statistics for England and Wales from 1945 to 1962 concerning male offenders dealt with before the courts, it is possible to describe the similarity between the crime patterns for each year of age (8–20) by the correlation coefficient. The correlation coefficient would take the value $1\cdot0$ if the two series were exactly similar and $-1\cdot0$ if they were in inverse association. If the crime pattern, as

157

TABLE 3

Correlations between age incidence of findings of guilt by juvenile courts for young offenders males in England and Wales in the period 1945–1962

	9	10	11	12	13	14	15	16	17	18	19	20
8	·97	·93	·85	·77	·50	·58	·29	·17	−·59	−·36	−·32	−·42
9		·97	·90	·82	·56	·15	·30	·12	−·91	−·39	−·36	−·43
10			·93	·86	·63	·25	·34	·12	−·68	−·40	−·36	−·37
11				·96	·82	·48	·57	·32	·16	−·12	−·15	−·13
12					·93	·64	·60	·30	·20	−·38	−·95	−·14
13						·86	·66	·30	·30	·16	·71	·22
14							·49	·11	·22	·31	·18	·44
15								·87	·83	·67	·66	·55
16									·94	·78	79	·60
17										·87	·86	·72
18											·94	·87
19												·88

TABLE 4

Squares of the correlation coefficients given in Table 3

	9	10	11	12	13	14	15	16	17	18	19	20
8	·94	·86	·72	·59	·25	·34	·08	·03	(−)·35	(−)·13	(−)·10	(−)·18
9	9	·94	·81	·67	·31	·02	·09	·01	(−)·83	(−)·15	(−)·13	(−)·18
10		10	·86	·74	·40	·06	·12	·01	(−)·46	(−)·16	(−)·13	(−)·14
11			11	·92	·67	·23	·32	·10	·03	(−)·01	(−)·02	(−)·02
12				12	·86	·41	·36	·09	·04	(−)·14	(−)·90	(−)·02
13					13	·74	·44	·09	·09	·03	·50	·05
14						14	·24	·01	·05	·10	·03	·19
15							15	·76	·69	·45	·44	·30
16								16	·88	·61	·62	·36
17									17	·76	·74	·52
18										18	·88	·76
19											19	·77

reflected in the persons dealt with by the courts, was exactly the same for, say, 8-year-old offenders and 9-year-old offenders over the whole period 1945–1962, the coefficient would be 1·0. If there was no association between the two patterns, the coefficient would be 0·0. Thus values between 1·0 and −1·0 represent the degree of similarity and dissimilarity between different ages in the crime pattern over time. As might be expected, adjacent ages show similar trends – that is to say, ages 8 and 9, ages 10 and 11, and so on reveal similar variations over time. The correlation coefficient found between the pattern at age 8 and that at age 9 was 0·97. But there is one important exception to the general rule that adjacent age-groups tend to be highly correlated. All the coefficients for adjacent ages are above 0·85 except that between the ages of 14 and 15 years for which the coefficient drops to 0·49. The age 14 is associated with the last year of full-time education for the majority of English boys. It is also the peak age for offenders found guilty of indictable offences.[1] In order to show the degree of association between each year of age and every other year, a triangular table may be used, as given as *Table 3*.

This table uses the conventional correlation coefficient, but it is convenient to think of the *square* of the coefficient as giving the percentage of the *variation* in one series which can be predicted from the other. The squares of the coefficients are accordingly given in *Table 4*. It will be immediately obvious from these tables that a knowledge of juvenile crime rates gives no indication of the pattern of adolescent crime rates; indeed there is a tendency for the later teen-age crime rates to be inversely correlated with juvenile crime rates.

The use of correlation coefficients or the square of the coefficients is helpful in suggesting the separate ages which are most similar and dissimilar, and in indicating ways of age-grouping which do least violence to the data. For example, if the *row* relating to 14 years of age (centre of tables) is considered, it will be seen that all coefficients are very small, whereas the *column* (rising above the centre of tables) shows generally higher figures. This means that 14-year-old offenders show a crime-rate pattern in the post-war years which is more similar to that shown by those *younger* than themselves. It is only a slight step from this to proposing groupings of ages which maximize the

[1] It is interesting to note, however, that it is the last year of full-time schooling which is associated with the peak age for adjudicated juvenile delinquency. The school-leaving age was raised in 1948, and prior to that year, the peak age for delinquency was also one year earlier. No explanation of this change in the peak age has been found.

similarities of the crime-rate trends for the ages so grouped. Foɪ example, if the ages 8, 9, 10, and 11 are grouped, the smallest correlation involved is that between 8 and 11, but this is still large (0·85); indeed the ages 8, 9, 10, 11, and 12 could be combined with the smallest coefficient (8–12) still remaining fairly large (0·77). The table may be examined in this way for all ages and all possible groupings and the best agreement (subject to the number of categories needed) can be selected. It appears that the main feature of the tables is the sudden drop in the correlation between contiguous ages (diagonal of tables) between 14 and 15 years of age. Clearly, it may be argued that these data suggest that 14-year-old offenders should not be grouped in statistical tables with 15-year-old offenders, but 13-year-old offenders might be grouped with 14-year-olds because the patterns in the variations in the crime rates are similar.

Whether groupings derived in this way for the particular purposes of statistical aggregates have any meaning in terms of other similarities which might be valid for physical groupings in training institutions is, of course, unknown. It might, however, be thought probable that where crime patterns are similar, similar treatments might be indicated. Optimum groupings in this way are obtained by considering the mean square of the correlation coefficients for the groups and the minimum value of any one coefficient; both should be as large as possible. If four categories are required to divide the interval 8–20 years of age, the best groupings seem to be 8–12; 13–14; 15–17; 18–20. These groupings are compared with similar but less homogeneous groupings below.

Best groupings	Mean	Min.	Example of different groupings	Mean	Min.
8–12	·81	·59	8–11	·86	·72
13–14	·74	·74	12–14	·67	·41
15–17	·78	·69	15–16	·76	·76
18–20	·80	·76	17–20	·74	·51
Mean	·78	·67	Mean	·76	·60

Somewhat more elegant methods are available than that given in the simple illustration, but the methods rest upon a similar system. The results obtained from this analysis may be compared with those obtained if the groupings used in the official Criminal Statistics are taken. The official groupings are, of course, related to the legal groupings for purposes of types of treatment which may be ordered by the courts. The mean square and minimum coefficients are:

Official groupings	Mean	Min.
8–13	·70	·25
14–16	·34	·01
17–20	·74	·51
Mean	·59	·26

No three-group classification can be as homogeneous as a four-group classification, but the main contribution to the heterogenity is due to the 15-year-old offenders. Prior to 1948, when the school-leaving age was raised, the classification used in official statistics (and legally) tended to agree with the 'natural' variations.

Analysis of this kind does not provide any answers to questions of 'cause', it serves only to assist the classification together of items of information which tend to go together so that an upswing in one group will not be masked by a downswing in a different group with which it is summed together.

Modern statistical methodology has provided many techniques, based on common-sense principles, which can deal with highly complex data in similar ways to that illustrated above, forming classifications which maximize the distance between groups and minimize the distance within groups. One further illustration with respect to crime data may serve to indicate that similar systems of analysis may be applied to data that are not numerical or related to continuous distributions like age.

A Classification of Types of Crime

It has often been remarked that 'crime' is not a unidimensional concept; many different acts are proscribed by law, and it is only the common fact of breach of law which defines 'crime'. It seems reasonable to ask which kinds of crime vary together over time and which tend to vary independently. If all crimes tend to increase or decrease together, it does not matter which individual type of crime is taken as an index of crime, but if different crimes vary over time in differing ways, there may be a masking effect as some tend to increase and others to decrease. It will be seen from *Table 5* that the numbers of different types of crime 'known to the police' during the years 1946–1959 tend to vary with time in different ways.

TABLE 5

Certain indictable offences known to the police adjusted for population changes (England and Wales) (base year 1946=actual figures)

Year	Murder*	Burglary	Embezzlement	Housebreaking
1946	131	4,220	799	31,270
1947	134·5	3,872	1,052	30,285
1948	146·3	4,153	1,732	31,417
1949	118·1	3,712	1,734	26,770
1950	121·2	3,592	2,153	26,057
1951	122·4	3,711	2,333	26,164
1952	134·7	3,811	2,894	28,195
1953	129·2	3,659	2,842	26,479
1954	134·5	3,126	2,981	22,782
1955	121·5	2,862	2,833	21,435
1956	142·7	2,836	3,091	22,705
1957	144·6	3,516	2,563	27,775
1958	118·2	4,316	2,756	34,569
1959	134·6	4,387	3,533	35,874

* Uncorrected for cases subsequently found to be manslaughter, infanticide, etc.

Crime and Indictable Offences

The definition of an indictable offence depends on the way in which an adult person accused of an offence may be tried. Special provisions for persons under seventeen years of age are ignored for purposes of definition. In England and Wales the police record as 'crimes known' only offences regarded by them as indictable. This excludes offences where there is a specific statutory provision for them to be dealt with either on indictment or summarily – that is, 'hybrid offences'. Perhaps when this criterion was devised the distinction between indictable and non-indictable offences was a reasonable one and related to some measure of public disapprobation. Today it seems a little out of accord with public opinion. It may be that continuity of statistical indices is important and that public opinion should not weigh too much in considerations of change. None the less, changes are introduced into the legal structure by reason of technological change which no attempt to retain comparability with the past can withstand. The horse was a factor to be considered in relation to criminal behaviour in the past, but it is very doubtful whether the transition from horse to horseless carriage is a sufficiently direct one for the continuity of legal definition and statistical counting tied to those definitions. For legal purposes, and not without good reason, there is a tendency always to try to make the existing structure suffice for the newer conditions for as long as possible. On the other hand, social research and sociological inquiry require indices which reflect the current structure of society. However, it may be argued that statistical continuity should also be sustained for as long as possible, but how long that is is subject to widely varying opinion. Changes in the law and related statistical data can be made only by discrete steps, while social and technological changes are a continuous process. Some items must, by reason of this fact, be out of step, no matter how often revisions are made. These gaps must be supplied by those who interpret the figures. For example, in England and Wales between the years 1954 and 1955 the offence of malicious damage to property dropped from 5,156 to 2,123. It is perhaps sufficiently obvious that the sudden drop in this category of offences is due to changes in the system of recording these offences. The discontinuity is apparent when we examine the detailed figures, and there is no satisfactory way of correcting or adjusting for it. The discontinuity of one sub-set of figures has, of course, an influence on the total or any other figures which include this sub-set.

A further difficulty in looking at crime figures over any period of years, which may at first sight seem simple to adjust statistically, is the fact that the population of a country or state changes. The total amount of crime will also be expected to change because, if there are more people and the definitions of crime remain constant and are constantly interpreted, more persons would be expected to commit more crimes. But is it sufficient merely to adjust for this factor by dividing crimes by the population? Is a meaningful crime rate provided by an allowance for the greater amount of crime expected if there are more people to commit it? Clearly, it must make some difference, and the rate per 100,000 of the population (the conventional index) is a better index than the actual number of events making no allowance for the population size. But the majority of crimes are committed, so far as is known from the persons identified as criminals, by younger male persons. Females commit little crime and persons over the age of thirty are far less likely to be found guilty of offences than are people under thirty. So, if only the population age structure were changing, if there were more young people in

164

the population, then even with a constant population an increased crime rate would be expected. The converse is also true. If a population is becoming on average older, the crime rate would be expected to drop, even if every person, age for age, were as criminally inclined as before.

Taking all points together, it seems very unsafe to make any statements regarding the *state of crime* over different years·or as between different countries, counties, states, or districts, except in the crudest possible terms. It would, of course, be possible and interesting to calculate an age-standardized crime rate, which made an allowance for the crime rate expected at each year of age, and to relate this to the population and the incidence of reported crimes (see Wilkins, 1963).

But such a standardization would have to rely on figures relating to *persons found guilty*. To extend inferences from *persons* to *crimes* begs a whole series of questions regarding the number of crimes cleared up for each age and many other difficulties which seem at present to be insurmountable. It is, for example, not unreasonable to suppose that young offenders are more likely to be caught, but there is no way of knowing how much more likely. It will be clear that the provision of a general crime index presents many difficulties; none the less, people are prone to make statements in a general way about the volume of crime. It is possible to suggest some crimes the figures for which are less affected by the difficulties to which reference has been made than the total of all 'crimes known'. It has been suggested that the number of offences of 'breaking and entering' provides such a good general measure because this group is restricted in its coverage, the definition is less likely to change with time, and the action itself is less likely to be seen differently by different persons. It may be argued that if crime (in the criminological sense) is increasing in total, the parts must be also, and thus, if breaking and entering offences are increasing, then other offences will be also. A comparison of the trends for offences of breaking and entering in relation to the total of 'crimes known to the police' in England and Wales is shown in *Figure 8*.

To a considerable extent the two sets of data support each other. But it is interesting to question whether all types of crime are likely to go up or down together. If they do, then it does not matter very much which type of crime is selected for the crime index, nor indeed whether all crimes known to the police are taken together.

FIGURE 8

Comparison of trends for offences of breaking and entering in relation to total of 'crimes known to the police' (England and Wales)

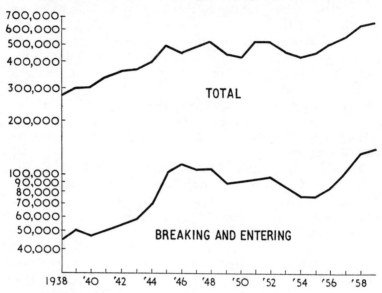

An Approach to a Crime Index

(a) Time Factors

Table 5 sets out the numbers of certain crimes known to the police adjusted for population changes for the years 1946–1959. It will be seen on inspection that the murder rate does not vary in any close relation with other crimes; years which had high murder figures were not high for burglary, nor were there any variations in the murder rate in excess of chance. But years which were characterized by high figures for burglary tended to show also high figures for house-breaking. It seems probable that correlation analysis might be of some value in studying the problem of crime indices. On the basis of the figures for the periods 1927–1938 and 1946–1959, fifteen types of offence usually regarded as serious crimes have been intercorrelated. The matrix of correlations is shown as *Table 6*. It will be seen that there is some tendency for murder to be associated positively with some offences and negatively with others. There is, however, no strong association between patterns in the murder rate and patterns for any other offences. The same applies to attempted murder and

166

TABLE 6

Relationships between trends in different crime rates
(England and Wales)

	Attempted murder	Manslaughter	Felonious woundings	Malicious woundings	Assault	Buggery	Attempted buggery	Indecency between males	Rape	Indecent assault	Unlawful intercourse	Burglary	Housebreaking	Shopbreaking	Robbery
Murder	·45	·10	−·42	−·15	−·15	−·20	−·36	−·29	−·11	−·28	−·28	−·03	−·09	−·09	−·09
Attempted murder	·	−·20	−·35	−·20	−·20	−·05	−·26	−·18	−·01	−·19	−·31	−·19	−·08	−·07	−·07
Manslaughter		·	·24	·34	−·02	·22	·42	·03	−·13	·28	·24	·11	·66	·27	·14
Felonious woundings			·	·82	·46	·70	·86	·75	·52	·84	·78	−·24	−·04	−·10	−·30
Malicious woundings				·	·46	·75	·87	·80	·55	·87	·93	−·26	−·09	−·09	−·20
Assault					·	·23	·46	·32	·25	·34	·55	−·20	−·18	−·20	−·21
Buggery						·	·77	·81	·42	·77	·68	−·56	−·20	−·19	−·06
Attempted buggery							·	·88	·43	·88	·61	·45	·79	−·05	−·19
Indecency between males								·	·38	·79	·72	−·45	−·02	−·02	−·11
Rape									·	·67	·62	−·60	−·36	−·30	−·28
Indecent assault										·	·86	−·41	−·09	−·09	−·06
Unlawful intercourse											·	−·36	−·01	00	·12
Burglary												·	·73	·67	·61
Housebreaking													·	·95	·66
Shopbreaking														·	·62
Robbery															·

Correlations over 0·80 are underscored.

manslaughter. But these three types of offence show different patterns of change from each other and also from almost all other types of offence. Manslaughter shows a fairly high correlation with house-breaking, but no correlation at all with either shopbreaking or robbery. Some of these correlations are of interest in considering the structure of a crime index. Clearly, in the case of murder, a crime rate based on any other crime would not give any information – the best estimate of the number of murders in any year is the average.[1] Thus it is possible to say that a 'murder rate' and a 'crime rate' are two entirely different things and bear little or no relation to each other. It would seem reasonable to require that for a rate to be meaningful the items included in it should not tend to mask each other in terms of their variations over time. The specific point made in connection with murder seems valid generally as a point for consideration regarding other aspects of crime rates.

Despite the logical difficulties, some grouping together of different types of offence in a crime rate seems essential. It does not assist the appraisal of figures to have more than is necessary; and separate rates for each crime, although useful for some purposes of analysis, will not serve for sociological investigation of general trends. It may seem reasonable to add together crimes which behave over time in a similar way, and the correlation analysis will assist in determining which offences may be taken together and which should be treated separately. In the correlation matrix, correlations in excess of 0·80 have been underlined. Not unexpectedly, shopbreaking and housebreaking tend to move together; burglary does not go with either in any significant way, but is more related to the group of breaking and robbery than to any other. Thus it may seem reasonable to group together shopbreaking, housebreaking, burglary (breaking by night), and robbery. It also seems reasonable to group together both sexual crimes and violent crimes, except perhaps assault. Murder, attempted murder, and manslaughter might have been considered, subjectively, to be a good grouping, but this is not supported by the analysis. There is no tendency for them to be associated either with each other or with other offences. It would seem that murder and attempted murder are different types of crime! Whatever the explanation, the fact remains that variations from year to year in these rates do not tend to move together. In practice, it might seem that attempted

[1] This does not apply in the U.S.A. where murder tends to be correlated with other crimes.

murder and felonious woundings may at times be difficult to separate in terms of the nature of the action. But again, over time, these crimes do not show similar patterns. The independence of the patterns of incidence of these three crimes may be surprising, but one thing is certain: if they are grouped together, then variations in one will obscure variations in the others. On the basis of this analysis it seems that separate indices are required for:

> Murder
> Attempted murder
> Serious crimes against the person
> Housebreaking, shopbreaking, robbery.

Although some assaults not classified as felonious or malicious wounding may be quite serious, the majority of cases taken under this classification do not involve the victim in any great degree of injury. It would appear that a sub-division of 'violence against the person' is needed which would make the distinction between fights and social disturbances, on the one hand, and the more serious attacks upon persons, on the other. Perhaps assaults which are premeditated, assaults carried out on strangers, or assaults which do not take place within the same sub-culture, do not form a homogeneous category – they are perhaps basically different types of crime.

The analysis of correlations which summarizes the patterns of variations over time does not yield a simple explanation. Some of the results are not in accord with subjective impressions that one may have of the relationship between different types of crime. Before any conclusions are based on these data, it seems desirable to examine some further evidence from other sources.

(b) Spatial Factors

Human ecology, which is concerned with the relationship between humans and their environment, is a method of study which has attracted criminologists from time to time. Very early attempts can be found to connect the causation of crime with community and geographical characteristics. It is possible that interest in this approach began, as Vold suggests, with Tarde (1886), who put forward what he called a 'law of imitation'. This is more likely to be an accurate reference if it is legitimate to argue a relationship between the application of ecological methods to criminology and the theoretical explanation of crime in terms of 'learned behaviour'. On the other hand, the application of cartographic methods in criminology may be traced to Guerry (1833) in the first half of the nineteenth century. Mayhew (1851) reported that the general crime rate seemed to be higher than the average in industrial areas in England and Wales. Other early work in this field was carried out by Quetelet. The majority of early studies in criminal ecology were based on the total crime rate, or selected types of crime, and were directed towards the comparison of urban and rural criminality. This is, perhaps, not surprising, since at that time the population was sharply divided between urban and rural communities. Very many references could be traced to work of this kind, but that of Jones (1959) agrees with the general pattern of evidence. He commented that, even in a small country like England with good means of communication, the differences in the pattern of community life are still very real and must have an effect 'in causing differences in both the distribution and the form of criminal activity'. In his study of Leicester, Jones compared the city with the county for the years 1935, 1946, and 1954, and found that the general tendency was for higher crime rates in the more urbanized areas. His results also agreed with the general findings in that he noted that crimes against property were more characteristic of the town, whereas crimes against the person tended to be more characteristic of rural areas.

In almost all large towns and cities there are well-known districts in which crime and vice are supposed to be particularly prevalent. The study of delinquent areas in big cities has become a favoured field of many criminologists, particularly in the period 1930–40. Shaw and McKay (1942) studied juvenile delinquency in Chicago and concluded that the nature of delinquency varied in different areas, and that some areas showed little or no criminal activity. In general, a higher degree of criminality was found towards the centre of the city and in the surrounding industrial areas. These features tended to remain constant, in that it was found that in those areas where criminality was high in 1930 the crime rate was similarly high in 1900, even although in the meantime the population and the ethnic group of the citizens had changed.

In a statistical analysis utilizing ecological methods, Calvin F. Schmid (1960) studied crime patterns and other variables in different districts of Seattle in 1957. Schmid was not concerned with the question of a crime index but with the relationships between crime and other social factors. He used the separate figures for each offence where there were sufficient numbers of cases in the category and omitted the remainder. Justifying this procedure, he remarks: 'Unlike most studies of crime and delinquency in which the entire gamut of violations is grouped into a single amorphous index, the various cases have been differentiated into relatively specific and precise categories.' None the less Schmid's correlation analysis based on geographic variations provides different information from that derived above using time as a base, but it may be studied from various points of view, including the problem of crime-index construction. Unfortunately, Schmid's work relates to a different legal system, and different types of crime classification were used from those we were able to include in the analysis given in *Table 6*. One of the correlation analyses used by Schmid is reproduced as *Table 7*. In our own analysis we have been able to include only indictable offences, whereas Schmid, by making use of both 'offences known to the police' and 'arrests', was able to cover a wider range of criminal activity.

It will be seen that Schmid found that 'bad' areas were generally bad, but bicycle thefts were *negatively* correlated with all other recorded crimes in his analysis except burglary (non-residence) and indecent exposure. This raises a general question of principle regarding the purposes of index construction. It may be that, as one type of crime goes up in one town or area, another goes up in a different area, whereas the incidence of the crimes examined may not be correlated or even inversely correlated. Thus, in comparing areas in terms of a general crime index, one is forced to equate many different and compensating factors. How many bicycle thefts and indecent exposures equal how many drunks or attempted suicides?

It must be emphasized that research work in one town, in one year, in one country, is not an adequate basis for generalization. But Schmid's work helps to suggest ways in which the problem of a general index of crime might be approached. His work does throw some light on the time-based analysis for England and Wales given above. In Schmid's analysis, six offence groups were highly correlated with each other. They were:

> Petty larceny
> Drunkenness and common drunkenness
> Disorderly conduct (fighting or other)
> Vagrancy
> Lewdness (not indecent exposure)
> Robbery – highway and car

TABLE 7
Correlations between crime rates, Seattle, 1949–51 (Schmid)

Column variables (X) and row variables (Y) are numbered 1–20:

1. SUICIDE – Attempted
2. SUICIDE – Completed
3. DRUNKENNESS – Drunk
4. DRUNKENNESS – Common drunk
5. DISORDERLY CONDUCT – Fighting
6. DISORDERLY CONDUCT – Other
7. VAGRANCY – Vagrancy
8. SEX OFFENCES – Lewdness
9. SEX OFFENCES – Indecent exposure
10. LARCENY – Petty larceny
11. LARCENY – Shop lifting
12. LARCENY – Bicycle theft
13. LARCENY – Auto theft
14. LARCENY – Theft from automobile
15. FRAUD – Cheque fraud
16. BURGLARY – Residence-day
17. BURGLARY – Residence-night
18. BURGLARY – Non-residence day and night
19. ROBBERY – Highway and car
20. ROBBERY – Non-residential

Y\X	1	2	3	4	5	6	7	8	9	10	11	12	13	14	15	16	17	18	19	Y
1																				1
2	.600																			2
3	.652	.461																		3
4	.491	.351	.975																	4
5	.673	.463	.950	.908																5
6	.634	.466	.972	.946	.960															6
7	.568	.398	.987	.990	.940	.970														7
8	.688	.480	.964	.921	.964	.963	.949													8
9	.185	.046	.018	-.071	-.079	.024	-.050	-.057												9
10	.668	.532	.971	.937	.936	.949	.958	.951	-.021											10
11	.713	.462	.431	.305	.488	.474	.394	.481	.138	.437										11
12	.192	.271	.194	-.157	-.183	.211	-.163	.229	.314	-.189	.038									12
13	.679	.620	.415	.273	.430	.401	.324	.419	.271	.459	.546	-.127								13
14	.890	.653	.758	.617	.759	.735	.682	.763	.168	.774	.688	.175	.801							14
15	.878	.438	.472	.301	.476	.435	.378	.505	.236	.490	.751	.100	.698	.824						15
16	.890	.398	.755	.628	.760	.720	.694	.775	.118	.744	.662	.144	.536	.852	.873					16
17	.894	.394	.628	.485	.656	.598	.555	.671	.127	.631	.680	.129	.541	.820	.911	.964				17
18	.151	.111	.134	.138	.053	.080	.115	.132	.191	.144	.046	.263	.036	.058	.139	.110	-.099			18
19	.716	.502	.962	.919	.957	.960	.951	.954	-.018	.951	.540	.175	.497	.814	.547	.801	.698	.090		19
20	.101	.189	.196	.189	.286	.254	.224	.251	-.024	.203	.145	.025	.032	.129	-.032	.095	.078	.364	.238	20

Negative correlations indicated

The majority of these categories would not be included in 'crimes known to the police' in English criminal statistics. The Seattle analysis also showed that burglary (residence – day) and burglary (residence – night) and cheque frauds are closely related, but these groups are not so highly associated with each other as are the items in the group above, nor are they highly associated with the first group. Perhaps it would be meaningful to regard the first group of offences as providing an index of 'social disturbance' rather than 'crime', if it were not for the items 'robbery – highway and car', or petty larceny. A transfer of the item 'robbery' from the first group to the group including burglary would not do violence to the Seattle data; thus, it seems reasonable to conclude (so far as the Seattle data go) that geographical patterns of offences suggest a crime index of three offence groups:

Crime Index	(i)	Burglary (residence – day)
		Burglary (residence – night)
		Robbery (highway and car)
		Cheque frauds
Murder Index	(ii)	Murder rate
Social Disorganization Index	(iii)	Drunkenness and common drunkenness
		Disorderly conduct (fighting or other)
		Vagrancy
		Lewdness (not indecent exposure)
		Petty larceny

According to the law of England and Wales, the first group approximates to housebreaking, shopbreaking, and burglary. The crimes of cheque fraud and robbery (highway and car) are not grouped separately in the figures for England and Wales and there are very few cheque frauds.

It is obvious that these data tend to support the argument that a general crime index, adding together serious and non-serious offences against property and persons, does not meet the requirements of a good index. Utilizing both the time-based and the geographically based data, it would seem that four indices are desirable:

(i) Serious crimes against property (e.g. burglary, breaking and entering, robbery)

(ii) Social disorganization (e.g. drunkenness, disorderly conduct, petty larceny)

173

(iii) Serious crimes against the person

(iv) Homicide (a) murder; (b) manslaughters

Unfortunately, the legal categories under which offences are classified for statistical purposes frequently do not distinguish the degree of seriousness. For example, the value of the property stolen is not regarded as relevant to the charge of larceny. Robbery may consist of anything from a bank hold-up making national headlines to a small boy tripping up another and stealing his pocket money. The dividing line between serious and non-serious violence against the person is one which may well vary from time to time and from place to place, according to the attitudes of the culture in which the event occurs.

Static and Dynamic Indices

Index numbers are very attractive. Their attraction is a potential danger, in that they seem to simplify complex problems – but they only *seem* to simplify them. There are many dangers of interpretation, even if index numbers are refined to the last degree possible. Clearly, an event which is not perceived today as a serious crime cannot be included in an index of serious crime, but the same event may tomorrow be perceived by the society of that time in a different way. Society is dynamic, and the problem of the extent to which an index of crime should reflect the changing attitudes of the culture is a thorny one. If events were to be defined in such a way that the classification of a crime indicated very precisely the nature of the action and the role of the actors in such a situation, some sort of fixed base index might be meaningful, but the purposes of social defence are doubtless best served by definitions which can be interpreted in slightly varying ways in order to take account of the changing attitudes of society without the necessity of revising completely the legal structure at very frequent intervals. Looked at in terms only of the nature of the action, the small boy who steals another's pocket money and the bank robber are behaving in an exactly similar way – they are both removing property from another with the use of force or threat of force. It is not the action which gives rise to different levels of social disapprobation, but the actors and the interpretation of the social significance of the action in terms of the culture of the society at the time.

At present there are both static and dynamic elements in the

174

criminal statistics, and it is not possible to separate these from each other. The situation is not very different with respect to any other data relating directly or indirectly to other social problems. Fixed definitions cannot take into account changes in the expectations of behaviour or achievement which are related to the social attitudes of the culture at any point in time. A person who may have been classified as highly literate in 1600 might be near the margin of illiteracy today; moreover, literacy may not be a unidimensional concept. In problems of health, perhaps because of greater investments in research over many years, a more satisfactory situation appears to exist, but there are many problems of data interpretation and of the relationship of different types of information to action strategies even in this area. Indeed, the illustrative discrepancy with which this chapter began was from the field of medicine.

The problems lie mainly in the area between research and policy, between science and administration, and they cannot be solved without cooperative effort.

Selection of Fields

For all that has been said in the current chapter, we do not seem to have thrown much light on the problems of selection of fields of activity to remedy perceived social ills. We began with the question, 'Does the problem exist?' and discussed difficulties of measurement. In the majority of cases there will be little doubt about the existence of the specified problem if the basic data have been subjected to the tests proposed and have passed them satisfactorily. But how is it to be determined that the problem selected is more worthy of attention than other problems? Perhaps the most valid purpose served by mass general social-accounting data (statistics), other than providing information for the provisioning, staff control, and accounting purposes of management, is to indicate the broad picture of social problems so that those requiring attention can be identified. In this regard, such data serve much the same purposes as the dramatic incident, the interest of persons in authority, the publication of research information that attracts public attention, the activities of pressure groups, and other mass communication and democratic processes.

The demonstration of the existence of the problem is the first step, but only the first step. Closer examination of the statistical data will most likely reveal some of the ways in which the problem might be dealt with, but there are no data which can help towards answering the question of whether the problems of old age are more or less serious than those of the young, whether it is the common cold or rheumatism, the educationally sub-normal or the unusually bright child, or any other possible claim to attention which should receive priority. We have no common bases for comparison of the claims on our attention of different types of problem. Each problem is measured in terms of its own factors and in terms of its own scales.

If measures were available which could tell us whether one problem was more worthy of attention than a different problem, the same system of measurement would provide a means for assessing whether one form of social action with respect to the same problem had been more or less successful than another type of action. If measures were available for solving the problems of selection of priorities, the problems of evaluation would be solved at one and the same time. Indeed, the problems of evaluation are easier, since the measures can be retained within the scales of their own system. If social action intended to reduce juvenile delinquency has reduced the frequency of acts normally agreed and classified as delinquent, then the action may be said to be successful within the system, without the need to show that it was more worth while to reduce juvenile delinquency by x per cent than to do something else for the benefit of other groups in society. It will be obvious that the problems of priorities cannot be solved until the problems of evaluation are tackled and some progress has been made.

REFERENCES

Annual Report of the National Institute for the Deaf (1960).

GREGORY, K. (1962). Unpublished monograph – reviewed as private communication.

GUERRY, A. M. (1833). *Essai sur la statistique de la France.* Paris.

HUFF, G. (1955). *How to Lie with Statistics.* London: Gollancz.

JONES, H. (1959). *Brit. J. Criminol.*, vol. 3, No. 4, p. 341.

LODGE, T. S. (1953). Criminal Statistics. *J. Roy. Statist. Soc.* A.

MARTIN, J. P. (1962). *Offenders as Employees.* London: Routledge & Kegan Paul.

MAYHEW, H. (1851). *London Labour and the London Poor.* London: Griffin.

SCHMID, C. (1960). Urban Crime Areas. *Amer. Sociol. Rev.*, vol. 25, nos. 4 & 5.

SHAW, C. R. & McKAY, H. D. (1942). *Juvenile Delinquency in Urban Areas*. Chicago.

TARDE, G. (1886). *La Criminalité comparée*. Paris.

WILKINS, L. T. (1963). The Measurement of Crime. *Brit. J. Criminol.*, vol. 3, p. 321.

CHAPTER 7

Problem into Model

TRANSFORMATION AND COMMUNICATION

From social ethic to objective – Accounting and needs – The two languages – A note on the philosophy of measurement – The unique personality – Intangibles

General statistical data, scientific theory, fears of the future, political pressures, many forms of information and types of belief may give rise to the statement of problems. Decisions will have to be made outside the framework of the scientific method before the scientific method can be applied to the problems highlighted by these means. Rational decisions have been defined as being concerned with the utilization of information in an optimum manner so as to ascertain which of the possible lines of action to deal with a problem is most likely to lead to a maximizing of some type of pay-off. At this stage somewhat different types of decision must be made and rather different problems solved. These problems are concerned with ways and means for 'getting into the model'. In 'getting into the model' the problems associated with the stating of objectives are central.

From Social Ethic to Objective

The scientific method cannot directly put forward criteria. At the beginning there exists only a general social ethic. The ethic is a reflection of the society in which we live, whether as scientist, administrator, or other citizen. The ethic, seen in relation to certain incidents or situations within the system, leads to the suggestion that something ought to be done to *change* specified situations or institutions, and the direction of the proposed changes is often phrased in terms of the perceived 'needs' of the people involved. At the point where 'needs' are discussed, theory and the ethic are closely related. The methods for problem-solving that are optimal cannot be isolated from the ethical considerations and the nature of the problems themselves.

It is probable, however, that the methods derived in connection with the solution of problems at a lower level of abstraction – that is, the methods of scientific inquiry – might throw some light on the ways in which problems of the criteria might be approached. At the level of the statement of the ethic, the language in which the operations will take place will doubtless be the 'language of administration' rather than the 'language of science'. Different levels or types of language will need to be related to each other throughout the process of 'getting into the model'. This process raises problems in the field of communication. The concept of communication provides a specific area for the application of the scientific method in its own right, and by this means several specific 'scientific problems' can add together to a statement of a general social problem. But since there may well be many specific scientific problems involved in any one general social problem, communication becomes a central issue. Communication involves not only the concept of language, but the media through which messages are coded, transmitted, received, and decoded. It is possible that different *systems* through which information flows, is coded, stored, and operated upon have an influence upon the outcome as well as the nature of the information itself. In the field of social action and research many of the systems of information-processing have been in operation for centuries. With any general social problem it is, therefore, not possible to accept the advice given to Alice and 'begin at the beginning' because society has been going on for a long time. The social scientist can begin only from where we are now.

A very large and wide variety of organizations are concerned today in stimulating social change. In many such organizations social scientists, social administrators, and social workers are involved together in some combined action to seek to remedy or alleviate some perceived social problems. The area of concern will differ between organizations, but one common element is likely to be an awareness of the need to evaluate current or proposed procedures with a view to assessing their effects. In any such endeavours certain common problems will be faced, and among them will be the setting-up of a criterion – a standard against which the achieved changes may be measured. It will be self-evident that evaluation must relate what is achieved to what has been attempted. How, then, can the social scientist, social administrator, and social worker best work together towards the solution of the problems of evaluation? How can the perception of the social problems be translated into measurement

179

suitable for the assessment of the outcome of different forms of action?

Any change in a social system which (if it could take place) had no impact upon individuals living within the system would be of little or no concern. We are concerned not only with the problem, but with the persons who experience the problem.

Accounting and Needs

The social ethic of our society is reflected in its social institutions, including those institutions concerned with social change. The link with the general democratic ethic and the general public is through the support the organizations obtain by means of the democratic procedures of government financial accounting or by private charity. It may be considered that these links are inefficient and do not reflect the ultimate authority of the society, but the question of who has the right to state the objectives of social research or social change is an ethical one. If a democratic society should provide its own self-regulatory systems, part of the social change desired by some social agencies may be in terms of the more effective operation of such systems, and this objective conforms to the general given ethic.

The institutions that are constituted to give effect to the democratic ideal will usually express their concerns in very general statements. Examples of 'needs' statements made by such institutions may be 'improve educational achievement', 'reduce juvenile delinquency', 'relieve suffering', and the like. Until such time as statements of this kind can be agreed by the organization and made public, money will seldom become available for either social action or social research. Once the objectives have been stated and money voted or made available from some source, the objectives *as stated* may be accepted as the starting-point for research or action, since such statements provide a guide to general policy. From this stage onwards, until a criterion suitable for use in a model can be derived, the process is one of continually increasing the specificity and definition of the statements, narrowing them down, sub-dividing problems, and working towards a system of rigorous measurement. In this process we move from the generalities of statistical data, which may have been used to assess whether or not the problem existed in the form specified, and from considerations of general strategies to consider more specific methods for the assessment of the size and nature of a social problem. We move from the area where rough counts and imprecise measurements of a social-accounting nature may be adequate to an area where more refined techniques become essential. The information which may have served to establish the social institution is not adequate or of the right form to provide an evaluation of the functioning of the institution.

For purposes of discussion in this chapter, some organization is supposed to exist having the necessary funds and authority to undertake social work and social research. The ethical foundation of the organization and its objectives are regarded as irrelevant to the methodology. Whether the social action which it is proposed to investigate forms part of a specific action-research design, or is seen as a self-contained social experiment, or has some other form is also immaterial. If the social problem with which we are concerned has been observed for some time it is very probable that something is already being done about it. Thus, there is always likely to be one alternative decision which might be assessed in any model we may devise – to do nothing about it. Whether what is being done is better, or even worse, than nothing is an open question with respect to much current social action. (By 'better' or 'worse' is meant only that which is or is not in accord with the stated objectives of the institution concerned in the action.) The necessary variance for the application of evaluation procedures exists within the systems as at present defined and operated. This does not mean that new experiments should not be set up, but it does mean that experimentation may not be necessary. No matter what type of research is proposed, no matter how it is considered that the evaluation of on-going social action should be carried out, ways for stating the objectives and reducing these broad statements to research criteria will appear as a common problem.

It will be noted that the methodology to be discussed does not deal with social changes which take place throughout the whole of a society or social system. We are concerned with different agencies for social change within a system which has a common ethic. Changes which take place over time between social systems are the proper study of historians. Historical analysis of the kind necessary for such operations is, in the language of the methodology used here, like studying very carefully an experimental group for which there can be no control group. Such analyses doubtless have a place, but in the main it seems that history provides good excuses for the existence of a social problem but no reasons for its continuity. If we are concerned with the business of social change, we must be influenced by the past, but we must also see the future as capable of modification through the methods we propose to use.

The Two Languages

Social scientists and social administrators often find communication difficult. The highly specific 'jargon' of the research worker does not seem to fit the 'real-life' problems which are the concern of the administration. The broad statements of policy cannot be taken into research designs. The social worker's concept of 'needs' seems to some to be the mere projection of middle-class values and to beg many questions. There is a tendency for the social administrator to think that the problems as he sees them should be the concern of the social scientist because they are real problems. The social worker has a feeling for those he perceives as suffering, and the cold approach of the research worker is, to him, irritating if not worse. The research worker regards the specification of the problems in administrative language as lacking specificity, and the social worker as more guided by his emotional involvement than by the logic of the situation.

But these differences are not 'real' differences. Social scientist, social administrator, and social worker are all concerned with the same problems of society, and the objectives of the different groups are the same. Only the language differs. And this difference is functional. Each language, each frame of reference has a place at the appropriate stage in dealing with a problem.

It is a mistake to attempt to force the statements based on the concept of social policy or 'needs' into too narrow a frame of reference until agreement has been reached at the level of abstraction at which the broader band-width language is functional. When dealing with broad policy concepts it is better to use a language of broad band width. Finding ways of reaching agreement on general policy issues is an appropriate field for the administrative art of compromise. This art must not be underrated. The scientific method is not superior to the art of compromise, nor is the art of administration superior to the scientific method. To use the one where the other ought to be used is inefficient. There are different roles for art and science and for language of broad conceptual frameworks and the more specific language. Art cannot replace science, nor can the language appropriate to deal with the concepts of the one be forced into the context of the other. Rather than a mixing of the languages there should be a development and a transformation from one to the other at appropriate stages. A translation and development are necessary before the administrative question can be turned into a question which can be taken into a model. The solution may be found in the model language, but again a transformation is required, after the completion of the research, into the language of general policy.

An indication of the stages leading from the general statement of a social problem to the specification of a criterion which can be taken into a research model is given as *Figure 9*. When agreement has been

FIGURE 9

A general indication of the different phases in planning a social-action-research programme

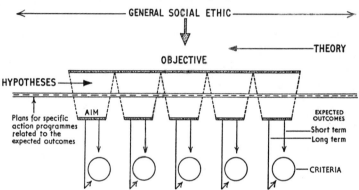

reached at the level of the general policy, more specific objectives can be stated; and when agreement is reached on these, the action proposed to reach the objectives will need to be sketched in. At each transformation stage there will need to be much communication and checking of one language against the other to ensure that the translation is adequate. Eventually the specific aims, both long and short term, of each proposed line of action must be explicitly stated. Long- and short-term aims seldom conflict, and in cases where they seem to do so, some stage in the transformation is suspect as the reason for this.

A Note on the Philosophy of Measurement

Before a concept can be used for evaluation, or even for most other purposes, it must be communicable. At some levels of operation it might not give rise to serious problems in communication if the person receiving a message and decoding it does not decode it into exactly the same terms as the transmitter. It is possible to move from one concept to another if there is sufficient agreement between the transmitter and the receiver. Exactly what degree of correlation between the transmitted and received message is necessary it might be possible to determine, but such estimation would be irrelevant to the solution of many problems. In evaluation a higher degree of correlation is necessary than in negotiation and compromise situations, probably because evaluation requires statements of order or magnitude to be made.

It may be that the difficulty of communication between different persons in different roles in relation to the solution of social problems is due in part to the failure to recognize mathematics and measurement as a form of language. Social workers often object to the use of mathematical models in dealing with problems involving human behaviour. Some writers have stated that though they can accept 'logical' methods in the study of human behaviour they cannot agree to the use of mathematical models. But the dividing line between mathematics and logic (especially symbolic logic) is not defined in this argument. It would appear, in fact, to be a distinction without a difference.

The objection to mathematical models is usually made on ethical grounds. But such persons are prepared to read case papers and discuss their experiences involving other individuals. Clearly, if a case is to be communicated from one caseworker to another, then words must be used. Only in this way can one caseworker learn from another. If verbal communication of information about individual cases is rejected, then each caseworker must be assumed to begin his work solely in terms of his own personal experiences unmodified by the experience of others. This idea will correctly be regarded as absurd. But the translation of events, emotional experiences, or 'needs' of clients into words represents a replacement of 'real' things and people by symbols, namely words. Words mean what by convention they have come to mean, and the majority of words may be defined in terms of other words. The effectiveness of words may be assessed by two criteria:

(a) how they convey meaning, that is, are they effective for communication?
(b) how they permit of manipulation by the processes of logic, that is, do they assist the thought processes?

A system of words with all (a) qualities and no (b) qualities would be deficient over all. The use of jargon, which grows around any specialist study, is an indication that normal language has been found to be deficient in either (a) or (b) qualities – usually (b). The development of symbolic logic is an indication that some persons have found the redundancy and uncertainty of normal language inadequate for purpose (b). It will be clear, however, that there is no fundamental difference between the use of word-symbols to describe things and people and the use of other abstract symbols. The difference exists mainly in that all persons have some knowledge of the use of words for communication purposes, and in general have found it possible to use the same system of symbols for (b) purposes also. If we require to communicate most effectively we should use the most common language consistent with the required degree of accuracy in communication. If we require to use thought processes we should use any system of symbols which proves most effective for this purpose. If we used one where it would be better to use the other we shall not communicate or think in the best way possible. Communication requires redundancy of language; analysis is confused by redundancy. As the process of evaluation moves from the emphasis on communication to the emphasis on logical processes, the type of language should change. At the criteria stage, language should become measurement, or as near to measurement as possible, having no emotional content or redundancy. Before the transition from communication of concepts to measurement criteria is considered in detail, it is convenient to look forward to the final stage of measurement, and to consider the nature of measurement applied to evaluation problems. Clearly, if we wish to be able to say that one type of social action is better or worse than another, it will be necessary to base these statements on some scale, and preferably a scale which enables us to say by *how much* one is better than the other.

The Unique Personality

In social action problems, we are concerned in the last analysis with the unique individual. It is often argued that 'the outcome of human action involves the dynamic interplay of many elements of personality and situation' (Ohlin, 1955) and, therefore, measurement of achievements in social work is not possible. It may be true that human action involves the dynamic interplay of many elements, but it seems to be possible to reduce the 'many elements' to a much smaller number of 'dimensions'. Some reduction of the number of characteristics that might be described is essential. For example, if we require one hundred characteristics to be described at five levels, say, 'none, very bad, bad, fair, good', then it would need 100^5 different categories (or 10,000,000 different individuals) if each category occurred once only. It is not difficult to suppose that by some characteristic or another which we could describe, any one individual would differ from all others, no matter how many individuals we may imagine. If we consider not only characteristics, and if we are not content with rough classifications into categories by levels, but require measurement, we arrive the sooner at the unique individual. Indeed, if we could measure any one thing, say height or weight, absolutely accurately, we should be able to define every individual as unique in terms of one measurement alone at any one point in time. We are only able to say that people are the 'same' height or weight when we are content to make measurements inaccurately – to the nearest pound, or inch, or some other limit. We know, however, that very small differences in weight between individuals may, for all operational purposes, be ignored. We know that people who are grossly overweight tend to have a shorter expectation of life than others, but there is no point on the weight scale which critically divides those with a shorter or longer expectation of life. This information could not be utilized if it were argued that no two people had exactly the same weight. It is only when we are prepared to classify that we can use the scientific method. To reject classification is to reject the scientific method and to provide nothing in its place. The result is not a better approach to human problems but an acceptance of complete defeat or an excuse for avoiding all forms of action.

That the social and psychological make-up of man is complex is not denied. It is accepted that every individual is unique when we consider the complex factors in his circumstances and personality. But it has been noted that if we could measure any one thing with sufficient accuracy the individual would be shown to be unique. Since the argument against measurement on the grounds of complexity is similar to the argument of uniqueness derived from the accuracy of one measurement, in that both lead to the concept of the unique individual, it is convenient to consider the latter case because of its greater simplicity.

The assumption of uniqueness from one accurate measurement may be related to a theorem of Dedekind, which states that number is infinite, that between any two numbers of which we can conceive there is always another number which may also be conceived. But this fact does not worry us. We operate with number sufficiently accurate for the purposes we have in mind. For example, we estimate circumferences of circles from their diameters using π, but we could raise the objection that the true value of π was unknown, and also object that we could not exactly measure diameters. No one would regard this argument as of much value. We use a value for π which, having regard to the accuracy with which we have measured the diameter, gives results sufficiently accurate for estimating the circumference. This is the solution we apply in physical problems. It may, of course, be claimed that our measuring instruments in this field are obviously highly accurate, but the analogy cannot be rejected on these grounds. Not long ago the accuracy of measurement was often a limiting factor in the physical sciences, and at the frontiers of knowledge may be so today. If measurement is rejected outright, there is very little likelihood of its being improved; if it is accepted and its possibilities appreciated, it is likely that advance will be made in the techniques of measurement. The joint interplay of improvement in measurement techniques and the use of measurement is important in the social sciences also. What we can do is limited by what we know, and what we know is also limited by what we can do.

If we measure persons to the nearest inch, we shall find many who are alike and can be classified together. This accuracy is sufficient for many purposes, and inadequate for others. In general, if we take one characteristic at a time and classify individuals into broad groups, we shall find many alike. We cannot reject the utility of this principle, but it seems that is what some critics of measurement applied to human problems would wish to do. They claim that measurement is too coarse and that they can measure or describe much more accurately than the degree of accuracy obtained by measuring instruments. They claim, in fact, that they know (can show?) that they can describe individuals with such precision that they are seen to be unique and go on to suggest that, because we do not untilize this information in measurement, measurement is inadequate. Logically they should also argue: number is infinite – I will not agree to use number which I know to be inaccurate! Clearly the concept of *sufficient* accuracy for utility must be accepted. This involves immediately the concept of use for *a purpose*. Not only are different degrees of accuracy required for different purposes, but information

187

which is useful for one purpose is not necessary for another. The number of measurements required as well as their accuracy depends upon the complexity of the task. This may seem obvious, but what follows from an acceptance of this obvious assessment of reasonable behaviour is often rejected.

Let us assume the acceptance of the above argument, which may be summarized:

(a) measurement is always approximate
(b) the number and accuracy of measurements should depend upon purpose.

Then it seems to follow that there is no point in demonstrating that individuals are unique or that measurement is likely to be inaccurate, without showing also that the 'inaccurate' measurements or those omitted are

(i) relevant
(ii) not sufficiently accurate

where both (i) and (ii) relate to a specific and limited purpose. This proposes a dilemma for those opposing measurement on the grounds of uniqueness or the complexity of the human personality, which are similar arguments. The proof of relevance and the degree of accuracy with respect to a purpose can, it seems, be found only in the use of measurement techniques. In any search for more information upon which to base measurements, we have to face the hard test of use-for-purpose. In any attempts to increase the accuracy of a measurement there will come a point where increased accuracy becomes unnecessary or where the increase does not result in any significant increase in the specification relative to the particular purpose. At some point, the contribution of further information will become so small that we shall not be able to distinguish any differences between increased accuracy and fluctuations due to chance alone. We cannot explain any unique case or once-for-all event since any event which is unique or once-for-all can be no guide to future action. It is not the uniqueness of the individual that concerns the clinician but the similarities between any particular case and prior cases in his or other people's experience. If a case is unique there can be no experience to guide the clinician.

Intangibles

Social caseworkers often concede that when 'facts' are being considered measurement and statistical methods are acceptable, but suggest that they are concerned with 'the significant intangible features of personality that they observe in the clinical situation'. But if these features are 'intangible' how can anyone know that they exist? How does the clinician take them into account? Can they not be described in words? If not, are they more than the prejudices of the observer? If they are describable they may be dealt with in logical models. How do we know that these intangible features, if they exist, do not overlap with observable features so that there is no point in including them? But these questions themselves cannot be answered until those who maintain that they can deal with 'intangible' features can reduce their claim to words in the form of a set of hypotheses of a kind which can be tested. Faith in intangibles, coupled with a scientific attitude, is an essential part of an approach to further development. It is not the intention to discourage faith, but only to indicate that it is not a substitute for, or an answer to, analytical methods. Science acknowledges the partial nature of knowledge, and looks always for better and newer explanations, but it can never reduce its rigour.

REFERENCE

OHLIN, L. E. (1955). Symposium on Prediction Methods. International Congress of Criminology, 1955. London.

189

CHAPTER 8

Target, Criteria, Ends, and Means

Needs: clients and agencies – Resources – Relevance of measurement – Attempted action and achieved action – The problem of consensus – Democratic definitions of objectives – Reducing juvenile delinquency – Vulnerable groups – Prevention problems – Selection of 'target areas' – Diffuse or concentrated action? – Criterion or criteria? – Contamination of criteria

If science can be inventive about other people's problems it should also be able to be inventive about its own. Attempts to rush into top gear with cooperative efforts in the social field are, perhaps, a little ahead of the abilities to organize a satisfactory communication system within and between the agencies concerned.

Needs – Clients and Agencies

Desires to meet the needs of deprived groups of the population and to operate upon the social problems perceived are not lacking; the techniques of measurement are still somewhat crude but are developing rapidly and even now are of considerable utility. What is lacking is a knowledge of how these different skills and resources might be marshalled most effectively. Agencies, systems, and organizations as at present constituted tend to settle into grooves. It has been remarked that social agencies which begin their life with a concern for social problems which is demonstrated with some effect, soon degenerate into systems where the major concern is with the preservation or expansion of the system itself. The emphasis moves from the external problems of other people to problems of the professional status of members of the agency. This means that there takes place a subtle change in the nature of the objectives which it is desired to achieve.

The majority of social agencies and even social research organizations are not dynamic, self-regulatory, and learning systems, continuously changing to adapt to the best means for obtaining their initial objectives. In present conditions special languages get built up within the professional systems, and communication across to other

190

disciplines or professions, also initially concerned with the same external problems, becomes difficult or impossible.

Recent foundation grants in terms of millions of dollars which have specified as a condition of the grant that cooperative effort between different agencies and research teams must be devised have the appearance of shot-gun marriages between mixed races! Perhaps the main achievement of some of these projects will be not so much in the area which has been specified as the problem, but rather in the solution of some of the problems of communication between the groups concerned. In order to obtain the money, many differently orientated persons have had to talk to each other and to try to establish some measure of communication. Once the grant has been given, however, power struggles can resume and result in unbalanced designs developing in the project, and staff resignations may tend to be selective. It might have been more effective, if, first, some study had been made at a higher level of abstraction in terms of problems of communication; and if, before more applications of 'science' were pressed into action, more effort had been spent in investigating problems in the 'science of science'. The position must, however, be taken from where it now is.

No matter what systems are evolved to deal with problems of social action evaluation, it will be necessary to work through from general statements of the major objectives to specific objectives or 'means' (sub-objectives), and some suitable strategy must be decided upon. When this is done the most difficult and important task has been completed. When it is known exactly what it is intended to do and how the action should proceed and with what effect, the problem of measuring the effects of the attempted changes becomes a technical problem where what is not known is known not to be known.

Resources

The objectives of any scheme must be realistic. What can be attempted is limited by the resources available. The resources for social change are people and knowledge. The number of people available for any social action project will be determined at the policy stage. The division of resources between action and evaluation of action is also a policy matter on which there is little information to serve as a guide to optimum allocation. It has not been customary to detail the costs of social research in relation to its results so that the relative pay-off can be assessed. Perhaps one of the objectives of any social-action-research design should be to try to obtain detailed cost data so that information is available for guidance in future planning. It seems to have been a feature of industrial and commercial processes that, as they have advanced, greater and greater proportions of the total costs of the enterprise have been deployed in research and development. Perhaps the same type of evolution will take place in the human science and administration field. At present, it can only be suggested that social accounting would seem to be as important as financial accounting. To do things and not to know the pay-off may be as wasteful as spending money and not knowing how it is spent; and perhaps equally unethical.

The balance between research and evaluation staffs and other staffs would seem to require a proportion not less than the ratio of financial-accounting staffs to other staffs. There is, of course, a major difference between financial accounting and social accounting or evaluation. In financial accounting the scales in which the measurements are to be made (money) are known and have been established over many years, whereas in the evaluation of social action the scales have yet to be derived. It is as though double-entry book-keeping had first to be invented! Moreover, different systems of book-keeping may be required for different types of social action pay-off measurement. In any event, and no matter what the ratio of evaluation to action resources, both sections of the activity must be integrated. The measurement must be relevant to the action.

Relevance of Measurement

The distinction between means and ends in evaluation studies is sometimes difficult to derive and maintain. When the general objectives of the project have been broken down into aims, the aims, although the 'ends' of some sections of the project, are only means to the general objective. For example, if the objective is to reduce juvenile delinquency, one of the steps to achieve this objective might be considered to be the improvement of reading ability, which may involve some modification in the school curriculum. Proposals to meet the sub-objective (aim) of improvement in reading ability are means to obtain the 'end' of reducing juvenile delinquency. Whether the means (sub-objectives) are appropriate to the ends is a matter for evaluation, as well as assessments of how well the sub-objectives are achieved. The stage of planning which involves the breakdown from the general objective to sub-objectives relies on resources of information and, particularly, on the result of research previously completed. Such activity is, therefore, an appropriate one for research-trained personnel.

In order to ensure the relevance of the measurement to the basic problem it would appear to be useful to state the evidence which is relied upon in the assumption that the sub-objectives (means) will assist in achieving the general objective. For any proposed action, even the day-to-day detail of social action, it should be possible to suggest what sort of behaviour on the part of the client, or of the target population, would be taken to indicate changes in a positive direction or changes in a negative direction with respect to the particular aims of the particular activity. If a person is travelling along a particular road towards a particular destination which he can specify, there should be some sign-posts or other characteristics of the country through which he is passing to enable him to know whether he is moving in the right direction. If it is not possible to spell out in detail those changes which are believed to indicate that the action is having the desired effect and, equally important, changes which would indicate that the action is having an undesired effect, then it would seem that insufficient is known of the action to justify putting it into effect. No sick person, no matter how deadly his ailment, is given medicine about which *no* statements can be made regarding its expected effects in terms of this kind. The same ethic should characterize social action. The detailed changes, either positive or negative, should be related to the desired change envisaged in the objective or the sub-objectives. It is, it seems, most unlikely that short-term undesirable results will give rise to long-term desirable results.

There is good evidence that learning theory offers reasonable explanations of many aspects of human behaviour with which social action is concerned. It is true that social workers usually claim that any evaluation of their work must take into account long-term effects – usually over several years or even a generation or two. There may be such long-term effects, but any attempt to assess them is likely to be extremely costly and very difficult to apply in practice. People tend to be mobile, and if even a small proportion of the initial sample, or target population, is lost, the results of evaluation are of dubious value. The claim to long-term effects does not seem to square with what is known of learning processes. All learning curves tend to be steep at first and to tail off rapidly. Of course, it may be that what one person has learned can only be transmitted in terms of social effect through other people. But if this is so, it should be possible to measure the learning achieved by the first person in the chain reaction and to state whether this has been in positive accord with theory or not. The theory should relate the short-term effects to the sub-objectives or limited aims, and through these to the general objectives of the social action. Each link in the chain reaction can be subjected to evaluation if the expected nature of the reaction can be specified.

If the nature of the reaction cannot be specified in respect of the short-term objectives, how is it that the long-term effects can be predicted with such precision as is usually claimed? It would seem that the precision with which expected outcomes can be stated should fall off as the distance from the action to the reaction increases, and not increase as some theses suggest. There may, of course, be processes which have long-term or cumulative effects, but it seems doubtful that these processes could be related to learning, and not at the same time show a discernible short-term effect of a related nature. The concept of long-term effects has further dangers. What sort of world will we be living in a generation or two hence? As has already been noted, change is now taking place in the technological fields at extremely fast rates. To what extent should we attempt to determine the sort of social situations which we now perceive as desirable for people, and project these to the social world of the future?

There may be spheres of social endeavour where it is meaningful to attempt to influence situations in the somewhat distant future. Any such attempts must take into account what is in the 'pipeline' for the future and carefully consider appropriate projections from other fields of science, technology, and human activity. The claim to long-term effects should not be used as a defence against the demand for evaluation of short-term effects, nor should it be used as an excuse for ignorance regarding the likelihood and nature of change to be observed in the immediate target population. If the relationship between long-term effects and short-term effects cannot be stated, there would seem to be some deficiency in the basic theoretical structure of the hypotheses upon which the action is proposed. It is particularly doubtful whether any action could claim to have zero short-term effects, but positive long-term effects. If the short-term effects are zero, it seems most probable that the long-term effects must also be zero in all cases where the process is one of learning.

Any social action related to long-term change should be examined to ensure that it does not inhibit in any way the 'means within society' . . . which enables it 'constantly to adjust itself to the alterations of technology and education and other social changes as they endlessly occur, automatically providing the basis for new advance' (Hailsham, 1962). In other words, *the future must not be mortgaged to the good intentions of the present.*

Attempted Action and Achieved Action

Related to the problem of separation of ends from means is the problem of assessing the extent to which attempted action is achieved. Obviously, attempted change is not expected to be achieved if the attempted action is not in fact carried out. The 'best-laid schemes' will not be put into effect in exactly the way they are prepared in the blueprints. As each modification has to take place in the field applications of the action programme, the potential and expected effect upon the outcome must be specified in detail. All social-research-action projects must, for obvious reasons, include means of assessing the nature of the differences between the proposals and the actual action. Indeed, it is desirable that the priorities for sections of any complex action programme be stated in advance. It is necessary to assess how much room for manoeuvre is available in the social-action proposals before the expected outcome has so deteriorated that it is not worth while to proceed further. It is futile and wasteful to claim after the event (although many instances of this claim appear in the literature) that the omission on practical grounds of a certain part of the endeavour, or some enforced modification of the scheme, provides the explanation of the ineffective outcome.

The principles underlying evaluation are fairly easy to state, and it is possible that they will command general agreement. The problems arise in the methodology rather than in the philosophy of evaluation. It may, for example, be agreed that it is necessary to have a large measure of consensus regarding the objectives and even the sub-objectives of the projected action, but how is such concordance to be obtained? It may be agreed that there are likely to be difficulties of language, and that broad concepts involving intangibles and imponderables must be reduced to specific expected consequences. But how may this translation be facilitated? Some techniques are available to assist in this process, and these may be illustrated with respect to the assumed objective of 'reducing juvenile delinquency'.

Again, the subject used for illustrative purposes is not intended to suggest that the methodology is restricted to application in this limited field.

The Problem of Consensus

In the initial stages of discussion the attempt to reduce the language of broad generalizations to more specific language in terms of aims and expectations seems to be dysfunctional. Experience suggests that there is a greater likelihood of success attending discussions at this stage if an identity of interests in terms of the general social ethic and its implications in the general objective can be obtained. If group solidarity can be achieved at this level of abstraction, it will be easier to move to agreement on the necessary detail. Discussion using broad band-width language – the general language of laymen with which all persons are familiar – will facilitate the gradual learning of the specific languages of the different interests and disciplines that may be represented around the planning-table. Research workers should be able to involve themselves in this discussion at the same level, using the same language as the others concerned with the action-research planning. At this stage research workers should resist verbalizing the particular logical processes of their own disciplines; phrases like, 'Well, it all depends on what you mean by . . .' or, 'Suppose that . . . then what?' are useful for research thinking, but may be interpreted as threatening to those emotionally involved with the problems of deprived or sick people. In any event, such questions do not have a place until the level of specification has been reduced following a fair level of consensus on the broader ethical issues. But the discussions in the broad band-width language of ethical considerations may be utilized by the social research worker to produce content analyses, and from these analyses to provide suggestions of more specific statements which embody the general ethic. Informal discussions can also increase the sample of information available. At this stage of the procedure we are not concerned with scientific measurement, but with the processes of 'democratic definition'. As soon as it is possible to bring in some formal research methods a number are available within the meaning of the democratic ethic.

Democratic Definitions of Objectives

The language of broad band-width concepts may be regarded as a language involving collective abstraction of events (Σe_i). If the language has been built up in this way, it seems legitimate to break it down again so that it can be used for research purposes, without such breaking-down of concepts changing in any way the meaning of the terms used in the higher levels of discussion. If, for example, an aim of a proposed change in the educational system is said to be desirable to increase 'initiative', it may be thought that the term initiative is one having a large band-width. Different people will interpret 'initiative' in different ways. None the less, most people will interpret initiative as being 'good', although the collective (Σe_i) to which they refer this concept of 'good' may differ. Suppose, then, that a sample of individuals from an appropriate population were asked to give examples of 'acts of initiative' from their own experience, the abstract concept 'initiative' would then be replaced by a sample of specific acts of initiative in situations to which the term is most usually applied (Belson, 1957). Since to 'increase initiative' was the stated aim of the action, and the term initiative is an abstract collective (Σe_i), the sampling procedure of democratic definition unscrambles the summation and at the same time provides a set of events which can be used as specific criteria. By this means the research worker is accepting a symbolic and highly coded term from the language of 'policy', on the reasonable assumption that the term is an abstraction derived from a collection of specific items. Abstractions may, it seems, be defined in terms of the particular elements which gave rise to the construction of the collective or abstract concept in the course of semantic development. *If words mean what by custom they have come to mean, then there is no difference in working with their meanings instead of working with the words themselves.* By the method of democratic definition almost all concepts may be replaced by samples of events; by samples of events which, by reason of their wide variation, may be supposed to have given rise in the course of semantic development to the need to invent the abstract term in the first place. From the sample events, it is possible to create a collective of specific elements which, together with their frequency distribution, may be expected to mirror the image in the minds of the discussants who used the term (e.g. 'initiative') as a form of summary of the underlying collective. Some abstractions may most appropriately be broken down by reference to a general population sample, whereas others may be more appropriately referred to special samples. It would be possible to deal with such concepts as 'happiness', 'maturity', 'adjustment',[1] and the like by this means.

The general case of 'democratic definitions' may be related to several forms of statistical analysis. Four types of research method[2] seem to be useful in deriving criteria from general statements of aims and objectives. These are:

> (a) rating scales
> (b) concordance measurement
> (c) Q-sort technique
> (d) semantic differential

It is not the purpose here to discuss how these different methods may be used, but rather when and why. To facilitate the exposition of why and when, one example may be given. If different persons who are authorized to state objectives cannot agree on a particular objective as desirable, such an objective does not provide a good basis for assessing the effects of social action. Before a concept can be used for evaluation it must be communicable. If some persons agree with respect to a particular objective, whereas others disagree, the principle of democracy may be applied in that the more idiosyncratic the objectives the lower the priority given in the total research-action design. This does not mean that concordance between all persons is essential before research or action may proceed, but where there is a greater measure of agreement, more funds might be considered to be legitimately spent.

The degree of communication achieved between persons can be measured by use of the coefficient of concordance (Kendall, 1948). Let us suppose that three persons are asked to rank in order six statements of objectives (devised perhaps from a content analysis of initial discussions of the project) as follows:

[1] The samples to be selected to provide the basis for the democratic definition of these terms would vary. Each term would need a different sample according to the frame of reference within which the term was seen as operationally valid. For example, 'adjustment' might refer to adjustment to an institution; in which case the definition might most appropriately be referred to institution staffs – namely those who habitually used the word. Those using it form the sample for defining it – if they put together experiences and impressions into the general term, they are the best people to unscramble it again! How is adjustment recognized in terms of behaviour? How is 'good' adjustment distinguished from 'poor'? What action is taken to remedy adjustment perceived as 'poor'? Such and other questions should assist the users of the term to provide guidance to the setting up of operational (democratic) definitions.

[2] With the exception of (d), these methods are described in any good general textbook of statistical methods applied in the social, psychological, or educational field. The semantic differential method is discussed in Osgood, Suci & Tannenbaum (1958).

TABLE 8

| Rater | Statement | | | | | |
	a	b	c	d	e	f
X	1	6	3	2	5	4
Y	1	5	6	4	2	3
Z	6	3	2	5	4	1
$\Sigma (R_j)$	8	14	11	11	11	8

The R_j gives the sums of the ranks. Clearly if each rater had agreed with the other two regarding the first placing, the R_j would be $1+1+1=3k$, and the second rank would be $2+2+2=6=2k$; if all agreed the various sums of ranks would be 3, 6, 9, 12, 15, 18, although not perhaps in that order in respect of the statements a, b, . . . f. If there were no agreement the R_j would be approximately equal. If a high value for the coefficient w (which may be obtained from the R_js) is found, we may assume that all assessors are applying much the same standard of assessment. If the standards of assessment are reasonably similar we may proceed further and attempt to build a scale, or we may select items as objectives to be used in the evaluation from those items which show high levels of agreement.

None the less, some of the items upon which there may be little agreement may be important, and the ranking differences may be due only to the different interpretation of the terms used in the description of the objectives. In such cases of disagreement, the semantic differential method offers a means for noting those items and concepts which may be perceived by different people as lying in different 'dimensions'. The application of this method enables a more specific terminology to be sought in respect of those items where it seems to be desirable. The simplest application of the semantic differential method utilizes a three-dimensional model of 'semantic space'. Different concepts are located on a three-dimensional graph, and their locations in this three-dimensional space may be compared, either in respect of different concepts or in respect of the same concept as perceived by different people. If, for example, two people have disagreed in regard to the importance or appropriateness of a certain aim or objective, it may be found that the particular aim is located in a different position in their 'semantic space'. The term 'mature' is used very frequently in caseworkers' reports, and although most caseworkers would agree that 'maturity' is an important factor in understanding any client, semantic differential analyses have revealed that different caseworkers locate the concept 'maturity' in different positions in their 'semantic space'. Although agreement may be obtained initially in discussions among caseworkers centring on the concept of maturity it would not be unexpected, therefore, if, as greater specification of the concept came to be required, differences began to appear.

Reducing Juvenile Delinquency

Some of the problems of measuring crime in general social-accounting procedures have already been indicated. The problems of measuring juvenile delinquency are even greater. If a juvenile delinquent is defined as any person under, say, sixteen years of age who has been found guilty of any offence which for an adult would be regarded as a crime (indictable offence), it will be obvious that it is impossible to measure juvenile delinquency from such indices as 'crimes known to the police'. Unless a crime is 'cleared up' there can be no way of knowing the age of the offender who performed the act. Thus the number of delinquent acts must be unknown. Immediately one speaks about juvenile delinquency one is speaking about *persons* and not *incidents*. To some extent it is meaningful to discuss the amount of crime in an area, but not the amount of juvenile delinquency. One may discuss the number of adult offenders *found guilty*, and the number of juvenile offenders *found guilty* or the number of adult *suspects* or juvenile *suspects arrested*, but the concept of juvenile delinquency is inseparable from the concept of the particular individual concerned, namely the juvenile. This is a very simple distinction, but it is quite often overlooked.

An area may show a high crime rate, but this does not mean that it has a high juvenile delinquency rate; it is in fact possible that no juvenile delinquents live in that area. Crimes and the disposals of offenders by the courts are usually referred to the area in which the crime was committed, indeed it is difficult to see how the figures could otherwise be recorded. A substantial number of offenders are persons of no fixed abode. It is, of course, possible to trace back those crimes which have been detected, and in respect of which some person or persons have been interrogated or detained, to the area in which the suspect or offender normally lived. This is the best measure that can be obtained of the delinquency rates in particular areas. It must be remembered, however, that these data relate to delinquency in respect of which some action has been taken and some person has been detained.

It is probable that the areas which contain the homes of many identified offenders also contain the homes of unidentified and potential offenders. If the requirement to 'reduce juvenile delinquency' is related to those individuals who have been identified as offenders, the problem is not strictly one of the prevention of delinquency, but of the treatment of offenders. It is much easier to consider questions relating to recidivism, because an individual will be identified, and at some time – at least for a short period – form a part of a 'captive population'. Action research related to this population is not strictly prevention work; it is treatment. The action is treatment carried out with a view to the prevention of *recidivism*, not the prevention of delinquency. This is an important distinction.

Delinquency cannot be measured with anything like the accuracy of the measurement of the effects of treatment. Moreover, there is evidence to suggest that factors which predispose individuals towards recidivism (once having committed an offence for which they have been detected) are often different from those which discriminate non-delinquents (persons who have not at any time been found guilty of an offence) from those found guilty of an offence (Power, 1963). In this area of research, certainly not less than in any other, the information which is relevant to the solution of one type of problem differs from that relevant to another, although both types of problem may be subsumed under the general phrasing used in the initial statement of the problem.

While there are problems in the field of treatment, these are different from those which arise in research in the open community where the 'target' population is not isolated by any administrative action or legal procedure. Doubtless the total problem of 'juvenile delinquency' is concerned with both recidivists and first offenders, but the fact that it is possible to state the problem in a collective phrase does not mean that it is possible to use the same collective when one is concerned with methods towards its solution. The separation of recidivism from delinquency that is not due to recidivists is only one of the divisions which may be essential in any attack upon the general problem. It is possible that non-offenders and one-time-only offenders are more similar to each other than are second offenders to first offenders.

It seems reasonable to try to concentrate action where it will have most likely effect – on the 'vulnerable groups'. If this is accepted as a strategy, it becomes necessary to define 'vulnerable groups' and to describe ways for detecting them and making them available for exposure to the treatment process independently of others.

The term 'vulnerable group' seems to have come to be used to mean two rather different things. On the one hand, it appears to have assumed some relationship with the social worker's concept of 'needy groups', whereas, on the other hand, it serves to indicate those groups that are most likely to benefit by treatment or other social action. The two groups may or may not be composed of the same persons. The term is used here to mean those groups where action is most likely to have a pay-off. This concept is related to the market-research field, where types of person who do not at present buy a certain product are identified as most likely to be influenced by advertising. Mass media are then chosen which are likely to be seen by the 'vulnerable group'. To some extent the analogy holds for social action; in dealing with crime we may be regarded as trying to 'sell' socially conforming behaviour. It is material, then, to ask which groups of persons are most likely to be influenced by our social action (sales) techniques to 'buy' the idea of 'good' behaviour – among those, that is, who do not currently 'buy' the idea. The analogy does not hold too well, because even the most criminal of criminals is not criminal all the time. Indeed, even our worst criminals must spend most of their time in reasonably 'normal' behaviour. At least in some aspects of social life and for a large proportion of their time, they conform to the demands of society. If they did not they would not be defined as criminal, but rather as mentally ill, and dealt with in quite different ways by society. Indeed, even the mentally ill do not demonstrate their illness in a continuous fashion, except in the small minority of cases. This is an important fact which is too often over-looked. Having defined a person as criminal or as deviant, we tend to forget that this definition rests upon a very small sector of the demonstrated behaviour of the individual. It is possible that there is an aspect of criminal behaviour which is continuous, and aspects of mental disorder which are continuous, but most of the defining actions of society do not rest upon these continuous variables and stable attributes of personality, whatever they may be, but on specific incidents.

These facts make it impossible to find out, for example, how many juvenile delinquents there are in any particular area, since it is not possible to identify them by continuous variables or attributes. Some continuous factors are known to correlate with the isolated incidents, but these correlates are not perceived by society as the defining variables.

Delinquency areas can be identified where known delinquents live, and this implies that in respect of those persons *some* action has already taken place. The action is inseparable from the identifition of the problem. The existence of known delinquents in an area (in respect of whom some action has taken place) is often used to suggest the existence of delinquency in the same area about which no action has been taken. But action to deal with *known delinquents* is not *prevention of crime* but *prevention of recidivism*, which may be a different type of problem. There would seem to be a basic difference between the problem of treatment (action to assist persons who have been found guilty of an offence by due process) and the problem of prevention (where the basis for action is either *persons* who *have not* been found guilty or some aspect of the social system which it is believed gives rise to crime).

There is also a very large difference between research and action related to *persons*, and research and action related to *systems*. The conversion of either of these types of problem into the form of the other raises many questions of social action and research methodology.

The majority of social-work skills have been concentrated upon individual or family treatment, and the conversion of the social problem of prevention of delinquency into an individual problem has been proposed by means of defining potential delinquents. Individuals not known to have committed crimes who show a number of characteristics similar to those who are known to have offended are classified as potential offenders. But attempts to identify 'potential offenders' are open to question on many grounds, and it seems that their identification may prejudice social action (see Chapter 4). Even if it were possible to overcome the objections to the identification of potential delinquents, investigations and social action in this area would need quite different approaches from other types of problems. Sub-division of the problem seems to be necessary on several counts.

The main sub-divisions seem to be:

(A) Treatment (i) first offenders
                  (ii) other offenders
(B) Prevention (i) potential offenders
                  (ii) other non-offenders

It seems possible that a sub-division of category A(i) into first offenders who are classified as potential second offenders and those whose characteristics seem to suggest that they are not likely to offend again (spontaneous recovery) might also be useful.

A study of recent research findings suggests that the four or five categories of 'target audience' will require not only different types of research and evaluation techniques, but different forms of social action, unless some general factor, at present unknown, should be found. Rather than more general factors being discovered, it seems likely that further sub-divisions of the population will be noted and shown to need specialized forms of treatment. Some of the evidence relied upon for these statements will be examined when it is appropriate to consider more detailed problems. At present we are not concerned to discuss what kinds of sub-division are necessary in any specific problem area, but only to indicate the need to consider types of sub-division as a method in problem-solving.

Vulnerable Groups

It is often suggested that the majority of serious crimes are committed by 'habitual offenders'. It is not clear what this statement might mean, because there is no acceptable definition of the seriousness of crime – it might depend on a circular argument whereby crimes committed by persons with long criminal records were automatically regarded as 'more serious'. Certainly the sentences imposed by the courts upon persons with prior criminal offences are more severe, but this does not indicate that the particular crime for which they were brought to trial was itself more serious.

Few data or none seem to be available to suggest which line of attack upon the problem of crime or juvenile delinquency would be the most likely to prove profitable. Nor is there any way of ascertaining which problem produces the more damaging effects upon society. This is, perhaps, a surprising state of affairs, but until criminal acts are viewed as situations and not merely as the wrongdoing of a person, it is improbable that information will be available which could effectively guide research strategy in this area.

Although it is impossible to consider the seriousness of crime, data are available regarding the criminal records of offenders dealt with by the courts.

Table 9 shows the number of cases of male offenders dealt with by the courts in England and Wales during 1956, who were seventeen years of age and over, having given numbers of previous convictions.

TABLE 9

Number of previously proved offences of male offenders found guilty in 1956 by courts in England and Wales (17 years of age and over)

Previous convictions	Number	Per cent
None	33,682	52
One	7,771	12
Two	5,196	8
Three or more	18,644	28
Total	65,293	100

Almost exactly half of the persons dealt with by the courts were, so far as was known, being dealt with for the first time. If, then, 1956 was a typical year, it may be assumed that approximately one-half of adult crime is due to 'first offenders'. These results seem to have some meaning for social action and research. Should scarce resources for rehabilitation be concentrated upon those offenders who are undergoing their first treatment, their second treatment, or subsequent treatments? Or should attention be directed to those who have not yet committed offences? The inferences which may be drawn from this single analysis are limited, but they may indicate that it is possible to obtain and interpret information which may assist in determining priorities in some relevant areas of concern. The interpretation of these data requires the assumption that 1956 was a typical year, i.e. that if any other year had been chosen the proportions of offenders who were first, second, or habitual criminals would be materially the same. It is not known whether this is so, or whether the increase in the total number of crimes detected and the number for which persons were dealt with in the courts in 1956 over preceding years was due to more first offenders becoming criminals or to the greater activity of those who had previously begun a life of crime; 1956 was a year with a high crime rate, but not so high as 1952 or 1957 or some later years; it was neither a peak nor a trough year in the 'crime wave' cycle.

The proportion of crimes of violence in 1956 was greater than in previous years, and crimes of violence are slightly more likely to be committed by first offenders than by habitual offenders. Crimes of violence, however, represent a very small proportion of the total of crime. If 1956 was typical in so far as the proportions of offenders with differing numbers of proved offences in their history were concerned, it may be supposed that every year would reveal 52 per cent of offenders dealt with by the courts to be found guilty of indictable offence(s) for the first time, 12 per cent to be second offenders, 8 per cent third-time offenders, and 28 per cent to have been found guilty on more than three previous occasions. If this is a reasonable assumption, it may be further assumed that the same characteristics would apply over the life span of current offenders. If the pattern of crime does not vary very significantly from year to year, it is possible to use the fact that all second offenders were earlier first offenders, and similarly all third offenders previously convicted for the second and a first time. This assumption permits of the use of the ratios of first to second, and second to third, findings of guilt to provide estimates of general recidivism rates for each degree of commitment to criminal activities.

Dividing the number of second offenders into the number of first offenders provides an estimate of the general probability of reconviction of first offenders (assuming stable conditions). Similarly, dividing the third offenders into the second offenders gives the general recidivism rate for those convicted for the second time. This provides a striking finding. The probability of a second offence, given that one has been committed, is 19·6 per cent, whereas the probability of a third offence, given that two have been committed, is 66·9 per cent. Using certain mathematical approximations, which are not unreasonable, it is possible to use these data to suggest that the probability of a fourth offence, given that three have been committed, is less than 72 per cent, which is only 5 per cent greater than the probability of a third offence given that two have been committed. Compare this with the probability of a second offence given that one has been committed – a difference of between 48 per cent and 49 per cent. Further, there can be little change in the probability of recidivism after two offences have been committed, since it is known that even offenders with

206

extremely long criminal records never reach 100 per cent recidivism (Hammond, 1963).

These ratios and percentages may be interpreted as follows. For every 100 offenders found guilty for the first time, only 19 or 20 will continue to a second offence; but of those 20, who go on to a second offence, 13 or 14 will continue to a third or subsequent offence. A large proportion of the 13 will have quite long criminal careers, although there is always a small chance that any offence will be their last. It should be remembered that these results relate to male offenders of seventeen years of age and over. The probabilities may be found to be rather different for juvenile offenders, and the slope of the rate of change in the probabilities between numbers of offences may change with the age of the first offence.

It would seem that, if it were possible to prevent first offenders from becoming second offenders, 50 per cent of the total amount of adult and adolescent crime which is cleared up by arrest would be eliminated. Indeed, the results might be better than this, because habitual offenders may be responsible for more than one event at any time that they are found guilty. This seems to be supported by the same data, although there is a chance that second and subsequent offences involve the offender with police methods which are rather more powerful in detecting additional offences than those available for detection of first offenders. For example, after a finding of guilt for an indictable offence, the fingerprints of the offender will be on the official files, but first offenders will not be so recorded.

Whether habitual offenders are responsible for more serious crimes is not known, but the number of offences dealt with at any one time by the court shows only a slight increase over the previous record of convictions. Of all male offenders over seventeen years of age convicted in 1956, rather less than one-half were convicted for one offence. Some had further offences proved at the same time, and others had offences taken into consideration in the disposal of the court. Including offences taken into consideration or proved at the same time, the following figures are obtained:

(a) Only one offence known or admitted	25,527
(b) More than one, but less than four, known or admitted crimes	17,202
(c) Four or more crimes known or admitted	22,564
Total (persons)	65,293

In terms of the number of crimes attributable to persons with different types of criminal record, the following analysis may be obtained if it is assumed that those having three or more offences may be considered to have on average four offences in the categories concerned.

	Persons	*Crimes*	*Mean*
(a) Only one known or admitted crime	25,527	25,527	1·00
(b) First appearance in court (no prior convictions)	33,682	50,694	1·51
(c) One previous conviction	7,771	13,197	1·70
(d) Two previous convictions	5,195	8,935	1·72
(e) Three or more previous convictions	18,644	35,788	1·92

These data are not primarily presented with a view to making any points specific to delinquency research or action, but as illustrations of the types of datum which may be obtained and used to throw light on the problems of selection of research strategies and action, and the problems of determining criteria in complex problem areas. It is probable that the interpretation of these data may vary between authorities, but it must be agreed that they provide some valuable evidence to guide discussions on the research process. Data of similar type to serve similar functions could doubtless be obtained with respect to other social problem areas.

In the particular illustrative case, it would seem to be reasonable to conclude that if research and action resources are scarce, research effort might be concentrated on the problem of identification of *potential second offenders* from among first offenders, and, when they are identified, action might be concentrated on means for their rehabilitation. The spontaneous recovery rate among first offenders is such that much effort could be wasted if attention were given to the whole group. Moreover, the identification from among those already classified according to the major category (i.e. 'offender') would seem to have a lesser probability of undesirable effects resulting from the classification procedure on its own account. Further, the problem is identified in terms of *persons* who are already selected (to some extent 'self-selected') and available for action.

Not all will agree that the needs of society for protection from criminal activities are best met by the concentration of effort on first offenders, and particularly on a small sub-set of first offenders. Some other or additional action will be demanded.

Prevention Problems

When action to prevent juvenile delinquency is proposed it is not only recidivism which is included in the proposals. There is a well-motivated desire to prevent youth from ever becoming connected with the treatment agencies for any infringement of the law. But good motivation is not sufficient as a guide to social action or research. No measures to *prevent* juvenile delinquency or crime can operate on the problem itself. It is possible only to operate upon the correlates. It is not possible to provide every potential delinquent, even if he could be successfully identified, with an externalized superego to withhold his hand each time delinquent acts began to be committed. The necessity for indirect action upon the problem raises many problems of methodology. The social action must deal with factors believed to be correlates (loosely termed 'causes') of delinquency, established for known delinquents in respect of whom some action has been taken in the course of identification. No matter how satisfactory the identification of the correlates, the action is indirect with reference to the problem.

Evaluation of such social action will concern itself in part with evaluation of the means to reduce juvenile delinquency which are, in fact, interim objectives. If lack of employment is believed to be a factor in delinquency, then an increase in employment facilities may be a legitimate interim objective. But the satisfactory development of a *means* is not proof that the *end* has been accomplished. Interim objectives do not provide a substitute for the general objective. If the general objective is not correctly stated, it should be amended, not replaced by a means. Moreover, the general objective must be related to a specific area – a city, county, or state. It is not possible to consider the evaluation of prevention of juvenile delinquency over a whole nation, because there would be no way of separating the effects of any total action from the general changes with time which may be due to factors outside the action programme. No action can be evaluated without *some sort* of 'control' system. Changes with time, independent of whatever action had been taken, will be expected to occur, and some areas or individuals must remain exposed only to these types of effects.

Action to prevent juvenile delinquency is usually proposed to be directed towards either:

    (a) specifically vulnerable individuals or groups (e.g. gangs);
    (b) specifically vulnerable areas ('grey areas').

The identification of pre-delinquent behaviour and the attempt to inhibit the development of delinquency through casework have been attempted in many action-research projects with doubtful results (see p. 96). Perhaps in view of these results it is now more fashionable to consider preventive action research beamed at particularly high-delinquency areas (Wilkins, 1962).

Selection of 'Target Areas'

The majority of research and action proposals beamed at the reduction of juvenile delinquency attempt to concentrate the resources in the high-delinquency areas. The identification of such areas is usually regarded as simple. Certain studies have shown, however, that areas which have a bad reputation among those who may be expected to know do not always turn out to be high-delinquency areas when rigorous data are obtained. In the United States of America the census tracts provide a very large quantity of social and economic data broken down for each tract, and even for blocks within tracts. Arrests of juveniles according to their place of residence can be related to the data in the census. In England and Wales the smallest unit area about which any social information is available is the ward. It would seem that data relating to juvenile arrests or other appropriate measures, analysed according to the census tract or ward of residence at the time of the offence, would provide good means for identifying suitable target areas for preventive social action. But census and similar data relate to a situation at a *point in time* (t_0) whereas delinquency at a point in time (t_0) is not meaningful. Delinquency rates, however constructed, must relate to some summation of incidents over a period of time. This fact immediately constitutes a problem of some significance. If the time interval is long enough for the number of incidents to be sufficiently large to have a small expected chance of variation, time trends will be obscured. On the other hand, if the size of the geographical area is increased so as to increase the number of incidents included, the area is likely to become more heterogeneous. Thus if the period of time over which incidents are collected is long, precision is lost, whereas, if it is short, the numbers used as the base for the delinquency rates will be small and subject to large variance. Similarly, if areas are grouped from census tracts or wards, precision may be lost owing to geographical heterogeneity. Some compromise between loss of precision (by time or geographical heterogeneity) and increase in variance due to a small number of delinquency incidents will have to be found. It is possible to solve such problems with mathematical elegance, provided sufficient basic information exists, but it is doubtful whether such data are generally available, particularly regarding the likely increase in geographical heterogeneity.

There are many unsolved problems involved in the selection of target areas. Only some of these can be noted here. The phenomenon of regression towards the mean presents a major difficulty. If only those areas are chosen for action which have shown, during a particular period, a very high rate of delinquency, it is probable that in a different period of time the same areas would show a lower rate due only to the 'regression' factor alone. The same applies to selected individuals who may, during a particular period, have shown a number of behavioural symptoms. To take the example of individuals who are defined as 'accident prone' because during, say, a one-year period they sustained an above-average number of minor injuries: during the following year, the larger proportion of them would not fall to be so classified, even although no measures were taken and they remained at exactly the same levels of risk. The reason for this will be seen intuitively if it is supposed that people playing a game with dice are identified as 'lucky' if, during a period of the game $(t_1 \rightarrow t_2)$, they have thrown a large number of sixes. Similarly, if the target areas are identified by reason of having the highest delinquency rates in a period (say, $t_1 \rightarrow t_2$), and social action takes place in the period following (say, $t_2 \rightarrow t_3$), and the results of social action are assessed later (say, $t_3 \rightarrow t_4$), the target areas would be expected to show some change for the better even if the social action had done actual harm!

It is also possible that areas which have high delinquency rates, and particularly areas which have a bad name, will be areas which are also seen as 'going downhill'. Thus there is a likelihood that during the period of social action, and during the period of assessment of its outcome afterwards, the factors conducive to delinquency may increase, even although the action may have inhibited the impact of these factors. The people most influenced by the social action to look to better things may, indeed, be the first to move away. The fitting of trends by statistical means does not seem to provide a very adequate method for explaining the expected deterioration in the target areas. This problem is very similar to that common to nearly all evaluation research; the nature of the 'output' of the treatment system may be influenced by the nature of the 'input' as well as by controlled (explained) and uncontrolled (unexplained) intervening variables. This problem has been approached by various techniques, one of which, and the most commonly misused, is the method of matching. There are objections to matching designs at nearly all levels of consideration, and these problems will be discussed in more detail later (see Appendices I and II).

Another method, somewhat related to matching, is known as the 'prediction' or 'base expectancy' method (see Appendix II). This method provides estimates of the expected outcome in terms of input factors. The method is completely general. It can be used to predict the outcome of individual treatment or, as is relevant in the present case, to determine the expected rate of delinquency in an area in terms of the social, economic, and other factors known about the area. Instead of matching in respect of those variables expected (intuitively) to have an influence on the outcome, the factors associated with variations in the output are determined empirically, then transformed into equations which (given that there is sufficient information) estimate the nature of the variation in the *output* which is due to variations in the *input*. These methods are described in statistical textbooks, and standard computer programmes exist to solve the necessary equations.

If satisfactory data can be obtained, it is possible to 'explain' a large proportion of the variation in delinquency (or other) rates between blocks, wards, or other geographically defined areas, in terms of other variables, such as age distribution, educational standards achieved, and economic factors. If the data are not adequate, this fact will be revealed by the analysis, in which case other methods must be sought. If the data are adequate, it would be possible to sort out the variations in delinquency rates within the 'target' area due to general social changes and those due to the social action. If a particular target area had 'gone downhill' during the period of social action, this fact would be reflected in other social indices that predict delinquency as well as in the delinquency rate itself. Thus an 'expected' rate for delinquency could be computed, having regard to the deterioration in other variables and compared with that actually observed following upon the action programme.

These methods are, of course, conceptually related to the experimental and control-group techniques and have similar limitations. The amount of control provided either by matching or by prediction methods cannot be better than the power of the data put into it. Prediction methods are expected to be more powerful in that they use more data than simple matching, and their action upon the data can be noted in detail.

The selection of the 'target' area can prejudice the effectiveness of the methods used for evaluation, and the selection of the area should be made with reference to the system it is proposed to use for evaluation. This feature of the method for selection and evaluation in social-action work in specific areas involves a number of technical issues, for which those interested are referred to Appendix I. For purposes of the present discussion, let it be assumed that the prediction equations have been calculated, taking into account the necessary technical refinements; it is then possible to draw a graph showing the actual delinquency rates within each of the areas of the city, county, or state on one axis, and the calculated (predicted by equation) rate on the other axis. A simplified illustration of how this might appear is given as *Figure 10*.

It is expected that the areas which it will seem desirable to select for social action will be those located in the top right-hand corner of the scatter of points, because they will have a high delinquency rate. Suppose, however, that some areas are 'outliers' – that is to say, they present a pattern of delinquency which cannot be well represented in terms of other variables (points marked in figure); the selection of one of these areas for the 'target' of social action would clearly be undesirable. Whatever the factors that may explain the high rates of delinquency in those areas they are not the same as those which explain the high rates in other areas. This fact has a meaning for social action as well as for research.

It may be supposed that in most cases some census tracts, blocks, or wards will cluster along the regression line. It would seem desirable to select as 'target' areas those located in similar two-dimensional space (predicted and observed rates) to other areas which might

213

serve as controls (as illustrated by points 'O' (control) and 'X' (experimental) on the simplified figure).

There are complex methodological problems in the selection of areas or groups of persons for whom special social action is proposed. Whatever the purpose of the selection, it must always be made

FIGURE 10

Regression matching for selection of experimental and control areas

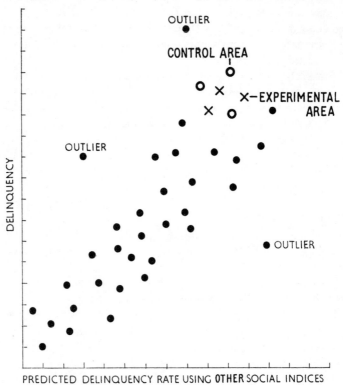

specific and carefully thought out in detail. It is not possible to consider the question of criteria of success of action until the basic dimensions along which change is sought are rigorously defined. Persons are not areas, and areas are not persons. If improvement is sought in an area, it is not reasonable to base the measure of improvement on the population of the area – it may be a different population; similarly, if the basis of the operation is persons, then it is not adequate to relate measurements of change to changes in the area factors. If areas are used as a means of obtaining access to people in the required categories, transitions in the thinking from areas to people are likely to prove difficult – it is not easy to separate means and ends even in this regard all along the line – but it is essential. And these problems can be met.

The most rigorous methods available that are consistent with the purpose of the action-research project should be sought out and used. The cost of the best methods is not much greater than the cost of poor methods; indeed, the cost of less rigorous methods may be greater. Rigorous methods have been adapted for computers, and computers work a lot faster and cheaper than humans, and are usually more efficient – if correctly told what to do.

Diffuse or Concentrated Action?

The nature of the strategy for action relates to the dimensions of proposed change, and relates accordingly to the choice of criteria. If a diffuse attack on the social problem is proposed, the separation of different components of the action will not generally be possible. Accordingly, it might seem appropriate to use a 'general net-improvement index' as criterion of success of the action. But an index which cannot be identified by its parts will always be of doubtful value. If the proposed action is concentrated upon several different and specific aspects of the general problem, and the specific aspects can be identified in terms of the expected nature of the attempted changes in the situation, it may be possible to obtain some index for each of the sub-problems and the nature of the change which could be combined into a general net-improvement index.

The majority of the research-action designs in the field of juvenile delinquency and crime prevention at the present time tend to concentrate all the preventive or remedial measures in one area or upon one class of person. The action is multi-phased, but the target population is restricted – many things are attempted in respect of the same persons. In such projects the effect of action which may be taken to deal with some specific sub-problem area will overlap with the action taken in other areas – in terms of both the physical area and the problem area. It is unlikely that specific criteria related to specific action projects within the total programme of action can be developed. How much one project has received of 'effect' spilled over from another project within the limited area or population will be confounded with specific effects. Indeed, in respect of behaviour which may be disapproved of, but is unrelated to any direct action, changes which may be perceived as improvement may be noted. This possibility is often claimed as one of the advantages of concentrated social-action programmes. This possibility cannot be denied, nor can the possibility that two types of action, both 'good', may have an undesirable effect if they interact together.

The studies at Haarlem, Lower East Side, Flint, and many other places provide examples of the multiple-action programme concentrated in one small area upon a selected population. It is questionable whether such a concentration of effort provides the optimum action design, and it is more certainly not an optimum design for assessing the effects of social action. It may be better to use one area as a demonstration and action area for one type of social problem and different areas for other types of research and action. The same may be true whether the basic unit is an area or individuals selected by other systems of classification than where they happen to live. The selection of a specific activity (in the case of offenders, say, a specific form of treatment for one type of offender and a different treatment for another type of offender) may prove more effective in terms of social action, and it would certainly facilitate research and evaluation.

Whether the problem is prevention, treatment, or preservation, alternative systems of action and research should be explored. At the present time it would be a most unfortunate decision if the few examples of demonstration-action projects which are in progress should be taken as models for further action. At the present time, and perhaps always, it is a poor strategy to restrict innovation. Flexibility of thinking and robust research designs are essential.

It might appear to those most concerned with social action that research requirements are likely to reduce the efficiency of the action. But obviously this cannot be known without research. The combination of research with action may reduce the efficiency of either action or research, but it cannot reduce the efficiency of both. If we have confidence in the direction we are travelling along a road, we may not spend time looking at the sign-posts, but a little time spent in checking the navigation appeals to the rational man. No one can claim to have travelled this road of social action before, and confidence in the 'right road' may be misplaced. Research (looking at sign-posts) may delay what we wish to achieve, *if we are by chance right in our assess-*

ments, but we must consider the risks – risks not only to ourselves but also to those for whom we wish to do 'good'.

Criterion or Criteria

The criteria used for evaluation depend both upon the strategy of research and upon action. The limitations of the 'mass attack' have already been noted (see Chapter 5). Objections were noted in terms both of research and of the probable effects of social action. A similar objection may now be made to any attempt to compress evaluation into one compounded measure of 'net effect'. Compression seems to be undesirable whether the proposed action is expected to influence one or many different social problems. Even where the effect sought appears to be quite specific to one factor or one social problem, multiple measurement of the outcomes may be suggested to be more likely to be of value.

In the field of measurement of human behaviour there are many systems which may be used for similar purposes. The different systems have different advantages and disadvantages. All forms of measurement begin by making some assumptions. Some systems make one kind of assumption, others different types of assumption.

No one method of measurement is absolutely rigorous and generally valuable. It is accordingly reasonable to seek to deal with the problem of evaluation by simultaneous attack using several *independent* measurement methods. All of the methods which can be employed are imperfect, but together they may be expected to give a more powerful answer than the one 'best' method. But the methods are not to be combined, nor should they be such that there is any possibility of interaction between them that cannot be directly identified.

Research evaluation strategy of this kind is similar to the 'panzer strategy' of social action and satisfies most of the requirements of a good strategy. To distinguish the 'panzer' social-action strategy from the similar strategy applied to research methods, the term 'grape-shot techniques' will be used to denote the latter. The term provides a good analogy – rather than try to hit the target with the 'big guns' we spatter the measurement dimension with 'small-arms fire'. If we are aiming at the right target, and the variance of the measuring instruments is large, this seems to be the best procedure at present known. If the variance of all instruments of measurement is large, it is obviously better to increase the size of (n).

The 'grape-shot technique' of research is particularly useful for dealing with measurements where the dimensions of concern are not very well specified. It has shown good results where the results of its application could be demonstrated by the correct prediction of human behaviour. It may indicate the nature of the method if one example is given of the measurement of an attitude which was related to subsequent behaviour.

At the end of the Second World War, a large number of ex-Servicemen were entitled to receive various medals and campaign stars (Wilkins, 1947). It was not possible to mint these until the end of hostilities, and the production of the several million needed to meet entitlements would take many months. During the period necessary for the production of the stars and medals, many of the entitled persons would have removed from the addresses to which they were demobilized. If they wished to receive the awards to which they were entitled, it would be necessary for them to advise the central authority concerned of their addresses reasonably near to the time that the awards became available. It seemed possible that a proportion of entitled persons would not trouble to inform the authorities of their addresses, and some might not wish to receive their awards. If the proportion of persons entitled to the different awards who would or who would not apply to receive them could be forecasted, scarce resources could be conserved. An accurate forecast would enable the Royal Mint to produce sufficient to meet the demand without waste of time and metal. Could the demand be predicted? This question was referred to the Wartime Social Survey.

Three basic dimensions were postulated, measurement of which, it was considered, could lead to a prediction. These were:

        (a) the amount of information
        (b) the strength of attitudes towards medals
        (c) inertia to form-filling.

If the entitled persons did not know that their awards were available they would not apply (information), if they did not want them they would not apply (attitude), if they forgot to apply or could not be bothered to notify their address, the authorities had no desire to press their awards upon them (inertia).

In view of the success of 'predicting' election results by the simple process of asking people how they propose to vote, it might have been decided to use similar methods for this type of forecasting; merely to ask a representative sample of ex-Servicemen whether they would apply for their awards. This was, in fact, done, but much more was also done. The separate measurement of the different dimensions postulated to be determinants of the behaviour were individually assessed for each member of a representative sample of entitled persons. The first analysis of the results of the data revealed that replies to the simple question, 'Will you apply for your medals?' did not agree with the results of more sophisticated methods based on the grape-shot technique. The grape-shot technique led to an estimate of 35 per cent of entitled persons making the appropriate application, whereas nearly twice that proportion said that they would apply. In fact the demand proved to be 34·7 per cent! Perhaps the greater efficiency of the grape-shot method is to be expected since it relies upon replies to a large number of questions and interrelates these according to a mathematical model based on the concept of dimensions. The 'dimension' replaces the simple result of a stimulus-response.

Several other tests of the grape-shot method in predicting behaviour of consumers after commodities were removed from wartime rationing procedures further demonstrated the power of the grape-shot method. In the particular case of the forecast of the demand for campaign stars and medals, the dimension of 'attitude towards medals' was bespattered with small simple questions (like small-arms fire). A large number of separate and independent questions were asked all of which were related to the postulated area of 'attitude'. The assumption was made that the 'dimension' along which these questions (shots) were most closely clustered was the basic dimension required. A weighted scale for attitude was built up from those questions which were not too distant from the general factor dimension. The linear scale of 'attitude' thus derived was related to the scale for inertia (willingness to get the necessary form and fill it in) and to information.

But calculations based on the three-dimensional model did not lead directly to the forecast of 35 per cent applications. If only one method had been used, whether it was the grape-shot technique or the polling method, either would have given the wrong answer. The fact that both were used enabled a cross-analysis to be made. This cross-analysis revealed a serious interviewer bias factor, and indicated ways whereby it could be adjusted.

This emphasizes the main point of discussion at this stage. Not only is it desirable to use powerful techniques, but to use a multiple approach through various techniques which can be cross-referred to each other.

Where no one rigorous and proven procedure is available it is desirable to seek to deal with the problems of evaluation by simultaneous attack using several independent methods. Each single question in a grape-shot technique will have a large error variation, and even a complete single technique will be imperfect. But each separate question interrelates with another if it provides a measurement along the same dimension, and each complete technique should be related to other independent techniques if they are measuring the same thing.

If two measures which are supposed to be measuring the same thing do not agree, then at least one must be incorrect. This is the reasoning subsumed under the term 'reliability'.

It is not possible to discuss validity (whether the measurement really measures what it is required to measure) unless and until two measurements agree among themselves. There is no reason why measurements based on quite different disciplines should not be made at the same time relating to the same social action and its effects. For example, measurements based on the sociological concept of 'imitation' and measurements based on the psychological concept of 'identification' will doubtless provide different measurements of essentially the same dimension. The sociological concept of 'imitation' and the psychological concept of 'identification' may, it seems, be regarded as identical.

The multiple evaluation approach commends itself, not only because it makes possible some assessment of the reliability of any measurements, but because it also makes possible a kind of scientific democracy. The different small-scale measuring devices used to assess the effects of social action may be designed by differently orientated scientists, and each may relate his special skills and interests to the problems independently. Separately the different techniques would be within the scope of small research organizations, whereas it would be difficult to find organizations large enough and with sufficiently varied expertise to make a good general measuring instrument or instruments. The involvement of several organizations should result in the work of evaluation as a whole being more widely acceptable. This argument invokes again the concept of scientific democratic principles. But there are other features which seem to indicate a multiple approach to evaluation. For example, some social action may result in change in some sectors and not in others, or there may be positive effects in some and negative effects in others. The multiple-evaluation approach seems more likely to reveal any such features. Another factor commending the multiple approach is that of simplicity. Large-scale complex evaluation designs are less preferable because with simple methods the deficiencies are likely to be more obvious. Large-scale complex designs may be so complex that their limitations will not be evident, and people may be persuaded to give too much respect to, and to assume greater power in, methods which they cannot understand. On the other hand, the attitude of 'not being blinded by science' may lead to a complete rejection of the results. Both attitudes towards research findings are unsatisfactory – the methods should be correctly appraised by as many persons as possible, and this means that they must be expressed in a manner likely to facilitate communication.

The nature of the basic data that provide the information suggests a further consideration in favour of a simple multiple approach. Not only are methods of analysis such as to indicate a 'safety in numbers', but the data that form the raw material for the models are also subject to difficulties of interpretation. The treatment of data must not be out of balance with the nature of the data themselves. It is possible to capitalize on error. No data, unduly weak at source, are strengthened by any form of analysis. In general we get out from analysis what we put into it. A nonsense input provides a nonsense output!

Time and the resources available are limiting factors which any realistic proposals for evaluative research must take into account. In most of the problem areas with which evaluation is concerned, elegant and rigorous solutions are not possible within the limits of existing knowledge. Rigour, of course, should be sought, but not necessarily elegance. We are concerned more with limited-reference, rational-decision models than with models designed for scientific explanation.

Contamination of Criteria

The difficulties that arise (if the target population is defined in terms of the geographical area in which the target families live) of relating problems either to the people or to the area have already been touched upon. It has been noted that any improvement in the population who initially live in an area may lead to the deterioration of the area itself by reason of their removal. Indeed, this is not an unexpected result, particularly in countries having a high geographical mobility. One of the most important correlates with social attitudes is area of residence, and upward social mobility and geographical mobility are very highly correlated. These factors present a considerable dilemma for social work concerned with the prevention of juvenile delinquency or similar social ills. On the other hand, the identification and isolation of the pre-delinquent individual, with the provision of individual therapy, raise social action if not social research difficulties. One thing is certain, whatever social action is proposed, and whatever evaluation is attempted, it is essential to take into consideration differences between the concepts of districts and of individuals and to ensure that there is no confusion of thought about the nature of the 'target'. The separation in respect of the model does not mean, however, that it is possible to deal with specific problems isolated in respect of individuals or particular areas. Social action aimed at individuals will have influences upon the areas in which they live – whether negative or positive, and action taken in respect of the social institutions or factors relating to areas will influence the individuals living within the areas. All social action will reveal two classes of effect: those directly related to the planned action, and those that constitute a bonus. Different types of social-action model will be expected to have different direct and bonus or indirect effects.

Two different models for social action seem to be indicated:

(a) where the persons or areas are already defined in terms of the on-going social systems
(b) where the social action may be regarded as the creation of a new social system, through the social-action-research project, making its own definitions.

In the particular case of juvenile delinquency, for example, the delinquent or pre-delinquent is already involved in many current social administrative systems, of which the police and the school may well be among the most important. Modifications in these social systems which are theoretically expected to have an effect on behaviour are of a different order from demonstration-action-research projects specifically created, publicized, and implemented in their own right, and which thus form their own independent social structures. The introduction of a new social system (that of the project) will produce its own definitions and its own specific impact upon the social systems of the area, influencing its culture and its sub-cultures.

The geographical areas covered by the different existing social administrative systems (school, police, and so on) differ in respect of the populations covered. Thus one of the first tasks of an evaluation project would seem to be a descriptive analysis of the organizations involved within the 'target' area or population. The interaction of persons with social systems must not be overlooked.

Perhaps the simplest method by which to obtain information about organizations may be through the population of the 'target' area. In any event, it is not sufficient to define the 'target' in terms of either its social organizations or the individual characteristics of the population, but to involve measurement and criteria in both dimensions.

The problem of 'bonus' effects of social-action research would seem to raise a serious difficulty in evaluation due to the contamination of the criteria. Such contamination is often referred to as the 'halo' or Hawthorne effect. But it must be remembered that existing social agencies also have 'bonus' effects. If it is possible to cancel out the two types of 'bonus' effect, the problem of evaluation is simplified. This fact, together with the general problem of conceptually separating people from factors associated with the agencies with which they come into contact and from factors relating to the geographic area in which they live, leads to the suggestion of a somewhat different strategy from that of the concentration of demonstration-action-research within a limited area.

A consideration of different types of social research and action as analogues of wartime strategy suggested that the 'mass-attack' strategy was not optimal, and we propose a model similar to the 'panzer' forces, probing along a wide front (see Chapter 5). It will be noted that in following the problem of evaluation a similar logical procedure has led to the rejection of the 'mass attack' (type (b), p. 222 above) on the grounds that evaluation of the outcome of such action programmes is not likely to be powerful or sound. In the present case, the 'mass attack' involves further unknowns, further problems of measurement, and a very much more complex research task than the 'panzer' approach. Indeed, a small but 'mass' type of social research and demonstration project could absorb far more money in the evaluation than in the action programme. It would seem that the worst possible situation, both for action and research, arises where a specific new social system is created through the social-action-research project itself, with its own definitions and publicity-created image.

The argument against the 'mass attack' is not an argument against the deployment of large resources of personnel and money – the solution of large problems requires a large effort – rather the argument is against certain ways of deploying such money and personnel. The investment is not questioned, but the investment policy – the strategy of attack, not the manpower involved in it. In terms of the analogue used previously, it may be observed that the same amount of armour may be used in a mass attack on a narrow sector of the enemy frontier as could be deployed along its whole length using panzer divisions. Not only do the latter types of strategy seem to be preferable on management, policy, and theoretical grounds, but they seem also to be essential in terms of sociological analysis, and to be the only strategies in keeping with our present state of ignorance of the effects of social work and our existing evaluation techniques. As was noted earlier in respect of social action, if a social system running across the existing social system and social definitions within a culture is set up for the specific purposes of a demonstration-action programme, it will be almost impossible to state exactly what action is expected to have exactly what effect and upon whom. It is true that there is mounting evidence that interactions (social system with types of person, and the like) may be important factors in explanations of human behaviour, but there is no point in knowing that this is so unless we can also know which types of action interacted with which other types of action or types of person and whether the total outcome was desirable or undesirable. At present, the evidence in the literature of criminological research is more in favour of negative than of positive interaction effects.

In research designs, unless they are highly complex, interaction effects become confounded with the effects of 'error' variance. There is no way of avoiding this feature, except by designing the studies so that high-order interactions are minimized. If modifications are made to existing systems the interaction due to new systems may be avoided. If existing definitions are used, the complexity due to two sets of definitions will not set up interaction effects, and thus there will be no need to seek to measure them. Although there are 'halo' effects, the 'halo' effect due to the new demonstration-action project may be expected to merge with the existing 'halo' effect of the existing social institution, if this is the basis for the action projects. If agency A is

224

'improved' for demonstration purposes, agency B may improve itself. In which case this is a 'bonus' effect for the programme with regard to agency A and it should be counted as such; but if, simultaneously, agency B is also 'improved', the total effect of modification of agency A will never be known.

It would appear that a step-by-step strategy is essential if it is to be possible to work from broad objectives to the statement of any criteria that can be used in evaluation studies. If evaluation is to take place, if we are not going to 'mortgage the future in terms of our present good intentions'; then a step-by-step approach is the only way to deal with our current problems. It may be regretted that the number of steps that we have been able to take in the past has been extremely small, but we cannot expect to make up the deficiencies of a century by major onslaughts on an amorphous, undefined, even if undesirable, 'enemy'. If, on the other hand, we adopt a step-by-step approach, or use learning systems and networks utilizing existing systems, existing definitions, and existing cultural and sub-cultural structures, and, whenever possible, even existing information, it would seem to be reasonably easy to say fairly precisely what it is intended should be done, exactly what each action is likely to achieve, and how these results are likely to be observed, in both the short and the long term.

A step-by-step strategy should facilitate the statement of goals, and give some indication of the nature of the 'sign-posts' that will help us to place our position, so that we can check that we are moving in a forward direction. If the proposals are laid down and described step by step, it should be possible to check whether each step has been achieved in the way expected or not. It should also be possible to divert future steps into more promising directions in the light of the information being currently obtained (i.e. a learning model).

It is essential to retain flexibility, because social situations are extremely flexible, and technical changes are taking place extremely rapidly. At each step we should aim to learn only a little, but to be sure that that little is based on sound methods of inference.

REFERENCES

BELSON, W. A. (1957). A study of the effects of television upon the interests and initiatives of adult viewers in Greater London. Ph.D. Thesis, University of London.

HAMMOND, W. H. (1963). *Persistent Offenders*. London: H.M.S.O.

KENDALL, M. G. (1948). *Rank Correlation Methods*. London: Griffin.

OSGOOD, C. E., SUCI, G. J. & TANNENBAUM, P. H. (1958). *The Measurement of Meaning*. University of Illinois Press.

POWER, M. (1963). Interim notes on research by Medical Research Council, Social Medicine Unit (limited circulation).

WILKINS, L. T. (1947). *The Demand for Campaign Stars and Medals*. Social Survey Report, London: H.M.S.O.

WILKINS, L. T. (1962). Juvenile Delinquency Research. *J. Educ. Res.*, vol. 5, no. 2.

CHAPTER 9

Measurement and Estimation of Pay-off

Prerequisites of measurement – General considerations in measurement of effects – Treaters and treated – Boundary conditions – Coding – Selection of methods – Critical evaluation of types of information – Input and output – Opinion, testimonial, expert opinion, public opinion, and attitudes – Actions (decisions of clients or treaters) – Time-intercept and similar observational techniques – Derived measures: cost, pay-off – Money as an ethic and a criterion – The 'as if' argument – Value transfer systems – The ecological model – Input-output models – Limitations of types of criterion

Different types of measurement, counts, and classification are appropriate at different stages in social-action programmes. Information has no value in itself, its value is only in terms of its purpose. There can be no generally useful measurement, because there can be no general purposes. Social-accounting data have a useful function in focusing attention on areas where problems exist and where further inquiry might be expected to prove profitable, or where the social ethic of a country may demand remedial or preventive action. Data that provide a general picture of health, education, crime, and other welfare and economic problems are essential, but they do not provide an adequate basis for measuring the effects of specific programmes of social action. There may be a tendency to try to make use of data that are not strictly appropriate to a problem because they are already in existence, and it is necessary to make whatever use one can of such information, but at the same time to be aware of the dangers of using 'semi-attached' figures. Some ways in which general social-accounting data may be used in connection with supplementary data obtained for the specific purposes will be considered in the present chapter.

Prerequisites of Measurement

The technical problems of measurement of specific effects of action programmes do not fall to be considered, however, until many other problems have been settled. The prerequisites may be summarized thus:

1. The objectives of the programme have been worked out within the framework of the general social ethic.

2. The sub-problems have been identified and related to the specific activity which it is expected will modify the particular behaviour or remedy the specified problems.

3. The ways in which the sub-objectives (means) relate to the general objective have been thought through and a rational strategy, including provisional priorities, determined.

4. The proposed activities have been devised, described, and standardized. Alternatively, variations in the activities have been identified and the expected nature of the differences in outcome associated with the variations in activity indicated. (Some pilot research projects may have been considered necessary at this stage to determine the likely variation in activity.)

5. The nature of expected change, both positive and negative, and long- and short-term, has been described in detail.

6. Use has been made of 'democratic' and operational definitions as necessary, and other pilot studies have made it possible to put forward all statements made in (1)–(5) above with reasonable confidence.

The problems now remaining relate to:

(a) Means for measuring the degree of change in the directions specified in (5) and

(b) ascertaining whether any changes were due to the particular action or to something else.

There are many techniques that can assist in these problems. Not all can be discussed here, and few will be possible in practice in any one project.

General Considerations in Measurement of Effects

If, after a demonstration programme is completed, we know only that 'health has improved' or that 'delinquency rates have decreased' and cannot describe the social action associated with this effect in sufficient detail to enable it to be reproduced, our knowledge is of an unsatisfactory kind. It is as important to describe the stimuli as it is to describe the effect. In general, too, the description of the social action will need to be continuous throughout the period so as to provide some form of quality control. If the quality or type of action changes during the demonstration, different effects should be expected.

Professional agencies may tend to be resistant to detailed studies and descriptions of their methods, but broad descriptions of their procedures, or, indeed, anything short of quite rigorous measurement, will not provide the type of information necessary. If we are to observe in a meaningful way the behaviour of the persons 'treated' we must also observe the behaviour of the 'treaters'. It is known, for example, that probation officers do not use exactly standard procedures with their clients – even when the clients have exactly similar problems. Although the general nature of the work of the probation service is described in appropriate training manuals, a time-study of officers in the course of their work (California Department of Corrections, 1963) revealed many large differences between members of the service, in the ways in which they perceived their roles, the ways in which they perceived their clients, and the methods they employed in their treatment. Some used long intensive interviews at less frequent intervals than others, who used more frequent interviews of shorter duration; some increased the amount of client contact after an initial period, whereas others gave more attention to those who were in the first few months of supervision; some considerably reduced the level of supervision towards the second half of the period of the order, whereas others continued the supervision at much the same level of intensity until the order was discharged; some were very interested in 'external' factors like employment and the environmental situation of the client, whereas others were more interested in the internal problems of emotional adjustment. Those who tended to give longer interviews would have preferred to increase the length of the interview still further rather than to increase the frequency with which they saw their clients; whereas those who tended to emphasize frequency would, if they had had more room for manoeuvre, have increased the frequency. Thus there was a strong tendency for attitude towards the type of supervision provided to be in line with the existing practice, and more latitude would seem to be likely to increase the differences observed between officers in the types of supervision they gave and preferred to give. (Which type of supervision was more effective was not investigated at this stage; perhaps both were equally effective, or perhaps one type was suitable for some types of client, and not for others.) There may be common elements in all forms of probation supervision, but there are certainly great differences between the ways in which it is applied by different officers. In the case of the

229

probation service, the clients who have contact with the officers are known, and cumulative records are maintained. To some extent it is possible to use these records as an indication of the nature of the treatment activity, but they are not ideally organized for such investigation. In other forms of social work, particularly in demonstration projects in communities, the connection between the client and the service agency personnel is much more tenuous, and greater degrees of variation between different workers become a possibility.

Treaters and Treated

The methods of data collection and analysis described in the following paragraphs may be modified to apply to treaters or treated; to individual client or officer. If we are concerned with the ways in which potential delinquents perceive authority figures, it is equally important to know how they are perceived by authority figures. If we are concerned with definitions of behaviour which determine action on the part of deviants, we are equally concerned with the definitions which the normal society uses to mark out the deviants. A change in either dimension could result in a change in the situation. Indeed, changes in opposing directions may well cancel out observations based on either one alone, or measures derived from external criteria. If behaviour improves, an improved standard of behaviour may become to be expected, and thus a new 'norm' may be formulated from which the same proportions of the population may still be defined as deviants, although according to the standard used at the commencement of the social-action programme there may have been a substantial improvement.

The necessity of considering both treaters and treated applies whether or not a deviation-amplifying model is proposed.

If the social change that the demonstration project is intended to produce is concerned with *systems*, then the method for collection of data and the data collected must relate to the *systems*. The system must first be defined, and information relating not only to the way in which it is intended to operate (rules and orders, etc.) but also to the ways in which it in fact operates must be obtained. Process analysis, individual interviewing, or observational methods, or all three types of method of inquiry, may be necessary. The distinction between individuals and systems must be most carefully maintained throughout both research and action elements of the programme. If individuals are fed into a system by a defining process that is *independent* of the demonstration project, and this defining process remains constant (a matter for checking), and if the demonstration is concerned with modifications of the *system* postulated to make it more effective in dealing with individuals, the simplest model is obtained. The system is defined, the input is defined, and the change expected is postulated to be limited to the impact of the system upon the individuals passing through it. Any effect which the modification of the system may have on other persons not having contact with the modified system must be regarded as a bonus effect. The action part of the programme for social change and the evaluation part must have the same boundary conditions.

Boundary Conditions

No problem can be solved that lacks boundary conditions. If the action programme cannot specify its boundary conditions the research and evaluation problems cannot be solved, unless, of course, there are set boundary conditions specified for the evaluation. It will be obvious, however, that if the research has boundary conditions that differ from those of the action programme, or if the latter does not stipulate any such conditions, the research can always be accepted or rejected according to the acceptability of the results. Research should never permit of any manoeuvring into such a position.

Another general consideration, irrespective of the subject-matter of the evaluation exercise, is that preference should always be given to methods which provide some satisfactory test of the null hypothesis, that is, methods which provide some test of the significance of the factors isolated in the measures against independent measures of the error variance. The factor of chance variation must be isolated and controlled. Within these classes of methods, preference should be given to estimation procedures that not only indicate the significance of the result (that it is better than chance variation), but also set out boundary conditions or confidence intervals for the results.

Methods of inference that indicate the likely effect of different types of incorrect judgement should be sought in all cases. No measurement of effect, and no decisions regarding social action, can ever be one hundred per cent correct. Knowledge will always be partial, whether statistical methods are used or decisions are made on the basis of various kinds of feeling. When errors occur, and they always will, different kinds of error will occur with different frequencies. Different kinds of error have different effects. Different kinds of error have different chances of being made, and the chances can usually be calculated. Not only should the chances be estimated, but the effect upon the basic criteria of the different types should be weighted whenever such weighting is possible. If it is not possible to make such weighting, the fact that it is not possible should be noted, and the reasons for its impracticability investigated.

Coding

No matter by what system information is obtained, it must always be 'coded' in some form of verbal system before it can be communicated or processed. Observations cannot be directly utilized, since the observer must use some code in order to communicate or manipulate the concepts. Methods for collecting data that can be repeated are to be preferred over measures that cannot be repeated because they rely upon the individual skills of the observers or interviewers. But the appropriateness of the information as a measure of what it is desired to measure is the more important consideration. Even assessments which rely upon the individual skills of the observers, but which relate directly to the situation, are often to be preferred to measures derived by methods that may be repeatable and precise, but do not relate to the situation in any direct way. Measures which have no demonstrated association with the situation, even although they may have a high 'face validity', are always suspect. Repeated measurements will provide safeguards in that if different measures are believed to measure the same thing they must relate closely to each other. But two *independent* measures, each of which is not repeatable in itself, but which relate to the factor that it is desired to measure, provide a similar or even superior check to a test-retest repeat of any single measure using the same methods of data collection and analysis.

Selection of Methods

Many different methods of measurement are available, and many different aspects of social change may provide the basic data. Many methods appear as alternatives to achieve the same objectives. Selections will have to be made. There is, it must be stressed, nothing in any method itself which can determine its selection but only its relevance to the problem. All questions of selection relate to the problem of describing the current or expected state of the individual or system and ways of relating this description to the observed or subsequent state of the individual or system. We are concerned with changes in systems and individuals, and hence our problem is to describe the input state and to relate this to the output state with efficiency, simplicity, and reliability. If this can be done, the further problem of separating the differences (changes) which may be due to the experimental variation from those which may be due to other factors such as the 'bonus' effects mentioned earlier, must be tackled. All methods for evaluation have one or other of these purposes as their objective.

Very few rules for selection among alternative methods or types of measurement can be indicated without reference to clearly defined problems, and a knowledge of the practical field situation involved in the individual projects. There are, however, some general headings under which the problems of selection of measuring instruments may be considered. These are:

    (a) type of information
    (b) method of obtaining information
    (c) methods of analysis and interpretation

in short, the 'what', the 'how', and the 'so what' of the problem! There are supplementary questions relating to 'when', 'where', and 'from whom'. The type of information may be sub-divided under three headings:

    (a 1) opinions (e.g. attitudes, expert opinion, testimonial)
    (a 2) actions (e.g. decisions, behaviour of clients or treaters)
    (a 3) derived measures (e.g. cost, pay-off).

The method of obtaining information is, of course, not independent of the type of information it is required to collect. There are also combined forms of the three types mentioned above; for example, opinions may be expressed by experts about the actions of clients, and attitudes may be related to action or latent action. It is, however, always important to distinguish information that is directly related to the variable (the 'thing' expected to change) from that which is only apparently related to it.

The methods for obtaining information may also be sub-divided into three classes:

    (b 1) observation
    (b 2) interview
    (b 3) self-reporting (questionnaire, test, etc.).

It is convenient also to break down the methods of analysis and interpretation into three categories:

(c 1) external criteria and correlation methods

(c 2) comparison of observed and expected results (internal criteria)

(c 3) simulation models ('causal' or mutual causal).

Some notes will now be given whereby types of information may be tested and factors in the selection weighed with respect to any specific case.

Critical Evaluation of Types of Information

It is not possible to say what ought or ought not to be done in any particular case, except that certain factors should always receive consideration.

The first consideration should be

Whether the type and nature of the data are appropriate to the specific problem at issue.

The following headings provide a check-list of what appear to be some of the more significant differences between types of information in so far as they influence selection decisions regarding appropriateness of the information:

(a) Consider whether the information related to

(i) counts of specific events where there is no doubt about the definitions, for example, the 'gate passages' discussed earlier; or

(ii) a continuum which has been classified or measured in some way.

(b) Consider whether the information was collected from existing records or directly from the people concerned.

(c) Consider the effect of the number of stages of summarization or interpretation that may have modified the original data or the information before they were published or produced in the form in which they now appear.

(d) Examine whether the data relate to the same population as the population selected for social action and whether such a population (or populations) remained stable throughout the period.

Data that are not reliable can never be valid. It is necessary to consider, therefore, the

Possibility of bias, whether conscious or unconscious.

The following check-list may assist in indicating features liable to give rise to bias:

(a) Consider whether the nature of the information was likely to have had an impact upon the persons responsible for collecting it. In particular, if the data concern human behaviour, would the recorders be likely to be shocked or pleased with any of the types of behaviour that may have been noted.

(b) Consider the controlling interests and policies of the collecting agency.

(c) Note whether the agency has publicly announced any standards of conduct.

(d) Consider the possible relationships between the agency collecting the data and the body to which the information was first reported.

(e) Examine the source of funds for the collecting agency.

(f) Note whether the collecting agency has any system of inspection of its staff, and whether the staff employed are likely to have special interests relating to the field investigated (e.g. reports on drunkenness by temperance or, alternatively, brewing interests).

(g) Examine the exact method of data collection. Copies of forms used should normally be given in any report or supplied on request. See especially which items were prompted in the question and which were volunteered by informants.

(h) Note whether in the stage of field-data collection, the information at issue is isolated from other items likely to have a biasing effect. Note that the answer to question (n) is influenced by the questions asked prior to question (n). Note and examine carefully any questions that relate to taboo subjects or emotional areas.

(i) Consider what experience the particular agency has had in the specific field of data collection at issue. Classification according to the four categories below may be useful in this regard

> (i) behavioural
> (ii) informational
> (iii) opinion
> (iv) conditions;

also consider whether the information was obtained by personal interview, observation, or other means. Self-completed questionnaires do not usually have any operational order (see (h) above).

(j) If personal interviews were used, how and when were the data recorded:

(i) by tape at the time
(ii) by writing at the time
(iii) later, from the interviewer's memory
(iv) or combinations of these – if combinations, which method was used for which items?

Although most of the tests that may be applied to data are applicable equally to census or sample inquiries, sample inquiries present some special problems. A well-conducted sample will often be more efficient than a poorly conducted census. A census may be regarded as an attempted 100 per cent sample taken at a fixed point in time. A 100 per cent sample of a small part of the total population of concern is *not* a census; indeed, it may well be one of the worst kinds of sample.

The following points afford a check-list of matters connected with the identification of the appropriateness of the sample or population concerned:

(a) If the data claim to be derived from a census is it reasonably certain that all items or persons are included?

(b) Were the data obtained from 100 per cent of the initially defined sample or population? If not, what proportion were lost and for what reasons. If any loss, consider bias and exact nature of reasons for loss.

(c) Examine the nature of the agency's reporting. Is the report made in such a manner that the possibility of bias can be investigated. If the report does not allow of detection of bias, it is likely to be present – the reporting has demonstrated that it is biased!

(d) Are full details of the sampling procedures given? If census, over what period of time were the data under collection? Consider possibilities of changes over the period. If sample, who selected the sample? Was the actual selection of the units made by the central agency or left to regional or local personnel? In particular, were the samples of individuals or units chosen by the persons who were also responsible for obtaining the data from them? If the sample was a probability sample, how many stages were involved? How has the error variance been calculated for *each* stage?

(e) If 'quota' sampling has been used, were all potential biasing factors covered? Note that sampling errors cannot be estimated for quota samples in any completely satisfactory manner.

Field investigators are used in almost all sample and census investigations. Field forces or others concerned with the initial stages of data collection can be a serious source of error or unreliability in the data:

(a) Consider whether information is available regarding the qualifications of the field force – are they full-time employees of the agency? Do they receive any training? What are the qualifications normally required?

(b) Consider how the interview was conducted. Was it by specific question and answer? Did the interviewer have any opportunity to add or modify questions or to edit the responses?

(c) If material was written by informants, consider whether the responses required were within the expected competence of the informants to record accurately.

(d) How was the informant identified by the interviewer? Was the informant interviewed alone or with others? Did any others also take part in the interview? Is any such intervention noted?

(e) If observational data were included, was there any check of the data by re-observation by different interviewers? If not, what other means of reliability checking are available?

(f) Have any checks been made on the possibility of differences between interviewers in the collection of the same data?

(g) What was the nature of the supervision of the field force? (A supervision ratio of 5 per cent is recommended by most authorities.)

(h) Were informants in the sample or census informed before it took place by means of any publicity? If so, what was the nature of this publicity? Is a copy included in the report?

Input and Output

It will, of course, be self-evident that the nature of the measures made at 'input' and 'output', or measures of expectation and actual outcome, must be in exactly the same dimensions and in the same terms if they are to be compared and related to each other, and, as has been continuously stressed, they must relate to the particular social action and its objectives. The latter requirement, besides being perhaps the more difficult to fulfil, means that even with the use of the most efficient measures of this kind, the priority cannot be assessed with respect to two different types of social action having two distinct purposes. It is, however, possible that the same action programme may have more than one purpose, and each of these purposes can provide a basis for input-output measurements. A further difficulty arises in many kinds of social action, namely that the action cannot take place with respect to the behaviour arousing concern in any direct way. For example, social action to prevent or reduce juvenile delinquency or crime cannot deal directly with crime itself, since crime is not continuous; the action must take place with respect to the individual who has been defined as a member of the target population or his environment. But it is not the indirect action which provides the basis for the measurement of the criteria but the end purpose. That is to say, if the reduction of delinquency is the objective for modified social action in schools or the community, the effects should be referred to the measurement of delinquency if this is the variable of concern. If it is not, then this fact should have been discovered before this stage is reached.

Social action may be regarded as testing causal or mutual causal theories. By 'cause' in this connection is meant nothing more or less than something which, if changed, results in a change in the outcome. But there is one further requirement, the outcome is desired in a particular direction which is perceived as 'improvement'. In social action it will be difficult to determine what is symptom and what is 'cause', but if modification of the symptoms modifies the outcome such modification provides the first step from which the next may be taken. The idea of causation in any other form is unsatisfactory both for scientific purposes and as a guide to action.

Some notes may now be given on the specific considerations in obtaining measurements of different kinds following the broad categories proposed above.

Opinion, Testimonial, Expert Opinion, Public Opinion, and Attitudes

It is improbable that a change in opinion or attitude would be set as the end objective of social action. These concepts may, however, be invoked as providing some indirect measures of the phenomenon that was the target for change. The assumption that a change in attitude or opinion in a direction perceived as desirable will be accompanied by or followed by a change of action in the same direction may be true or not. In general, expressions of opinion and attitude do tend to correlate positively with behaviour to which the opinion relates, but this is not necessarily so. There are a number of examples of attitude measurements which proved to be uncorrelated with the apparently associated behaviour and some examples of negative correlation. For example, a study of blood donorship revealed that people who expressed a very positive attitude towards the idea of donating blood were less likely actually to give it than people who expressed a less strong attitude (Slater, 1947). It appeared that there were stronger associations with the dimension of knowledge. It was as though there was a given amount of goodwill towards this form of good works and people were able to express it either orally or in terms of their blood. If they were able to satisfy their emotions by oral expression, it was less necessary for them to take action. Thus it might be supposed that a change of attitude in favour of blood donorship might be associated with fewer donors!

Though the positive correlation between attitude and behaviour cannot be assumed, any social action aimed at a change in behaviour should, it seems, be accompanied by measurements of changes in the relevant attitudes. The measurement of attitude and opinion can give indications of the nature of the perceptual processes, and it may be as important to know how the social action is perceived as what in fact the social action is. Measurement of attitude and opinion can provide an intervening variable between what is in fact being done and what is (in fact) the outcome. Such measurements, as we shall see later, are particularly useful in controlling for the 'bonus' or 'halo' effects.

Opinion and attitude measurement is a highly specialized field, and a field in which a lot of very poor-quality work is to be found.

There are areas of description where techniques of measurement may not yet be applied. In such areas the trained social observer, the cultural anthropologist, and the clinical psychologist cannot be replaced. Description must precede measurement. The use of expert opinion may be the only technique available for descriptions of parts of the on-going process of social action. The court-of-inquiry method of testimonial also has its merits and uses in this field, where one is concerned with description or with filling in the background of measurement devices. However, description is not measurement, and preference should always be given to reproducible measurement, but where the validity of measurement has not been thoroughly tested, the use of the techniques of skilled observers, expert opinion, and even testimonial will provide highly desirable cross-checks and perhaps point the way to further developments of measurement.

At the present time there is a need for the use of many techniques in parallel.

One form of expert-opinion/testimonial type of information is always readily available in respect of any social action or social phenomena which attract public attention, namely press reports. In the assessment of social action the mass media should not be forgotten or treated lightly. Content analysis provides a scientific method for assessing the nature of the comment by the mass media, with respect to either the phenomena to which action is directed or the action itself. Moreover, newspaper editors have a specific policy regarding the type and nature of their coverage, and hence even quantification in terms of the number of column inches is not a measure to be ignored. Although many social policy and social action agencies would claim to be attempting to maximize some perceived good, much of their action may be interpreted as an attempt to minimize the amount of adverse mass-media comment and to maximize the quantity of favourable coverage. For example, a 'rational' or 'ethical' policy for the parole of prisoners might be expected to be based on the probability of recidivism. But such a policy would lead to the earlier release of sex offenders than of breakers-and-enterers. Yet parole boards are notably more reluctant to release sex offenders. The underlying reason may well be that the subsequent reconviction of a sex offender while on parole receives much more adverse press comment than would the recidivism of a paroled burglar. This would be so even where the subsequent sex offence was no more serious than the subsequent offence of the burglar, where the degree of seriousness applies both in law and in public opinion. It is merely that sex is greater news value than offences against property. But may not attention given to the mass media on the part of parole boards and others concerned with social action be realistic and even ethical?

Subject to the policy and the particular market of a newspaper, the content provides a quick indication of the expert opinion (editor's) of the public opinion demand. But there are many other more scientific and important reasons why a study of the mass media should run in parallel with social-action projects, particularly where the mass media are concentrated upon the same population as provides the target for the social action, or are available to persons concerned with that target population. Prior to the commencement of the

Youth Opportunities demonstration project in New York City the turnover of teachers in schools serving the target area and other socially deprived areas was extremely high. Certain action was taken in the schools in the target area, but it was noted that the teacher turnover rate in a number of other schools, some remote from the target area, dropped radically after the inception of the scheme. The probable explanation for this might be that teaching in a socially deprived area, owing to the publicity given to the Youth Opportunities project, became prestigeful. In other words, the 'job image' of teachers employed in schools in lower-class areas was changed through information in the mass media, both for themselves and for their peers and other persons significant to them. Whether the reduction in the teacher turnover in such areas would tend to reduce juvenile delinquency – the purpose of the demonstration project – (or even increase it!) is not known, but the change in teacher turnover was one of the bonus effects of the social activity possibly taking effect through the communication systems provided by mass media.

Actions (Decisions of Clients or Treaters)

The stated purpose of most social-action programmes is to change behaviour which is perceived as dysfunctional into functional behaviour. Measurements relating to opinion or attitude are useful only as intervening measures which may indicate the processes of change and enable modifications of the programmes or research to be made quickly – perhaps ahead of manifestations of behaviour. Evaluation is obtained by measurement of the difference between what is attempted and what is achieved. It may be regarded as necessary to attempt to change attitudes as a means for changing behaviour, and assessments of attitude change will then have a place in assessing the *means* towards the end – the sub-objectives. Successful achievement of the sub-objectives is not, however, proof of the achievement of the objective.

Various techniques are available for observing behaviour. The simplest have the disadvantage that in the process of observation the behaviour observed may be changed from that which it would be if not observed. Time study, with its symbol of the stop-watch, has a useful place if carefully planned. But the stop-watch is a threatening symbol to almost all workers and is likely to give rise to behaviour change. Workers may go faster or slower when observed, depending upon the results which they believe will follow the measurement. But the relationship between different parts in a task is less likely to be changed consciously. Any modification of behaviour under observation will normally be confined to a general adjustment, and the correlation between parts of the behaviour tend to remain constant. In fact, the higher the order of the correlation, the less likely is it that it will be consciously changed. This gives a clue to methods of observation. There is no reason why different parameters of behaviour should not be assessed by different means. The higher-order correlations between components of behaviour may be adequately and simply assessed by direct (even stop-watch-timed) observation, while the mean and variance may be measured independently by more gross measures.

Time-Intercept and Similar Observational Techniques

The time-intercept technique is used extensively in measurement of television viewing in countries where the majority of the population are available on the telephone. A random list of persons is drawn from the telephone directory and asked by phone what they are viewing or listening to at the time of the call. Road-traffic studies are made by driving around circuits at certain times and noting the flow in the opposite direction. Samples of persons exposed to shop-window displays can be obtained by interviewers moving in prescribed order round the area of display, counting individuals moving past them. interviewing every *n*th person, then themselves making a prescribed walk at a prescribed time and further counting persons standing still or moving in the opposite direction to the walk. Machine-idle time in factories can be measured by noting the condition of machines at random intervals – a method due to Tippett (1941) and generally known as the 'snap-reading technique'.

The snap-reading technique and similar methods of sampling behaviour have the advantage that the persons observed do not have time to adjust their behaviour, since the question is 'What is X doing now?', where 'now' is an instant of time of very short duration. Studies using this system have been made of the work of nurses in hospitals without interference with their normal routines. The basic idea of 'time sampling' or 'location sampling' follows the same general statistical principles as any other form of statistical sampling. The method could be used for such diverse purposes as measuring delinquent gang behaviour and police activity!

Perhaps one of the most interesting adaptations of the snap-reading method was that applied by the Case Institute of Technology (1960) in a study of the reading habits of physical scientists. An electronic mechanism was designed which emitted a signal with a mean interval that was adjustable, but having a random distribution of such signals. The use of transistors made it possible for the apparatus to be no larger than a match-box so that it could be carried throughout the day by the sampled scientists. When a signal was heard, the sample were required to note whether they were reading at the time and, if so, what they were reading. The snap-reading method provides the sampled person with an escape excuse – he may have done a lot of reading of the type believed to be desired, but, at the particular time that the instrument sounded, he was not so engaged. Moreover, if the records are collected at very frequent intervals, so that only a few observations are recorded before they are removed by the investigator, the observed person has no means for building up a knowledge of the pattern of his total behaviour and making adjustments which he may think would present a more acceptable picture, unless, of course, he maintains a duplicate record and analyses this himself sequentially.

The Wartime Social Survey, which was concerned with problems of de-rationing after the end of hostilities, made use of observational techniques in order to estimate the likely demand for rationed goods in a free market. In addition to asking for information regarding the buying habits of the housewives sampled, interviewers examined their ration books and asked for permission to check the contents of their larders. In nearly all cases permission was given, and the state of the ration book, together with the content of the specific goods in store, provided a form of snap-reading method which could be used to supplement and check the attitudinal information obtained from the more conventional interview. The same organization, in a study of the use of hearing-aids, required the interviewers to note when they had made contact with the informant whether, at the initial contact, an aid was being worn and, if so, in which ear. If it was being worn, then the state of the batteries and some other technical details were noted. If it was not being worn, they asked the informant to produce it, and its state was again checked. Observational data were again supplemented by conventional interview methods.

In addition to direct observation of the particular behaviour which it is the purpose of the social action to change, observation of related behaviour will provide checks upon attitudinal data.

Sampling of time and space with observations of behaviour distributed in terms of these dimensions may require more thought and inventiveness than merely asking questions of a population sample, but the data are harder and more likely to be valid. Observational data should always be sought, whether for direct use or as supporting evidence of other data.

Derived Measures: Cost, Pay-Off

It has been noted that measures which relate directly to the purpose of any study or project cannot be used to determine priorities for different types of project because the necessary comparisons require the measurements to be in the same terms. Derived measures that can relate the social benefit obtained from different types of project directed at different types of social problem have the advantage that they enable something to be said about priorities between projects as well as providing measurements of the effects of any one specific project.

Money as an Ethic and a Criterion

Cost or value has many advantages as a measure of social phenomena. Physical injury and even death have an actuarial financial value. It seems surprising that this common denominator has not been used to standardize some basic social indices. It is possible, moreover, when cost measures are used, to provide a constant basis over time by reference to such economic concepts as 'gross national product' or the value of the pound or dollar at the time.

It is interesting that the murder rate is conventionally related to the population and hence to the potential number of victims, although this might be fortuitous owing to the nature of the relationship between the offender and the victim or victims. But the number of thefts of motor-cars, money, or other valuables is not related to the 'population' of motor-cars, money, or valuables available as items offering opportunities. The constant nature of the murder rate over a large number of years is often commented upon by criminologists, but might not similar constants appear if other crimes were related to the opportunities available for committing them? The relationship of values to cost makes such comparisons possible. There is some indication that such constants do appear, but absence of value and cost data makes it difficult to interpret the results. Even crimes of violence against the person seem to be more meaningfully interpreted when the injury is related to a cost basis. Physical injury can occur in many ways, in the home or factory by accidents, as well as by road accidents and criminal attack. Injury in the factory is subject to compensation – that is to say, a cost figure is placed upon the incident. It would seem more satisfactory to compare the cost of industrial injury than merely to count the reported cases, and such a view is generally accepted as reasonable, but crimes of violence against the person are counted without reference to the injury – indeed the victim does not appear as a significant factor in the statistics of crime. This may be because crime is related to ethics, and not to financial considerations. But ethical considerations cannot be measured either by counting or by costing.

It has been maintained that ethical considerations are orthogonal to information, decision, and pay-off – one may be rational but unethical. Indeed, until rational decisions can be stated, the ethical considerations must be restricted. But, it was at one time asked, 'What will a man give in exchange for his soul?' This is an ethical question proposed in financial terms. Is it unreasonable to suggest that a measure of our social and personal ethic is given by how we are prepared to spend our money, and how we assess the cost of things or people? We often deprecate the past by the phrase 'life was cheap then', or we refer in similar phrases to cultures which we perceive to have lower ethical standards than our own. Could it not be suggested that the answer to the question, 'What will a man give in exchange for his soul?' is not only an ethical matter, but an exact measure of a man's ethic? That is to say, the interaction between the ethic, which cannot be directly measured, and the value in money terms of different actions provides an obvious vector from which the unknown may be assessed. We may express the ethic as (x), but we may rank other factors in terms of (x) using the vector of money value attributed to the other factors. If the ethic changes, the resultant vector would change in terms of money value. Money has no real value, it is merely a means of exchange; it is a way of saying and showing that a person or a society prefers one item over another because they are prepared to 'pay' more for it. Society pays for its offenders to be kept in confinement, and presumably it regards this cost as justified by the additional safety for normal citizens; the cheque-fraud offenders who are locked up help to maintain an easy credit system for the remainder of the population, which would not be so free if more difficulties were placed in the way of obtaining credit, although such difficulties might reduce the numbers imprisoned. Society indicates which way it desires itself to be organized by its preferences in payment. Society is prepared to spend a certain amount of money on juvenile delinquency research, but less on many other social issues, which, it must therefore be concluded, are considered to be less important in terms of the social ethic.

Whether this argument is regarded as philosophically sound, or whether other dimensions could be found that do not fit the transposition of value for ethic, it would seem that more data based on the concept of social costs would enable decisions to be made in more rational terms than at present. It is not desired to extend this point beyond the suggestion that counts of numbers of incidents, according to the definition as perceived at the time, are statistics of less utility than data based on the concept of 'cost to society'. The concept of cost has the great advantage that its base is adjustable to the level of gross national product, cost of living, and other economic indicators. By relating social issues to the cost-to-society concept, comparisons may be made in a meaningful way both over time and over different types of social issue.

What, then, is the cost of crime? What is the cost of crime prevention? What are the costs of treatment or punishment of offenders? How much does society pay for the security provisions in prisons? Remembering that part of the cost of security provisions in prisons is the cost of loss of liberty for the offender, is the cost worth it? We cannot say whether a thing is worth it until we know what it costs. If society, knowing the cost of imprisonment and of maximum-security provisions, still considered them worth the money, we could assume that the locking-up of prisoners was in accord with the ethic of society. But until a society knows the cost, it has no real foundation for its ethic. The cost or value of a life is not infinite – no one behaves as though it were, even although they may verbally claim that this is so. If the value of anything is set at infinity, no rational decisions can be considered; but we do make decisions, and hence we do not in practice believe in values of infinity. If, for example, we really believed a human life to have infinite value, we should have to ensure that every person was trained as a fire-fighter, because people do get burned to death in fires. What we might do about the motor-car if we were really to assess a human life at infinity is difficult to imagine!

Clearly there are risks in all human activity, and even in human inactivity. We test atomic and hydrogen bombs and argue that the background radiation (the natural existing risk) provides some ethical standard. In fact, logical inferences from the ways in which our society behaves would lead to the suggestion that we do not value human life very highly. Perhaps, in many cases, we value it at rather less than its economic worth in terms of expected contribution to the gross national product.

Possibly it would be highly desirable for social administrators and even for social workers to become more cost-conscious, provided that such costing is accurately carried out. It may, of course, be pointed out that with our present techniques we cannot place a cost on a number of items that we value. Such an argument is merely an argument against our ignorance of methods, not against the principle.

The 'As If' Argument

We do not know the cost of lives lost on the road, and we cannot relate this unknown cost to the other unknown of the value of roads to the economy and the standard of living. None the less, we behave in our everyday business of driving and transporting goods and people as though the loss of lives on the roads had a value. It is possible, therefore, to use the 'as if' argument, and to infer the costs of various 'ills' or 'evils' from the ways in which people behave. Insurance rates and compensation paid to victims and such types of datum could provide the answers to the 'as if' questions. It may be that we are able to behave in certain ways that are unethical or even uneconomic only because we are unaware of the balance of costs. Similarly, if we knew exactly the cost in waste of manpower of retaining in our penitentiaries certain types of offender, it might be possible to make better decisions regarding alternative dispositions. The statistical 'as if' argument is extremely similar to the ethical points raised by the question, 'What will a man give in exchange for his soul' – one infers the value by what is given in exchange!

If social problems are related to economic concepts in some such way as this, the complexity of social research and social action becomes all too clear. Expenditure that may begin with the purchase of one small item will have effects, attenuated to greater or lesser degrees, throughout the whole economic system. Money is not the same as 'value', although values may be expressed in terms of money. Money as a means of exchange can be likened to the concepts of movement or 'motion'; and a concept rather like that of relativity also holds. Money may be said to be 'saved' or 'spent wisely' or 'wastefully' only with respect to the reference-point of an observer who may or may not be the spender. What is wise spending for an individual may be foolish (dysfunctional) for a corporation or a state, and what is wise spending for a corporation or state may be foolish for an individual. If offenders are kept in unnecessary detention, the cost of the detention represents only transfers of goods and services in a different form from that which would take place if the offender were not detained. In detention he helps to keep the institutional staff employed, his absence from the labour market enables other workers to be employed ... and so on. The attachment of money values to social actions (such as detention of offenders) makes possible the attenuation of the effects of the social action to be described. But there is no point in discussion of cost with any other point in view. Cost is no absolute measure; it is a measure of potential movement of goods and services. Thus the apparently desirable objective of reducing to a minimum the cost of retaining persons in penal establishments is not a simple objective limited to the system under study. It is now generally assumed by economists that some measure of unemployment is necessary in an economy, although there is disagreement about what is a desirable percentage. If this is a correct assumption, then moneys paid in unemployment benefit are not wastefully spent but represent in some degree a payment for a service – the service of doing nothing, which is functional for the economy particularly if the unemployed are available for work. By the same token, research that is useless (in terms of its own evaluation, value-less) may be functional for the economy! Perhaps the same may be said of much social action, and even of some administration.

Value Transfer Systems

Perhaps the simplest way to regard the problems of evaluation of social action is as problems in the transfer of value – as questions of distribution. Assessment in terms of money of the pay-off of certain lines of action is a means of assessing the nature of the transfers which can take place. Money, the transfer medium, provides a measure of the exchange systems which could be utilized. Absence of the knowledge of the transfer code means that transfers cannot be considered in any other terms – money is the transfer code and the only transfer code available in our society. The code is implicit in the acts of transfer by definition. If more money were to be transferred to those who wish to look after the interests of the deaf rather than those of the blind, more of the welfare services could be attracted to the former tasks. If the value of one programme to reduce delinquency could be compared with another programme in terms of the pay-off expressed in money terms, the two programmes could be compared and thus 'evaluated' – more, the effect of the programmes could be compared with the saving in social costs to be obtained from quite different investment of social services (the transfer argument).

It will be clear, however, that in this discussion we are not concerned with money values in the accountancy form. The simple accounting is a means to an end, not in any sense an end in itself. If the accountant claims to save money, he means by this that he has prevented its use in the form originally proposed. This one-way measurement has no meaning, except as the first step in the direction of multiple measurement and as a language in which value transfer may be considered.

An artist may create a picture from almost valueless materials, but once the value has been created it becomes a potential of transfer. Part of the work of the artist can be adequately assessed only in terms of the potential transfer created by his work – it cannot be assessed by the concept of the 'value of the picture'. Unless it appeals to some other persons who may wish to have it for themselves, it is not a creation of value. It is, in fact, the expression of the desire of others to possess the picture which represents its assessed value in the market. This type of model of the economic system has an impact upon the criteria we may consider in social action. A successful campaign to stimulate church attendance will stimulate the sale of hats as well as hymn-books. The output of goods and services from one sector of the economy becomes the input at other places. This network of transfer of values is being studied by econometricians using matrices of *input and output*. Econometrics is concerned with the utilization of natural and human resources through the medium of transfers of values expressed in money terms.

It would appear that a similar model of *input and output* would have application in the field of social action. But in this area the first requirement of the value-transfer model is not satisfied – we do not know the nature of the attenuation of transfer values. That is to say, we do not know in what ways moneys 'saved' in one direction are likely to be applied in others, or in what ways moneys move throughout the system. Of course, we cannot begin to apply any model of this kind until the basic transformation of the concept of value into money terms has been attempted.

The Ecological Model

If the model afforded by the econometric input-output system can be successfully and logically opposed, the nature of the model still persists. The interdependence of individuals and systems can be demonstrated in terms of ecology without reference to economic concepts. The error of introducing the rabbit into Australia or the eucalyptus tree from Australia into California, and many other instances of the disturbance of the balance of nature by well-meaning but inadequately informed persons, is now fully recognized. The difficulties which these actions started may be said to be due to the error of attempting to deal with one variable without reference to its interactions, which were, of course, unknown. In present-day language we could say that those who made these errors were operating with a model which was too simple. If this analogy should be seized upon as support for the 'mass attack' in social work, let it be noted that a similar mass attack would have meant cutting down all the trees in California and replacing them with a cross-section of the trees in Australia, or removal of all the animal life in Australia and replacement by a fully representative sample of animal life from countries where a balance of life including the rabbit had been achieved. No other solution would be possible without knowledge of which variables were and which were not of importance.

Whether we work with the econometric model, the ecological model, or with some other model which seems more satisfactory, we are dealing with an interactional situation, and the model must take account of the interactions. Thus the scales in which we operate must have some validity across the types of problem and relate to the concept of values over the total field. Money has the necessary characteristics. The concept of subjective utilities has similar characteristics, but, it seems, provides a scale which is a simple transformation of money values (Sellin & Wolfgang, 1963). Despite the direct transformation of money and subjective-utility scales, many persons reject the concept of money, but accept the concept of subjective value. Sellin and Wolfgang have shown, for example, that crimes can be ordered in terms of seriousness, and since most crimes involve money, money values are implicit in the difference between crimes that are identical except in involving greater or lesser sums of money. The scale being determined with respect to the difference in money, and the concept of 'seriousness' acceptable to samples of the public (judges, police, sociologists, and students), it can be inferred that the concept of money values is rejected only when the scales presented for rating are directly related to money; people can accept a transformation of the money function (which they do not recognize as money) but reject the concept of money value for actions which involve the idea of ethical value. This would seem to be the result of a layman's idea of money as having 'value'. And since it is difficult to change people's orientation towards money, it may be preferable to deal with the concepts in terms of subjective utilities – that is, to invoke directly the idea of comparisons or potential exchanges, and to relate the comparisons to the utilization of natural resources and human skills.

Input-Output Models

If the reader feels that this argument has taken us too far away from practical issues, he is perhaps right. The value-transfer argument has as a first requirement some measure of the nature of the attenuation of transfer values. In terms of money, we need to know how money which is 'saved' in one direction is likely to be applied in others; that is, we need to know the ways in which money or the equivalent of money moves throughout the system. The output of goods or services from one sector of the economy becomes the input at other places. This network of transfers of values at present used only in econometric input-output analysis, would appear to have applications in the field of social action. Indeed, econometrics is concerned with problems of the utilization of natural and human resources, and these problems are studied through the medium of transfers of values expressed in money terms. It is by the means afforded by better economic models and better measurement that the disastrous slumps and booms of the past can now be subjected to some measure of control.

The interdependence of transactions is recognized in the economic field, and recognition of this interdependence has enabled progress to be made in the development of models for the study of economic systems. The models have, in turn, provided information for use in rational decision-making regarding economic problems.

In the social field there is also an interdependence between actions and transactions. Interdependence is revealed through studies in human ecology and in the recognition of the 'multi-problem family'. But another way of regarding the multi-problem family is as a multi-agency family, and the problem as a multiple-agency problem. In New York City there are over 600 social agencies known to the Commissioner for Social Welfare! How much of the activity of any one agency is stimulated (or even generated) by other agencies, and how much by the social problem, is an unknown quantity which is likely to be greater than zero. In the terms used above, part of the input-output is taking place between agencies and not with respect to the problem which the agencies would claim to be their objective. A two-way table showing agencies on one axis and clients on the other could be derived by surveying methods, and might reveal much of the internal transfer of effort, which, from the viewpoint of an observer concerned with the welfare of the problem family, would be regarded as wasteful. The problem of the multiple-agency family is not unique to New York; it is a common problem wherever social work is an acceptable form of endeavour. The problem seems to exist mainly because some of the criteria explicitly or implicitly used by agencies as a measure of their success are internal criteria. The approval of colleagues is sought, adherence to 'professional standards' (internal criteria of behaviour) is an essential feature of the activity, and these, rather than the external criteria of the pay-off, become the standards by which the work is assessed. The test of the surgeon's success is not whether the students around the operating-table exclaim with approval of his skill at making incisions, but whether the patient recovers; whether a life is saved from suffering or an early death.

Perhaps the suggested criteria of pay-off in the form of subjective utilities or in terms of money values are not the best measures of the success of social agencies, but they are better (more functional) than are internal criteria. If these criteria are inadequate then it seems clear that the top priority should be given to finding other more satisfactory criteria. In the meantime it would be rational to work with the best criteria we have.

Limitations of Types of Criterion

Derived measures (cost, pay-off, and subjective utilities) are, of course, measures of gross effects. Like general statistical data, derived measures do not indicate the nature of the changes taking place in the system, but provide a comparison between the system before change and the system after change or a means of assessing differences between systems. No research or action programme would be adequately assessed by measures which considered only the social-cost factors. To assess the nature of the changes which took place, to compare different systems for obtaining similar objectives, and for descriptions of interactions within an action project, specific measures of attitude, behaviour, and opinion would be required. All types of measurement that are sound have a potential place in research methodology. The special function of derived measures is their validity for comparison across different fields. If the problems of measurement relate to within-field differences, more powerful and varied measurements are possible and would have a place even if pay-off could be measured rigorously in money terms. Indeed, as has been indicated earlier, cost measures limited to within a field may be very misleading indices of change. What may show as a saving within a field may be a costly waste when taken into consideration with its interaction with other fields.

Changes in attitude may give rise to changes in behaviour, changes in behaviour may lead to changes in attitude, individuals may change systems, and systems may cause changes to take place in individuals who are involved with the systems; all levels of personality and social factors are interrelated. Measurements of attitudes, measurements of changes in systems, observations of changes in behaviour patterns, and, indeed, the whole psychometric and sociometric armoury of techniques, as well as derived measures based on an ethical concept like 'social costs', may need to be explored in connection with any one project. Social problems do not follow the hierarchy of academic disciplines but run across them with differential impacts. Communication is the key issue in any social problem: communication between those who can measure and those who are concerned with moral philosophy and politics; communication between those who would prefer to measure phenomena in different ways and those who would prefer to act in different ways. The ethical basis relies upon two concepts – responsibility and tolerance.

REFERENCES

CASE INSTITUTE OF TECHNOLOGY (1960). An Operations Research Study of Dissemination of recorded Scientific Information. Cleveland.

DEPARTMENT OF CORRECTIONS (1963). Research Monograph Probation Time Study. Sacramento: State of California.

SELLIN, T. & WOLFGANG, M. E. (1963). *The Measurement of Delinquency*. University of Pennsylvania.

SLATER, P. (1947). *Blood Donorship*. Social Survey Report. London: H.M.S.O.

TIPPETT, L. (1941). *The Methods of Statistics*, Third edition. London: Williams & Norgate.

CHAPTER 10

Groups, Loops, and Hierarchies

DECISION-MAKING NETWORKS

Groups with role-interchange potential – Decision groups, other types – Two case studies – Social engineering? – Learning systems – The informational feedback loop – Mechanical aids to decision-making – A model organization

It has been maintained throughout the discussion that social problems cannot be dealt with effectively without cooperation between the social administrator, the social scientist, and the social worker. Nor can any of these interests ignore the public – the consumer of their products.

It will be obvious that cooperation is not something which can be achieved merely by wishing for it. It will be necessary to develop techniques to assist cooperation through communication. It has also been held that 'society must bear within itself the means constantly to adjust' to changing conditions, and that the models used to solve social problems must be flexible and dynamic, taking into account the fact of continuous social progress (or regress). The mechanism of social evolution was related to communication; indeed, it might appear that social evolution is not in the same class of concepts as evolutionary processes in the remainder of the animal kingdom. Man can interfere with the evolutionary process, and progression does not seem to be inevitable.

It has been shown that what is perceived (and acted upon) as 'good' (functional) or 'bad' (dysfunctional) information depends not only upon the content of the message, but also or even mainly upon the perception of the person giving the information. The network through which the information is received is, in the case of human beings, not an inert substance.

The perception that the social administrator has of the social worker, and the perception that the social worker has of the social scientist, are important factors in the communication between them.

Perhaps the perceptions are built upon residues of prior information received and encoded into the experience, but it seems that if prior information is postulated, then prior distortions of information through earlier perceptions and through the effect of the 'channels' must also be postulated. We cannot begin at the beginning, we can only begin from where we now are.

In addition to the interpersonal perceptions each person in the informational network has of others in the network, the construction of the network itself may be an important factor in the efficiency of message transmission.

To date, there have been few studies of decision-making and information-processing in administrative systems, and the more complex interdisciplinary team does not really exist to be studied.

Groups with Role-Interchange Potential

In the majority of decision-making systems the persons involved in the weighing of the evidence could exchange roles, or have been trained in essentially the same 'language'. Communication leading to decision-making within such systems is likely to have different characteristics from decision-making in systems where the main actors cannot change roles because the background of their experience differs.

Consider, for example, the decision-making structure of the higher courts (Christie, 1963). The main actors involved in the decision regarding the disposal of the offender are the judge, the defence counsel, and the prosecutor. Each of these persons could change roles with the other, and they frequently do appear together in different roles when dealing with different cases. The judge, prosecutor, and defence counsel and, indeed, other minor actors in the legal proceedings have been trained in the same basic information-processing methods. Each has knowledge which enables him to evaluate the performance of the others, and each knows that the others share this ability and this knowledge. In such a system the ways in which information needs to flow and be processed differ from those obtaining in other systems lacking the role-interchange potential. The criteria by which information is assessed will tend to be the same in systems where the main actors could exchange roles, and there will be no need for many items of information to be explicitly stated. Explanation of the system of operation or of ways to obtain information will be unnecessary between the main actors, and the distance between those 'within' and those 'without' the exchange potential will tend to be considerable.

Systems having role-interchange potential will tend to be professional groups with codes of standards of behaviour which may be quite complex. There will, therefore, be a tendency for internal standards of behaviour to become, at times, even more important considerations than the external criteria of the objectives of the system. Goffman (1961) has noted how medical doctors, when surrounded by medical students, come to pay greater attention to the expectations of the in-group (role-exchange potential) than to the patient (external criteria). It may be, of course, that potential role-exchange groups can perform certain tasks more effectively than more complex groups lacking this characteristic. It could be that a change in any group's structure from one type to another could change the nature of the information-processing which would take place within the group and thus result in changes in the types of decision made. It would appear that decision groups and informational systems are worthy of study as a means for facilitating certain forms of social action. The system, as well as the nature of the information in the system, would appear to be important in considerations of achieving a desired objective.

Decision Groups, Other Types

As yet there has been insufficient study to make possible a proposition of types of decision-making group and their characteristic information flow systems. It would appear, however, that there are at least two major factors which would need to be taken into account in any typology. We may distinguish systems where there is a definite and permanent leadership function (H) from groups where the leadership function may change among the actors according to the task or some democratic principle ($\bar{H}$). Either type, (H) or ($\bar{H}$), may or may not possess the potential for role-exchange among its members. We may denote groups having role-exchange potential (E) and those without this characteristic ($\bar{E}$).

Some examples may be given:

1. H.E. (Hierarchical group, possessing role-exchange potential.) This would seem to describe the legal decision-making group of judge and learned counsel. It may also describe many professional 'in-groups'.

2. H.Ē. (Hierarchical group, not possessing role-exchange potential.) The surgeon and nurses with other specialists who make up the operating-room team would be one example, and a number of types of military group could be described thus.

3. Ĥ.E. (Non-hierarchical group, possessing role-exchange potential.) A jury provides one example, particularly because they are required to behave as citizens and those having special skills are, in most countries, specifically excluded from lists of jurymen. Other types of citizens' group would also fall to be classified in this category. A doubtful group in this category would be university members in one faculty; the seniority of professors is not supposed to constitute a hierarchy which would in any way influence the free exchange of information and opinion, but some traces of a hierarchy exist in salary differentials and in status.

4. Ĥ.Ē. (Non-hierarchical group, not possessing role-exchange potential.) Perhaps this is the ideal classification for a multi-disciplinary research team. The leadership role should fall to whoever was most qualified to deal with the matter at issue at the time, irrespective of role or status.

It will be observed that certain primary groups, like the family, have tended to change from one type to another. The Victorian hierarchical family under the headship of the father has become more of a type 4 group, or perhaps, in some cases, the term group has also ceased to be applicable. The courts have recently shown a tendency to change from a type 1 group towards a type 2 group with the addition of specialist medical advisers to the decision-making system.

Certain statements can be made about the type of information flowing within the different decision-making group systems. In groups with role-exchange potential, the total amount of information available to the group will not tend to be very much greater than the amount possessed by each member. In the case of the jury, this requirement is regarded as an essential feature of the decision-making system. In hierarchical groups there will tend to be a formalized routine for information flow which will be supported by discipline or encodification of rules of procedure. Information in such systems will tend to flow up and down, and decisions may be plotted to look rather like a family tree, because, once a ruling has been given, it may not be challenged. Such systems will lack informational 'loops'. It will be more difficult for hierarchical systems to adjust to change or to build into their own structure any learning devices for self-adjustment, except adjustment from the top of the hierarchy.

The technological revolutions have forced many systems to change from role-exchange potential with fixed leadership to leadership-exchange potential without role-exchange. In many areas of knowledge there is too much for one man to know, and knowledge has to be shared. In some groups the responsibility remains at the top of the hierarchy, but in others it is also shared among the decision-makers. Where responsibility is not shared, the higher ranks in the hierarchy must be briefed by those holding lower ranks within the system whose role they cannot themselves fill. It seems logical to suppose that in such systems the information available for decision-making will have to pass through more channels and transformations, and the process of information flow will be slowed down.

Two Case Studies

The difference between hierarchical and non-hierarchical groups, and between role-exchange groups and those where this potential does not exist, may explain some of the differences found by Marples in his study of the decision-making of design engineers. His study is one of the few in this field and, although it does not relate to social problems, it seems to provide data very similar to those which might be obtained from a study of different decision-making systems, no matter what the subject-matter. Marples (1960) examined closely the development of a design for ducts and valves in an advanced gas-cooled reactor of the Atomic Energy Authority and a problem in the production of an industrial powder in a commercial organization. He suggests that the types of decision-making system he found would be likely to apply where the problems required novel solutions, and not where the form of the solution was known.

Taking first the Atomic Energy Authority problem, Marples discusses in the form of a diary of events the progress towards a solution of a most interesting engineering problem. He summarizes the diary of decisions in a table which is reproduced as *Figure 11*. In this case, the tendency for the pattern of decisions to look rather like a family tree reveals the hierarchical nature of the system of decision-making. Similarly, tracing the history of the 'powder problem', Marples provides the chart of decisions reproduced as *Figure 12*. The difference in pattern will be immediately evident. Of course, the two problems were quite different, but the teams making the decisions

FIGURE 11

Decision hierarchy of ducts and valves problem
(broken lines are alternatives, vertical lines are sub-problems)

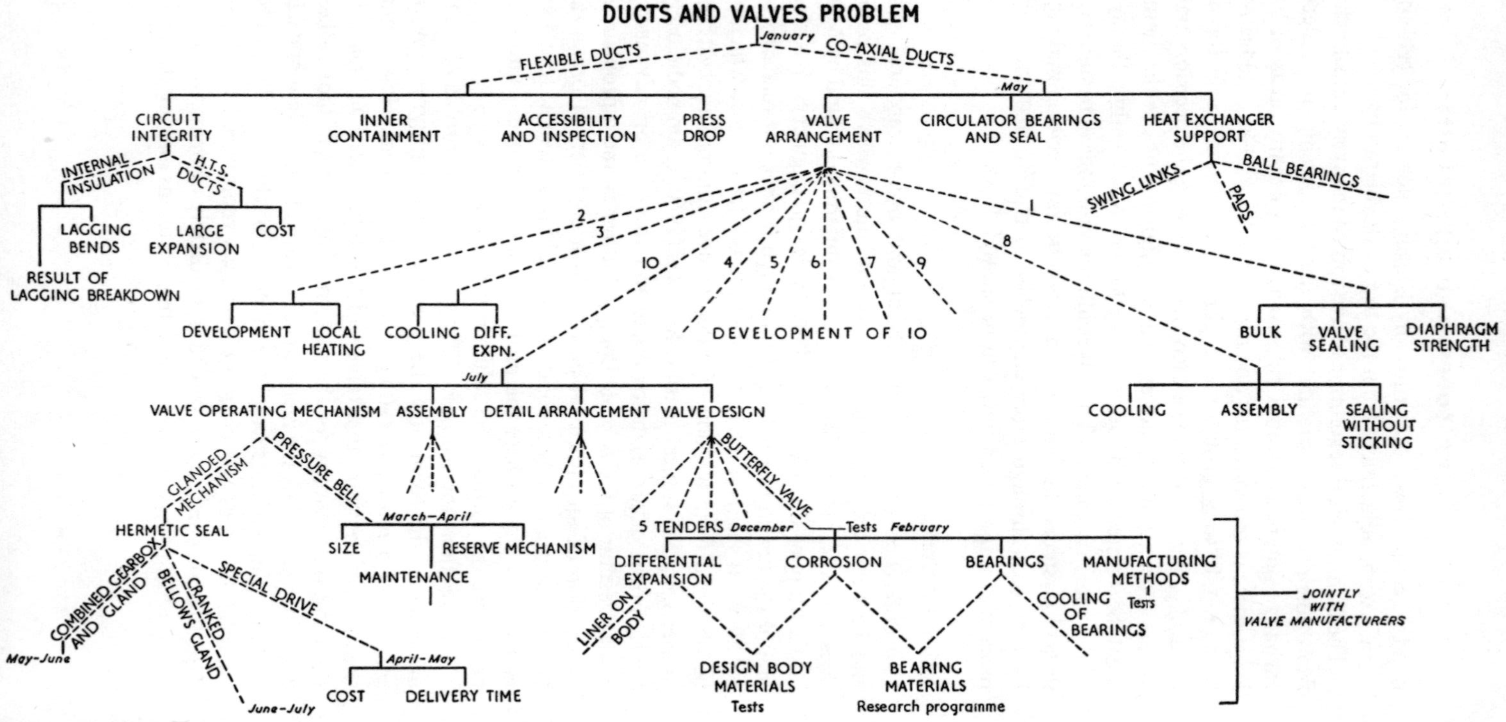

DUCTS AND VALVES PROBLEM

FIGURE 12

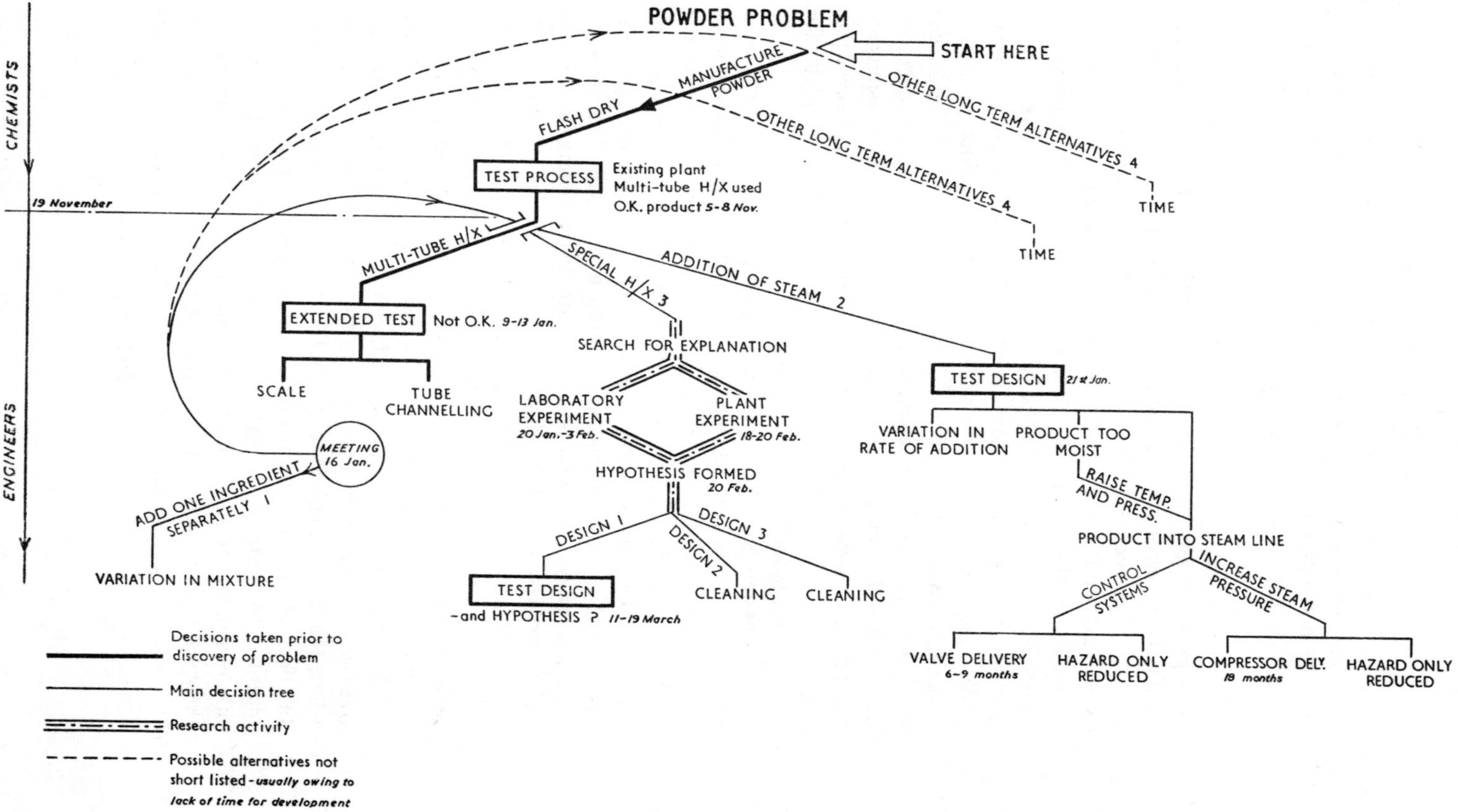

Alternatives, sub-problems, tests, and research in the powder problem were not drawn from very different disciplines. Many of Marples's comments in interpreting his results fall so close to the methods advocated at different times in earlier chapters that they can be reproduced without modification. The following are extracts from his report.

'These studies,' he writes, 'are used to illustrate a generalized description of [engineering] designing as a sequence of decisions leading from the original statement of the requirements to the specification of the details of the "hardware" to be manufactured.' 'As we move down the tree [the decision process] the level of abstraction decreases. At the top the problem and its solutions are described in relatively abstract terms. At the bottom we envisage detailed bits of hardware made from particular materials. The result of all engineering design activities is "hardware"; manufacturing techniques, standard parts and assemblies constitute a set of means which have been previously devised for carrying out a variety of design decisions made at a higher level of abstraction. All new high level decisions are made in the knowledge of the existence of these means. All new detail designs and methods of manufacture increase the means available for carrying out more high level decisions.'

In discussing how the engineers examined proposals for the solutions of their problems, Marples notes that 'two methods seem to be possible. One to attempt a ranking of the proposed solutions in the order of judged feasibility, and examine them in this order, searching for intractable sub-problems. When one is found, try the next solution and so on until a feasible solution is obtained. The other, to attempt a ranking of the proposed solutions in terms of the advantages which may accrue, and examine them in order of desirability, searching for intractable sub-problems, and so on as for the first method.'

The two case histories studied by Marples provided examples of both methods. 'In the Ducts and Valves problem [the Atomic Energy Authority problem] the first method was applied to the flexible co-axial ducts choice; if the second method had been applied the alternatives would have been examined in the reverse order . . . . On the whole the second method seems preferable unless time is very short. In effect, the greater the advantage of any proposal the greater the incentive to master its sub-problems and the more important it is to discover them early so that as much time as possible is available for their solution. It is clear that however great the advantage of a given scheme, it is a non-starter if it also involves an intractable sub-problem. Once, therefore, a proposal has been made, attention should be directed to discovering the sub-problems and solving these. Evidence as to the advantages of the solution is of little value – except as an incentive.'

'This method,' he continues, 'has other advantages. No one will deny that a problem cannot be fully formulated until it is well on the way to solution.' (Here he is clearly referring only to engineering experts' concordance – it is doubtful whether such agreement could be assumed in the field of behavioural research, although the statement remains equally true for this area.) 'The real difficulty . . . lies somewhere among the sub-problems. . . . The nature of the problem can only be found by examining it through proposed solutions and it seems likely that its examination through one, and only one, proposal gives a very biased view. It seems probable that at least two radically different solutions need to be attempted in order to get, through comparisons of sub-problems, a clear picture of the 'real nature' of the problem' (see Chapter 7). 'In addition, of course, a designer is apt to become enamoured of his own solution. This make him liable to underestimate the severity of the sub-problems it involves. The designer will be helped to an objective assessment if he makes a practice of examining a problem through at least two solutions and of comparing the solutions . . .' If this is true for the reasonably exact sciences, how much more so for the problems of social behaviour?

Noting the relationship between subjective certainty and research procedures, he goes on to observe, 'the sooner a proposal is rejected correctly, the less the work required, but as long as that proposal is feasible, the greater the uncertainty that the best proposals have been retained. If it were not for the fact that the examination of inferior proposals leads to a better understanding of the problem or even to ideas for superior solutions, the work done on them could be considered useless . . . rejecting proposals early could improve efficiency but only at the expense of certainty.'

Even the role of theory was noted in these two case studies, and the lack of glamour in research was apparent. Research, it seems, is more a matter of technical competence than of flashes of genius. 'Little evidence of this kind [flashes of inspiration] is forthcoming. . . . Nevertheless the difficulties of the problems demanded innovation. More often than not, the initial proposals for a solution were comparatively pedestrian and taken straight out of the stock-in-trade of the engineers concerned. Such proposals were used to high-light or uncover the real difficulty of the problem, and, when this was revealed, some well established techniques could get around it. By the time this had been done with a number of sub-problems a result was achieved which is extremely ingenious and properly commands our admiration. But it had involved far more hard thinking and argu-ment than inspiration.' One incident of 'inspiration' was, however, noted in the commercial problem. The moment of inspiration oc-curred when the hypothesis was formulated. 'This was an instant of enlightenment which, I found, could be placed to within a few minutes. Evidence of behaviour had gradually accumulated and the engineer reviewed it again and again searching for an explanation in terms of hydrodynamic and thermodynamic theory. Some extra evidence provided a clue, and then a hypothesis was formed which explained everything. But, having this knowledge, his design to over-come the trouble became simple and logical deductions from it, although when completed, they are sufficiently ingenious to be patented. It is almost as if an appropriate description of the sub-problem contains the genesis of the solution.' 'Calculations . . . can only be applied to problems whose nature is perceived. For example, a structure may be stressed to carry expected loads, but if it is not perceived that the conditions of the load will lead to fatigue, the wrong calculations may be made. There is no way of being sure that all the sub-problems of a given design have been perceived and the necessary calculations and tests made. The ability to perceive sub-problems is one of the major contributions of experience . . .'

Social Engineering?

Of course, even although some aspects of social work have been termed 'social engineering', there are large differences between engineering and social science, but there are also similarities. In engineering the objectives may be initially stated in language on a high level of abstraction, but they can be clearly and precisely stated. It is known exactly what the 'hardware' is intended to do, and a large body of theory and other hardware exist. Engineers have, in mathe-matics, a common language which they share with the related sciences; the information upon which decisions are made can be noted in unambiguous terms, and there is a quick feedback of the results of decisions made.

Despite the similarities between the engineering research decision networks and those of social research, there seems something unsatisfactory about the use of the concept of social engineering. Perhaps this inadequacy is related to the inadequacy of the analogue used earlier of wartime strategies. In designing a piece of hardware, the function desired can be stated, and the creation of the apparatus does not interact within itself. Social research is carried out within the social system and forms part of that system. There are, of course, sub-problems in social affairs where the engineering model may stand up well, but there is the overall problem of interactions. Society is dynamic, and the systems of research and action should be dynamic or learning systems. Research and action are, at present, two types of operation but they cannot be independent, and assumptions of independence for purposes of applying existing techniques present some serious weaknesses.

Learning Systems

It might be possible to develop a system of self-evaluative action – a kind of social evolutionary process with its own built-in learning and re-directive mechanism so that the distinction between research and action within the social ethic of the culture became blurred in a unitary organization.

There is already some indication that such a model is possible. Factories can be built in such a way that they are best described as self-learning systems. They can be told what they are required to do, in quite general terms, and thereafter they never relax. They are always trying to do better through the continuous study of their current achievements, and, from information derived from previous experience, they adjust their behaviour (processes) in a manner calculated to be that most likely to increase their efficiency. The process and the objective must be understood in a dynamic way before it is possible to lay down the programme for such types of factory. In the chemical industry some plants are already working which embody the principle of a self-regulating control directed towards a dynamic objective, and plans are nearly completed for steel production along similar lines. The system consists of informational loops of process variables and the results of production related to an information-storage system which provides the 'memory' and the basis for 'learning'.

In such a model the evaluation is continuously related to the action in a loop which provides no specific separation of action from evaluation. Cause and effect also become blurred in such models, as they do in the simple case of the thermostat. The evaluation changes the behaviour (processes) and the behaviour (processes) changes the evaluation.

Social processes are, of course, by no means so well understood as are the processes of chemical production or of metallurgy. None the less, some models of social action have some characteristics which are similar to the evolutionary processes models provided by the 'learning factories'.

It will be recalled that in the discussion of the difference in 'information sets' of members of village and urban culture, it was remarked that the village system was characterized by a communication system in which information about the system was fed back into the system – each member of the village culture had information regarding the functioning of the culture. But the quality of the self-regulatory mechanism depends upon the quality of the information and its valid processing. The village's information 'loop' will consist of direct observation as well as opinion. And yet it seems that the village communication system had some qualities which helped to offset the modern malaise of anomie and alienation. It might be asked whether the type of 'village' communication system might not be improved and used as a vehicle for social change through increased knowledge of a wider set of variables regarding persons in different roles within society.

The Informational Feedback Loop

Some recent methods aimed at promoting social change have developed information loop systems, although the inspiration for the model is more likely to have been derived from some of the postulates of psycho-analysis than from the village culture. Groups of people who work together in different roles – say, probation officers, judges, police, and prison staffs – are brought together to discuss quite freely their problems, and particularly their problems in working together. No particular goals are provided for this method of informational feedback, that is to say, it is not a training system modelled on any system for instilling certain attitudes which are perceived by the *trainers* to be good or functional. The process is not without objective, but it is without any fixed plan. The underlying philosophy seems to be that the information feedback will assist with the processes which the representatives of the system who are involved in the discussion sessions are concerned to carry out. It would appear that the system provides a means for speeding up the normal processes of the development, that is, the *evolution* of the system is expedited. Presumably if the system is evolving in the desirable direction, the informational feedback loop will speed the processes in the desired direction, but if it is not moving along in the right direction, the process of dysfunctional change will be similarly expedited.

Although the method of informational feedback may have its inspirational roots in the methods of psycho-analysis, the logical model which it affords is very different. Psycho-analysis uses similar methods of non-directive discussion, but the objective in analysis is to lead the client to a realization of 'truth'. Psycho-analysis proposes an external criterion of truth which may be attained by self-realization or through insight, which is assisted by the group discussion processes. In the logical model of the informational feedback method there is no external criterion – or there need not be. There is no supposition of truth giving or truth revealing. Instead of truth, the information which passes and the emotional exchanges relate to *perceptions* of 'truths' or situations, not to 'truth' or presumed 'realistic' situations. If either 'truth' or 'good' are presumed to lie anywhere, the way towards the goal is expected to be realized through mutual trippings.

The informational feedback method may be viewed as a small replication of the processes of our general democratic institutions. It may thus be viewed as a model of the general social ethic itself. Evaluation of such demonstration training programmes poses a different problem from evaluation of other methods. If the method embodies within itself the general social ethic, it cannot be validated without questioning the general social ethic! The only open question is whether the social sub-system created for purposes of the method is a reasonably true reflection of the larger democratic process. Since the system of feedback itself provides its own goals, these cannot be stated in advance, unless they are stated by some other authority outside the group. By hypothesis, the goals stated by the other authority are the goals of the democratic social institutions; hence, if the sub-group is a representative sample of the general authority, the goals will be the same. If, on the other hand, the group is not a representative one, the goals it will set for itself will not necessarily accord with the goals desired by those who have the right and duty to state them; they may or may not be the same. If the goals are not the same, then the group will be working itself towards goals which are not 'right'.

It would seem that the informational feedback system of 'training' presents some interesting philosophical problems. None the less, training schemes based on models of this kind have a great attraction, particularly in fields where formal training methods would be likely to be rejected by those who might be perceived as in need of further training.

It seems clear, however, that though the procedure can prove useful in assisting the progress towards objectives which are considered as desirable, it may also lead to results which could be seen as negative. Whether the general motivation of the participants towards the desired goals is normally sufficient to ensure that training systems based on this model will always prove to have positive effects has not yet been tested. The ways in which research information might be built into informational feedback models have not yet been worked out, nor has the optimum composition for such groups. Each group will 'programme' its own informational flow system, and hence the information flow is not under control, nor can the same flow system be expected to occur with different groups. Each group will certainly have unique aspects, and without experimentation it cannot be stated whether these will tend to be so numerous that the variance between groups is too large to permit of measurement of the effects of the 'method'.

Perhaps more effective methods might be evolved from some hybrid system, where part of the information was 'programmed' into the system from outside the groups themselves, and part was permitted to arise from within. It might be possible to overcome some of the problems of 'information overload' (where an increase in information available to a group reduces the effectiveness of their decisions) by programming the input of information in certain ways.

More experiments with groups of this kind are needed. Pulling oneself up by one's own shoe straps may be one of the best ways for systems to develop towards greater effectiveness. More is known about small group dynamics than about other social systems, and this knowledge could be harnessed into social change programmes of this kind. It seems that informational feedback systems have great promise. Perhaps initially somebody ought to know what is likely to represent progress in the desired direction and what is no more than a Rake's Progress. If the method begins to prove too dysfunctional for the performance of the participants in their roles in the larger society, then some controls should be exercised.

Mechanical Aids to Decision-Making

It seems desirable to say something about the factors which may determine the group's efficiency, and this would suggest that evaluation of (a) the quality and relevance of information, (b) the quantity of information, (c) perception of channels for receipt of information, and (d) the processing efficiency, would be essential for the development of these methods. It seems questionable whether the human mind can process information of any complex form with any real degree of efficiency. Of course, only humans can know what humans *want*, but they may not be well equipped to produce it by traditional processes. Man can get from place to place by walking or swimming, but he can get there quicker and he can get to places otherwise inaccessible if he uses the technical aids he has developed – ship, aeroplane, or car.

Man can process information directly and unaided, but not so efficiently as by use of the technical aids he has developed. Ship and aeroplane do not determine *where* and *when* a man should go – not even when fitted with self-regulatory devices!

Groups of people singing and marching together may get further than if they travelled alone without mutual support. Without technical aids, groups, even using informational loops, may develop only a more positive and satisfying inefficiency. The role for human groups is not in providing inefficient replacements for mechanical aids, but in finding ways of utilizing aids to achieve the ends desired by human groups. Their effort is better directed towards keeping the machines in their place than towards replacing them.

We must learn to live in a four-dimensional world – three dimensions of rationality, and the fourth of ethics, where the fourth determines the way we operate with the remaining three, and, in particular, sets the criteria which we seek to maximize or minimize. Of course, the scientist, operating as a scientist, cannot accommodate ethics within his methodology, but this does not condemn science as unethical – it is as though one were to blame the dimension of space for not measuring time. Yet W. Macneile Dixon (1962) could claim much more support for his views when he wrote, 'Science is the view of life where everything human is excluded from the prospect. It is of intention inhuman, supposing, strange as it may seem [sic], that the further we travel from ourselves the nearer we approach the truth, the further from our deepest sympathies, from all we care for, the nearer we are to reality, the stony heart of the scientific universe.' What limited dimensional nonsense! This is saying that a location described with respect to the x-axis does not define the location with respect to the y-axis. And of course there are other people who can see only along the y-axis; although these seem to be fewer and less vocal.

Whence come the scientist's strictures on the behaviour of those guilty of misrepresenting their findings who would claim membership among his ranks? From where does he obtain his belief in the free publication of results – a matter upon which he often comes into conflict with non-scientists? It is usually the scientist who is first to claim the superiority of truth over expediency. It is the scientists who are among the first to advocate an open society, not the moral philosophers and the priests. In fact, is there any group more ethical than the scientists with respect to the scientific ethic? Science, it would seem, is far more aware of ethics than moral philosophy of science. But scientists do not claim any superior knowledge or rights in any field which they know they have not studied with great care and rigour. Perhaps they have not claimed enough? The war against science is no righteous war, it is generated by ignorance and limited thinking. The scientist admits that others live in this world too – he too is a member of our democratic institutions.

The scientist is right in regarding ethics as orthogonal to his methodology. Ethics is, or should be, orthogonal also to social administration – that is the meaning of the concept of the 'public servant'. The social administrator is charged with ensuring *social* good, not *ethical* good. Of course, if the ethic of a society changes, so also will the perception of social good which should guide the social administration. The social administrator is not in charge of the social ethic, he is its servant. It cannot be otherwise in a democracy; indeed, when this has not been so there has resulted the dictatorship of the Church or some other 'religion' like Nazism or Communism, and it is then that the people have perished. The ethic must remain orthogonal to science and administration, but society is not a simple structure. The different dimensions must be related through the ethic of responsibility by means of communication.

Machines do not guide themselves by ethical considerations. Machines do not have a concept of responsibility. Machines do not determine ends or objectives. Machines do not negotiate with each other, nor do they invent systems. These are roles for the human intelligence.

There is no separate world for the scientist, statesman, artist, philosopher, or 'common man'. There are not even different societies; all are concerned with the ways in which we govern ourselves and the ways in which our systems are administered. How can we harness the power which is *ours* to best achieve those ends we perceive are ethical and functional for our society? How can we best ensure that our society 'bears within itself the means of constant change ... adjusting itself' as a continuous learning process to meet the needs of the times? How can we unblock the channels of communication, freeing them from misconceptions and misrepresentations, and overcome the difficulties of language between disciplines and different experience groups?

A Model Organization

In the belief that our society can only obtain the needed means of change through communication and cooperation, an essay in administrative systems has been made. The objectives of the system are to facilitate those types of interaction and information-processing which appear necessary to ensure constant change in continuous contact with the social ethic and democratic principles. If the model does not achieve anything else, it is hoped that it will make somewhat more clear some of the ideas and arguments of the preceding chapters by reducing them to proposed 'hardware'.

This model is doubtless not the only model nor the best that could be designed to achieve the purposes which constant change requires. Much thought, trial and error, investigation, and experimentation will be required before any system can be set up. There is only one characteristic which is new in the model proposed – it has built into it a learning 'device' – a self-regulating control. It is not intended that, once set up, it should remain in the form in which it is established; indeed, if it is to cope with change, it must itself change. The proposed model system is illustrated in *Figure 13*.

It will be noted that the central core organization consists of four sections linked closely together. Ideally, it would seem that they should be housed in the same building and have some common services. The organization is not under the direct control of any governmental department, local authority, or even a university, nor is it a 'social agency'. This is because each of these bodies presents a specific 'image' and has its own particular role as a social institution. It seems essential, however, that the organization should have very close links with universities, governmental agencies, local authorities,

FIGURE 13

Example of a problem-centred organization for action research

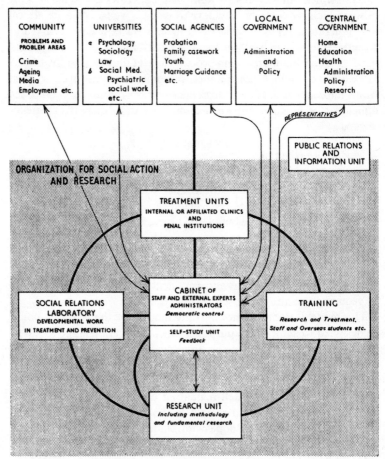

and other institutions and bodies, but particularly with the community itself, so that it can keep in direct touch through its 'central nervous system' with community problems.

It is suggested that the policy of the organization is determined

272

by democratic principles – a sort of parliament or cabinet of equals – recruited from representatives of government and other 'user' interests in its services, as well as from the four sectors of the organization. The operation of the 'Cabinet' will, of course, be a critical feature of the system. It should certainly not be an hierarchical group, but be composed of persons who are all potential leaders. The leadership should be determined not by status but by the nature of the problem in relation to the skills available among the members. Any leader should be able to yield up his leadership to another without loss of prestige – indeed prestige might be gained by insight as to when it was desirable to yield up the leadership to another. How well the leadership changes were accomplished would be one of the functions of the 'Self-study Unit' to determine by observation and the application of research techniques.

The Self-study Unit is not superior to other units but is charged with a different responsibility and may develop special skills with regard to this duty. This unit is intended to provide an insurance against bureaucratization of the total system, keeping its focus of concern upon external criteria. It is possible that this role might best be achieved by the personnel in this section having tenure of office rather like the Fellows of some of the senior universities and colleges. It would appear that it must be independent of the four remaining sections of the organization and must never become a large unit. It should be composed of mixed disciplines and the personality characteristics of its members could be of supreme importance. (They would certainly need a sense of humour!) In addition to being concerned with the effectiveness of the central nervous system of the organization, the unit would be required to provide continual assessment of the effectiveness of the organization in its contact with the external agencies. It would be able to feed back information which could be used to direct the organization towards ways of continually improving its functioning. This is the mechanism 'within itself' which provides the 'means for constant change'. Once the organization is set up, its course should be determined by rational considerations of information, objectives, and its room for manoeuvre. It is like a 'self-homing missile' directed at the 'enemies of society'.

The initial act of setting up such an organization will have to be an act of faith on the part of all the groups concerned. The will to make it work will make equal demands upon the scientists, administrators. and social workers involved. No one speciality can perceive itself as

273

superior to the others, and all must share a real drive to see society advance towards its goals. If the argument derived from normality theory is accepted, it follows that the organization must tolerate deviance within itself, since change and deviance are often similar in appearance. The whole system must constitute a learning network, and remain throughout its life a learning system.

Some indication of the impact of the organization upon social administration and social agencies may be given. The results of, say, research developed first in the research unit may be tried out in the 'Social Relations Laboratory', in much the same way as medical developments achieved by medical research teams are given clinical trials in a hospital having special connections with the research laboratory. If the trials are successful they should be released for further use and evaluation in the Treatment Units affiliated to the organization. Eventually, new methods would be regarded as having demonstrated their utility, and, having passed the stage where continuous checking was desirable, they would pass out to the social agencies and the community, or, through the governmental agencies, be applied throughout the country. The close link between the different levels of trial and evaluation should ensure that the delay between the discovery of a useful technique and its general application was minimized.

The 'Training Unit' of the organization would provide another channel of communication between the different interests. Training in both treatment methods and research methods would be available. Indeed, an interchange between treatment and research personnel would seem to be a profitable operation in increasing or maintaining good communication. It might be possible that training for action might take place through research and training for research take place through action. It is hoped that this close integration would resolve the difficulty postulated in the diabolical hypothesis (those who know are inhibited from action, and those who act do not want to know!).

The 'Treatment Unit' might be the first to observe some problems, and these could be rapidly referred to the laboratory or the research unit, whichever was the most appropriate. There must be effective two-way communication, indeed an all-round communication between all sections within the organization and outside. If this communication should begin to break down, it would be the concern of the Self-study Unit to point it out and to seek remedial measures.

The breaking-off of this role from the other roles seems to be the best way to ensure that it is given the attention it needs.

It is to be hoped that after an initial period where considerable difficulties with 'language' may appear, the different unit personnel would become bilingual. The research staff would learn the language in which social action and treatment personnel expressed their concerns for their cases and clients, and the social action staffs would gain insight into the power and limitations of research methods. The end-goal of the organization – the integration of social action and social research (with social policy determined according to the best available information) seems to be in accord with the general goals of our society.

The model is capable of adaptation to other problem areas. It would seem that little modification would be required to provide a suitable system for the study of the mass media. Research and Training Units would remain much the same, the Social Relations Laboratory would be replaced by a laboratory in the more conventional form, with closed-circuit television, mock-up press facilities, audience-reaction rooms, and the like. The Treatment Units would be replaced by the organization's own transmission system, or an affiliated system where large-scale trials could be made of new forms of entertainment or informational programmes. The links with the community would be similar, except that instead of, or in addition to, some of the agencies represented in the Cabinet for the social-work model, newspaper and other mass-media interests would be involved. The Training Unit would bring together different technical training facilities including television, sound-radio, and newspaper reporters and other staffs. There would seem to be as much need for cross-stimulation among mass-media groups as among social-work groups. The Self-study Unit would be similarly charged with prevention of the bureaucratization of the organization and with directing its focus upon its external objectives.

It must be emphasized that the main purpose in setting forth these models is only expository, as first illustrations of a type of organization which might meet the requirements of a 'learning organization'. In the science of science, in the strategy of research and the organization of creative environments, there is so little information to guide us. The proposed system is not put forward as an ideal, it is put forward as an organization with a mechanism that may enable it to pursue continuously changing ideas of ideals. An organization which has a built-in 'pursuit mechanism' should be able to keep in advance of systems which lack such a mechanism. If it is suggested that the model savours of building a bureaucracy to abolish bureaucracy it may be retorted that that may be better than building a bureaucracy to build up bureaucracy!

REFERENCES

CHRISTIE, NILS (1963). Paper presented at University of California Department of Criminology seminar, August 1963. (To be published.)

DIXON, W. M. (1962). As quoted in *Man Alone*, ed. Josephson E. Dell. New York: Laurel Books.

GOFFMAN, E. (1961). *Asylums*. New York: Doubleday. London: W. H. Allen.

MARPLES, D. L. (1960). *The Decisions of Engineering Design*. Monogr. London: Institute of Engineering Designers.

Appendices

Selection of Target Areas

The demonstration techniques which involve intensive or extensive social action in a limited area or with respect to a limited selected population afford a useful tool for the examination of the effectiveness of different approaches to social problems. There are, however, many pitfalls which can result in serious errors of inference.

If the similarities between 'matching' designs and 'target area' designs are considered many problems will become evident. Matching requires the samples compared to be exactly similar with the exception of the particular variable under study (see Appendix II). Only in ideal laboratory conditions can such requirements be fully met. The degree to which the actual conditions fall short of the basic requirements leaves room for error, and this error cannot generally be measured. There is a sharp distinction between stratified sampling and matching as the latter is usually practised. Stratified sampling has known properties, whereas there may be many unknown factors in a matching design, although the best matched designs are, in fact, stratified samples by a different name!

The assumption is normally made that a demonstration project which provides data with respect to a specific area or population is also a sound basis for generalization. But target areas are usually selected *because* the particular social problems which it is proposed to attack are particularly evident there. In fact, neither purposeful nor haphazard selection of target areas is a satisfactory procedure. In the last analysis, any procedure which does not rest on the basic factor of randomization is suspect, but some designs are more robust[1] than others and some are more powerful than others.

A method for selection of target areas is proposed below which has the advantage of utilizing existing information as fully as possible. The method is similar to the regression matching (or 'prediction') method.

Suppose that the particular proposed social action is aimed to reduce 'juvenile delinquency' (although it could be almost any other social problem with little change in the method being required).

Almost all large cities and towns can provide general statistical data relating to many social factors. Many of these indices will correlate with juvenile delinquency (or other social problem which is itself the subject

---

[1] A technical term referring to the degree to which conditions may fail to be satisfied without distortion of the estimates.

of a social index). For example, the proportion of young persons having a record of some proved offence(s) in any area will tend to be correlated with the infant mortality rate, commuting ratio, population change, income levels or indices based on the value of residential property for purposes of local taxation, and many more social factors. Thus it is possible to 'predict' or estimate, for each area for which social indices are available, the delinquency rate (or other x variable) from the other factors (or y variables).[1] The different areas may be described in terms of the accuracy with which it proves possible to estimate the delinquency rates (x) from information about variations in the remaining data (y). Some areas will have *observed* delinquency (x) rates which do not differ very much from the *expected* rates (i.e. rates estimated in terms of other data). It may be helpful to convey the meaning of this method to think of some areas as following certain 'laws' (predictable delinquency rates (x)) and other areas which are not following the same 'laws'. Some areas with high delinquency rates may fit in with the estimation equations, as may some areas with low rates.

It will usually be desired to carry out demonstration projects in areas having a high incidence of the social problem (e.g. x = delinquency), but some of these areas may be atypical in respect of the association between delinquency (or x) and other factors (y). If this distinction is unknown when selection is made of the target area(s), clearly, useful information is lost. If, for example, after a demonstration project had been carried out, (a) a typical area had become atypical (unpredictable), or (b) an atypical area had become typical in respect of the association with the y-variables, different types of inference would seem to be called for. Indeed, it is not at all clear what inferences might be made if a change were to take place in the form of either (a) or (b) above. The inferences to be drawn from change are more direct if the areas selected as target areas are 'typical' (i.e. predictable). For example, a change may be observed in the x-variable during the demonstration-action period, but this change might be explained by changes in the y-variables – in which case there is no evidence for the *direct* impact of the action on the x-variable. It would then be necessary to question whether the demonstration project had an effect on *any* y-variable(s) and then, indirectly, an impact on the x-variable.

The analysis proposed makes it possible to select target areas and *similar* 'control' areas at the commencement of a demonstration project and to consider the outcome of the social action in terms of the change in x or y variables. *Figure 10* (see p. 214) shows a possible position at the commencement of a project with outlying observations (areas which are not related in x and y variables in similar ways to the majority of areas – they are atypical in the dimensions covered by the analysis) and areas

[1] Transformations may be necessary for some variables to ensure that the conditions of multiple regression or other forms of estimation may be used as may be appropriate.

which are typical. If high-delinquency (or x) areas are selected for action it is clearly advantageous to select areas as targets having high (x) rates which follow the general pattern in y and to reserve some similarly typical areas (in x and y) for control purposes.

Evaluation of the outcome of social-action demonstration, even with this model, is not completely rigorous, but the use of the information from related dimensions adds power to any analysis of the outcome. At best, this model clarifies the difficulties of inference where, as has usually been the case, the target areas have been selected without reference to the relationships between the x-variable and y-variables. An area which is an outlier in this model (atypical in respect of the relationship between the x and y variables) may be expected to respond atypically to the social-action variables.

Perhaps the strongest feature of the proposed model is in the degree of control it affords over factors which may change with time. For example, unemployment may be related to delinquency and unemployment may increase generally during the demonstration project. If the relationship between unemployment and other y-variables and the x-variable (delinquency) is measured it would be possible to show, say, that despite expected increase in delinquency because of a rise in unemployment (inferred from 'typical' control areas) no increase had taken place where the demonstration-social-action had been put into effect, namely in the target areas. If, however, the relationship between, say, unemployment and delinquency in the target area was atypical before the demonstration began, this type of argument could not be made. Further, it may be that there will be a general tendency over time for atypical areas to become more typical and for typical areas to become more atypical, but some areas may be exceptions to this pattern. Comparisons of trends of this kind will also provide some further light on the evaluation of demonstration projects.

Although methods for evaluation of large-scale demonstration social-action programmes will always fail to carry a conviction of proof, it is economic to seek to use the information available to obtain maximum power. There can be no reason to select target areas blindly or in the light of information about the x-variable alone. Prior analysis of existing data is clearly an essential requirement of reasonable efficiency in the final evaluation, and it is to illustrate this point (rather than to provide a perfect model) that the dimensional approach has been suggested here.

Are Matching Designs Satisfactory?

It may be an overstatement to say that the current practice of sociologists is to standardize by matching persons on psychological factors, and of psychologists to standardize by matching on sociological factors, and thus to try to avoid considering explanations of their observations which derive from the other's field of theory. To some extent this practice may be not as bad as it sounds – if, that is, matching can be justified at all in the human behavioural sciences.

General Statement of Conditions

The idea of matching relates to the classical experimental method of the physical sciences, which assumes that all variables are held constant except the experimental (one single) variable. Perhaps in some simple problems in the laboratory this assumption is justified, but even where it is, since this is only under the strictest laboratory conditions, inferences to situations outside the laboratory are often attended by considerable uncertainty. Many laboratory-developed processes in the advanced physical sciences fail to stand up on pilot plant tests or in production lines for this reason. Highly controlled laboratory experiments enable generalizations to be made in terms of the materials or processes, but not in terms of different situations. In the human sciences it is important to be able to make statements about situations. Even in the physical sciences complex experimental designs are usually necessary if valid and useful inferences are to be safely made.

Where it is impossible to hold the relevant factors absolutely constant, random allocation procedures may be used. Randomization has also the advantage that it may not be necessary even to know what the relevant factors are, but, where knowledge is restricted, inferences which are valid are also restricted. The methods whereby maximum knowledge may be obtained with the minimum of untested assumptions, or whereby the impact of assumptions which may be unwarranted is reduced to the smallest possible amount, are often highly complex. The selection of the best design will often involve some element of subjectivity, or some attempt to assess the relevance of experiments or data in a field believed to be analogous to that now the subject of experiment. If no assumptions can be made, little will be achieved. The very strict statistical approach would frequently lead to the requirement of quantitative, continuous normal variates – conditions seldom satisfied in real life. Departure from normality is, for some statistical measures, less serious than for others. Robust statistics[1] are, however, often less powerful than those which require the assumptions to be met quite strictly. This is intuitively obvious since inferences must relate to the amount of information. If the nature of the distribution is unknown except in terms of limited information, this limitation must be carried through to the end-product, namely legitimate inference.

Let us see how these general principles apply to matching designs.

Matching and Stratification

If certain information is already available to the experimenter it would seem desirable to use it. This is certainly true. The difficulties in matching do not arise from the use of more information, which is, of course, legitimate and desirable, but from the incompleteness of the information or its incomplete use. In its legitimate form 'matching' is not in fact matching, but 'stratified sampling'. If, for example, we wish to estimate the number of cars owned by private householders in England and Wales it would *perhaps* be more efficient to use a sample of households which overweighted the upper-income groups. This could be done by use of the rateable value of homes or by use of the juror qualification; both factors correlate highly with income. Thus some stratification by income is obtained by use of known correlates of income which are available in the sampling frame data. But whether stratification is more efficient than completely random sampling depends upon the degree of correlation between car ownership and the stratifying factor, as well as other operational considerations. Furthermore, and perhaps more important, it is seldom that only one estimate of one unknown (e.g. car ownership) is required. The stratification may help with one item, but what of the others that may be estimated at the same time? It is possible that other estimates could be less efficiently derived. But stratified sampling covers the *whole field of reference*; it adjusts only the proportions within the subpopulations, and sampling within the sub-populations is random. It is the basic element of randomization that permits statistical inference to be made.

Matching in Practice

The term 'matching' is used to cover a wide range of procedures, some of which are more reasonable than others, but none is completely satisfactory.

A typical problem for which matching is often proposed as a solution is the evaluation of some form of treatment.

For some purpose or another, one group of persons has had a form of

---

[1] A 'robust' statistic is one which is not materially affected by some departure from the basic assumptions, usually normality, in the distribution of the variables.

treatment and a control group is looked for after the event. In such cases the 'experimental group' (treatment) is seldom, if ever, randomly selected; in most cases there will be a 'volunteer bias'. Thus the *ex post facto* experiment does not allow of randomization. Indeed, most matching studies present this same problem. The 'experimental group' is fixed and an attempt is then made to find another group which has the same characteristics as the treatment group except for the fact of treatment. Of course, this can never be achieved, and factors which are believed to be important are selected as the basis for matching, and other factors are not utilized. Common matching factors are social class, intelligence, age, sex, ethnic group, and generally other factors believed to be related to the hypothesis underlying the treatment. But the common matching factors, and, indeed, in general, any factors used in matching will be correlated with others not so used in unknown ways. For example, a group selected for matching on the basis of intelligence will usually be matched in some degree on ethnic group and social class. If then subsequently some factor is found not to be associated with treatment (say, ethnic group) it may be because matching by intelligence has removed this evidence.

It will be obvious that the removal of unknown correlates of the treatment by unknown correlates of the matching factors raises many problems of inference. Conflicting results are to be *expected* from studies using different bases of matching. If sociologists standardize out (by matching) all important psychological variables – either directly or by accident through the effect of unknown correlates, they should not be surprised or pleased when psychological variables fail to appear in the analysis, and of course, conversely for psychologists. Smuggling the rabbit out of the hat before performing the trick is no better (but perhaps more sophisticated) than smuggling it in, as in the classic music-hall turns!

Where knowledge is incomplete, estimates of error variance can be obtained *only* by some basis of randomization. Tests of significance cannot otherwise be used, and where tests cannot be used, legitimate statistical inference is *impossible*. This worst case is limited to the *ex post facto* 'experiment' based on matching. Matching in other treatment studies on a number of relevant factors is justified and may add information if the individuals are allocated as matched pairs to the control and experimental situations, *at random*. But even in this type of design there are problems. Freedman[1] reports that when he matched 58 per cent of a treatment group he obtained different results from when he matched 89 per cent after obtaining access to more 'controls'. He remarks 'it appears that the difference between pairs which matched most easily is not the same as the difference between pairs which were more difficult to match'. Since matching requires the rejection from the matching group of cases which

---

[1] Freedman, R. Incomplete Matching and ex post facto Designs. *Amer. J. Sociol.*, vol. 55, pp. 485–87.

are not 'sufficiently' similar, the population remaining changes in uncontrolled and unknown ways, according to the degree of similarity in the *direct* relationship with the few selected factors.

Prediction or Regression Matching

It has been noted above that there is usually a correlation between variables selected for matching and other relevant variables. If, then, variables are added until the multiple correlation between the dependent variables and the independent variable (criterion) shows no significant increase, the control and experimental groups might be matched by their regression weights. This method is in some ways more efficient than matching by selected items with rejection of cases not providing a 'good' match, but it has other difficulties. It may be that the estimates of the criterion derived by this means are making heavy use of chance values, especially where a large number of factors are used. In no matching technique can we be sure that all the relevant information has been taken into account, but regression matching has one advantage over simple matching in that we know how much of the variation is explained by the equation. In designs (or 'models') of this kind, the validity of any inference depends upon the amount of information in the total matrix, and also upon the degree to which the assumption of linearity may be satisfied – even where other necessary assumptions are sufficiently satisfied. Non-linear models increase the degrees of freedom and thus increase the error variance relative to any test of the experimental control hypotheses, until we are back at a situation very much like matching by combinations of variates or similar systems.

Perhaps the basic problem is that almost all statistical models make predictions about groups of persons according to some measurements or classifications, and individual differences are the same as 'error' – indeed differences between individuals within groups provide the basis for estimates of errors of estimation about individuals derived from information regarding the class(es) to which the individuals belong.

Regression to the Mean

In the discussion of problems in selecting experimental areas (see Appendix I) the effect of regression towards the mean which will occur between two or more compared periods of time and two or more samples was noted. A similar effect can occur in matching designs, where it may be less obvious. Perfect matching cannot .be achieved and the two groups (control and experimental) cannot be taken from the *same* population – not even where the individual provides the experimental and control data. In the latter case the regression effect could be estimated if there were sufficient data about the whole population. But matching rejects the cases which do not fit with respect to the selected factors, and thus a different population is created which will tend to regress towards its own mean. In this case, absence of data regarding the whole population from which the controls are a selected sample makes estimation of the regression effect a very uncertain procedure; indeed, the control group as constructed is even more artificial than the experimental group.

Input Partitioning

Perhaps the best solution that can be adopted at the present time is to define a population by means of some 'input' system, outside the control of the experimenter. Thus we may define as a 'population' all boys sent to borstal training, and all persons adjudged as in need of some form of therapy. The population must be defined at *input*. If then variations are made in the treatment to which allocation is made at random from this rigorously defined population, it is possible to use this element of randomness to make inferences about the whole 'population' so defined, provided that the input mechanism remains constant. If, however, the input mechanism changes, the basis for the definition of the 'population' will have changed and inferences again become uncertain.

One type of solution to the problem of matching has received very little attention in the field of human behaviour research, namely, the use of simulation techniques. In other words a hypothetical 'population' may be constructed and various procedures tested against the model, and the 'model' population may be compared with 'real' populations in terms of a quantity of information. Inferences may then be made together with reasonable estimates of confidence limits. Designs which allow of simulation techniques may be more difficult to deal with in theory, but are likely to be more acceptable in practical situations. Information about 'situations' as well as 'persons' may be taken into the 'model', and checks on its power and efficiency may be built into the design. In general, however, such models will require a larger amount of information than is usually regarded as required by the matching design. But this is not unreasonable. Information cannot be used for support for inference if in fact it does not exist. It must not be forgotten that assumptions once incorporated into a research design will behave in the *same way* as 'real' information. The power of any system of inference is based on the quantity (and 'quality') of information. Assuming that information exists gives only the illusion of a power of inference. Assumptions may be imported to enable a step to be taken, but they must not be forgotten when the end-product is set forth.

Perhaps one way to increase the available information for purposes of evaluative studies is to obtain additional measures of within-individual variation so that reliance is not placed only on the within-group variance as the measure of individual variation.

One thing seems reasonably certain, that an information approach to the study of human behaviour presents a better possibility of development than reliance on experimental designs where the assumptions and conditions are never satisfied in practice. If informational approaches are combined with experimental designs in the limited areas where these are possible (e.g. small group studies) this strategy represents the best at present available.

Evaluation of Training Programmes

Evaluation may be defined as assessments or measures of the degree to which what it is desired to achieve is in fact achieved.

In training programmes it would seem to be fairly generally acceptable to suggest that the objectives are:

(a) increase of appropriate knowledge

(b) increase in willingness to use knowledge in decision-making (attitudes)

(c) increase in ability to use knowledge (that is, to make logical inferences from facts in an efficient manner)

(d) decrease in 'prejudice' (that is, blocks to efficient assessment and use of information should be cleared)

(e) increase in willingness to accept responsibility, perhaps related to an increase in confidence in ability to handle information and possession of more information (as (a), (b), and (c) above)

(f) increase in flexibility of thought or decrease in rigidity (see also (d))

(g) increase in critical ability, particularly positive critical ability in the weighing of evidence.

Measurements can be made with respect to all of the above and not merely the conventionally measured first two items. Moreover, the conventional methods of testing students after a training programme do not provide data to evaluate the programme, since different amounts of the knowledge used in passing the examination may have been possessed before the students' entry to the training course. Evaluation must relate the nature of the situation at 'input' to the same types of measure at 'output', and, of course, all measures must relate to the objective(s) of the system.

Evaluation as Part of Training

Since evaluation requires measurement of the state of the 'material' at both 'input' and 'output', evaluation techniques can make a positive contribution quite directly to the training operation. Clearly, efficient training programmes must be geared to the state of mind (knowledge and attitudes) of the students. Information regarding the 'input' state is, therefore, relevant to both programming and evaluation.

It is also possible to work out systems and devices for measurement which in the course of their administration can serve the training function as well as the measurement function. For example, criterion (d) (reduction in prejudice) requires tests which not only could reveal the prejudices of the subjects to the tester, but later might be used to reveal them to the testee. Measuring instruments may be constructed to serve multiple purposes with efficiency and economy. Subjects may, in fact, construct their own tests as a part of the training system in such a way that they can be used for evaluation. In evaluation of training programmes it must always be remembered that two things are being tested – the subjects and the training system. Tests which are independent of the system or independent of the subjects will not serve the required purposes.

An Example of a Method

It may assist the exposition of this thesis if one specific example is given. This is not necessarily an ideal method, nor is it by any means the only method, but it serves to illustrate the means whereby tests and training may be serving a common purpose. The training programme to be evaluated is, for purposes of this illustration, taken to be a short programme using management training techniques, of from a few days' to a few weeks' duration. The topic assumed is one related to the treatment of offenders or problems in the prevention of crime and delinquency.

Step 1

Subjects (students), at the first opportunity after preliminary orientation, are asked to write down all forms of social action they can think of which, in their view, would help to reduce delinquency recidivism.[1] The time allowed for the free-association exercise should not exceed 30 minutes. Each separate idea should be noted on a separate slip of paper.

Step 2

Classification of the ideas for action or concepts noted will, after content analysis, provide an initial statistical distribution. (Each type of concept or idea for action can be described by its frequency of mention.) This information can be made available to the instructors, with or without identification of the students.

Step 3

If there is found to be a wide range of items following Step 2, sample five to ten of the items.

Step 4

Select pairs of items or arrange items so that each may appear in com-

[1] The procedure would be exactly similar for other topics but, of course, the material requested must be directly related to the subject-matter of the training programme.

parison with every other (paired comparisons, or some partial set according to size of test). For example

item a – b
a – c
a – d
b – c
b – d
c – d

About twenty pairs with partial sets of comparisons or full set (6 items =15 comparisons, 7 items=21 comparisons in full set) appear to represent a test of sufficient length, with test time not exceeding 20 minutes.

Step 5
Prepare cards representing the comparisons in the form illustrated below.

If *A* better tick → ☐	*A* Provide more boys' clubs	*B* Increase school-leaving age	If *B* better tick → ☐
Degree Number ▭			Degree Number ▭
Ease of Decision }	very easy	almost impossible	

Step 6
Present cards as specimen above prepared from subjects' own material provided by Step 1 as early as possible. It should be possible to do this within 24 hours of Step 1. Administer with following instructions:

(a) If you think A is more likely to be effective than B, put a tick in the left-hand side of the card in the box provided. If you think B is more likely to be effective than A put a tick in the right-hand side.
(b) Now try to think how *much more* – how many times more – effective your choice is likely to be than the other item. If about twice as effective put '2' in the lower box. Note '1' means equal, '1½' means 50 per cent more. Do not be too cautious in your selection of the number – number is used in this way to represent ideas we usually put in words like 'little more', 'very much more'; pick a number rather like picking odds, which means 'very little' or 'very much' in whatever way *you* think of number. Do not compare with anybody else.

(c) Now indicate on the line below how difficult you found it to make the decision.[1]

The material derived from this test can be compared with an exactly similar rating of the same cards at the end of the training programme. It is more profitable to relate two similar tests both given at the beginning and end of the course.

After completion of the procedure for the first topic (in this illustrative case, action to prevent delinquency) a similar routine might be applied to the concept of causes of delinquency.

It then becomes possible to cross-analyse 'causes' by 'action' thus:

Cause

	1	2	3	4	5	6 ...
a						
b						
c						
d						
e						

Action proposed

It may be assumed that action should relate to types of belief about 'cause'. Similarly, for other topics any two dimensions which it is postulated would reasonably be expected to be correlated might be selected. The raw material used to form the test scales and comparisons may be of many forms; for example, students might mention types of information they believe to be helpful in making various types of decision. The objective of the procedure is to obtain measures of the starting-point for each student in a standard form, but one which is directly related to their frame of reference *and* to the objectives of the training programme.

Uses of Basic Material

'Before' and 'after' training programme measures can be obtained from the data in many ways, serving to provide assessments of several factors. Some examples follow:

(a) does the relationship between 'cause' and 'action proposed' (or other related concepts) show a more logical pattern after training?

[1] Whether the scale of difficulty is related to the dichotomy or the scale will depend on the subject-matter and the subjects (students). The reference is chosen by the experimenter to ensure variation in the scale. A spare card not used in the test itself is retained from Step 5 to serve to illustrate by example how cards are to be marked. From subjects' response to the illustration the reference point can be set.

(b) what changes, if any, have taken place in the 'difficulty' scale? It might be suggested that the range of the difficulty scale ought to increase, revealing an increased awareness of differentiation.

(c) do the comparisons show fewer circular triads (mutual inconsistencies) after training? (More logical evaluation by students.)

(d) It is probable that different types of person may select different values and that this provides a measure of 'prejudice'. See Galanter, E. (Derived Measurement of Utility and Subjective Probability. *Amer. J. Psychol.*, June 1962, pp. 208–20) for interpretation of degree scores.

(e) have degree scales different variance for 'causes' and 'action' factors (or other related concepts used) and how does this compare in terms of the 'before' and 'after' tests? Some assessment of 'rigidity' is provided by this comparison.

Most of the objectives of training can be related to some measures derived from the comparisons between tests, scores, persons, and time. But perhaps the main value of a system of this kind is in the fact that it makes a feedback loop of information possible, and this loop can be used to improve training.

For example, some subjects like delinquency, management techniques, and indeed most areas involving human behaviour, are usually discussed in imprecise (broad 'band-width') language. It is possible, and even probable, that when Step 6 is put into effect, students will reject the test by saying that the concepts are meaningless! It is then a case for tactful reminder that they had themselves produced the statements from which the experimenter has simply sampled some items. They are encouraged to 'have a go' by the experimenter pointing out that part of his statistical procedures will reveal this problem and make some measurement of it. It is, in these circumstances, difficult for students to regard the task set as 'answering a lot of foolish questions' – a typical reaction to many forms of attitude-test procedures.

Some Technical Comment on the Method

It will be recognized that this test procedure provides 'ipsatively based' measures and the variance between different groups of students (different courses) is not a factor. Standardized general tests have some advantages, but the variance between groups (different course intakes) may swamp the variance due to change with time. Standard tests, used in any specific situation, will contain much material which is redundant in any particular case and this reduces motivation of testees. In evaluation of training, we are more concerned to provide information of value to develop training methods than to make general statements about groups of persons in different training situations, where the training situations cannot be rigorously described.

The purpose of proposing the evaluation of training in the course of training is in accord with the general theory of feedback. Measurement in the abstract is not meaningful – even the most abstract measurement must be related to some practical consequences before it serves the purposes of the scientific method.

Of course, methods which have the greatest generality should be sought, but not at the cost of too much loss in the power of the measurement. Measurement which is only marginally useful over a wide range of problems is not always preferable to measurement which is more useful in a more limited area. It is seldom that we can have it both ways.

Confidence and Competence in Decision-making

The theory set forth in Chapter 4 proposes the central importance of 'information' among the various factors which influence human behaviour. Both the quality and the quantity of information, as well as the channels through which it is transmitted and the manner in which it is processed, were regarded as important areas of study for those concerned with social change.

The majority of techniques available for the study of information handling in the process of decision-making are not well developed. The majority of studies either are unsatisfactory in terms of the degree of control exercised by the experimenter or have failed to simulate 'real-life' situations at all closely. This note reports the results of a study[1] of the decision-making of probation officers in relation to information about their cases. A simple piece of apparatus is described which enables the experimenter to observe the subjects' methods for the use of information and to relate the type and quantity of information to the types of decision made and to the degree of expressed confidence in the decisions. The results obtained derive from a small pilot study in a very limited field, but the description of this work may provide a suitable vehicle for suggestions which may lead to some general hypotheses regarding decision-making by human subjects.

The first consideration in this project was to construct a situation as near to that met in the day-to-day work of the subjects as was consistent with the need to obtain good observations and controls. The apparatus used 'real-life' information from actual case histories written up in reports made by staff from the same office as the subjects whose decisions provided the data. The decisions to be made in the experimental situation were of exactly the same kind as those normally and frequently made in the ordinary work routines of the sample of subjects.

It is generally believed by social workers that the more information they have about the cases with which they are concerned, the better are the decisions they are able to make. It is known, however, that different case-workers give higher priorities to different types of information. In practice, the amount of information upon which decisions are made is limited by considerations of time and cost. It is to be expected that too much information may cloud the issues, and, instead of decisions improving with increasing information, the increased complexity of the task may lead to less

[1] The fieldwork of this study was carried out by Ann Chandler.

efficient use of the information and to less efficient decisions. Probation officers are frequently required to make recommendations to the courts at quite short notice, and accordingly have to be selective in their search for data or in the questions they ask of their cases in their interviews.[1] In general, the information which may be sought in interviews and used in making decisions or recommendations is not predetermined; the officer may spend whatever time is available in obtaining the information he deems relevant. (Previous studies have passed information to the case-workers in a sequence determined by the research worker.)

Apparatus and Method

From the files of the probation office which provided the subjects for the study, a case history was selected which was believed to be one of the best examples of case-recording available. The assessment of the quality of the record was made by a probation officer. The selected case history was subjected to content analysis and the material classified under 49 subject headings. The terms used for classification were commonly used in the particular office. Each item of information was then reproduced on a $6'' \times 4''$ index card with a title describing the nature of the information on the card printed on the lower edge. The cards were then arranged so that only the lower edge (showing the classification title) was visible, and all the 49 edges with titles were visible at one and the same time. The content of any card could be identified by the visible edge title, and the material on the card could be read by flipping the card with the thumb. Each card of this *information board* was numbered for reference purposes.

The subjects were required to utilize the information in the information board in making the decision whether or not to recommend probation as a suitable treatment for the particular case. The information could be read by them in any order they chose, but they were told that the purpose of the study was to see how quickly, that is, using as little information as possible, they could come to a correct decision.

The remaining apparatus consisted of a quantity of sheets of paper on which the subjects were to record their decisions, together with the ratings, on two scales. Each scale was represented by a ten centimetre line: the first providing for an assessment of the 'ease' or 'difficulty' in making the decision, ranging from 'dead easy' to 'almost impossible'; and the other for recording the degree of confidence the officer felt in his decision, ranging from 'no confidence' to 'complete assurance'. After each decision and rating the officer handed the sheet to the experimenter.

Officers (subjects) were informed of the nature of the study and were given ample time and opportunity to examine the total coverage of the information board by referring to the visible edge titles. They were per-

[1] The subjects for this study were probation officers in a large city on the east coast of the United States.

mitted to turn up *no* card until they expressed satisfaction with the system and understood the nature of the available information. Subjects seemed to regard the experimental conditions as a fairly realistic model of the conditions under which they had to consider information in the practical day-to-day work of the courts. The subjects were prepared to agree that they often had to make decisions on limited information. They were told that they would have an opportunity of saying how difficult they found it to make decisions as the amount of information to which they had recourse increased, and to say what level of confidence they felt in their decisions. There was, as has been noted, pressure to make the best decision, in the minimum of time and with the least information. The experimenter was able to observe the order in which the subjects selected information, and to relate this to the type of decision, the assessed difficulty, and the degree of confidence expressed in the nature of the decision. Subjects could indicate at any time that they had referred to sufficient information.

The Pilot Study

In the pilot study reported here, the subjects were seventeen probation officers with varying degrees of experience and with different background training, all of whom were actively engaged in probation work in a large eastern university city in the United States of America. Their experience and the numbers by which they may be identified are shown below:

Subjects Ref. No.	Experience in probation work	Final Decision
1 (F)	Little experience (under three months)	No
2 (F)	6 years	Yes
3 (F)	5 years	Yes
4 (F)	6 years	Yes
5 (F)	6 years	Yes
6 (F)	1 year	No
1 (M)	Supervisor 5 years	No
2 (M)	2 months	Yes
3 (M)	Assistant supervisor	No
4 (M)	5 years	Yes
5 (M)	7 years	Yes
6 (M)	$2\frac{1}{2}$ years	Yes
7 (M)	1 year (M.A. Psychology)	Yes
8 (M)	4 years	No
9 (M)	$4\frac{1}{4}$ years	Yes
10 (M)	1 year (2 years institution)	Yes
11 (M)	$1\frac{1}{2}$ years (M.A. Sociology)	Yes

It will be apparent that there is no relationship between the type of decision made and the sex or experience of the officers in this sample.

Probation was not recommended by either of the two officers at the supervisory level. During the course of the experiment (as information increased) ten officers changed their minds (four of the six females, and six of the eleven males).

After the subjects had turned up four cards they were asked for an interim decision and completed the two rating scales.

The classification of the information from the case history was as shown in *Table 1* below. The reference numbers in the table identify the information and relate to the same items throughout the discussion. It must be emphasized that the content of the case history was not determined by the experimenter nor was the classification of the information. The officers making the decisions on the basis of the information provided through the medium of the information board were accustomed to these headings. The case history was selected by an officer in the same office as a good example of case recording.

TABLE 1

Classification of information from case history
(titles appearing on the visible edge of the cards in the information board)

Ref. No.	Description
1.	Charge
2.	Complainant's account of incident
3.	Co-defendant's account of incident
4.	Offender's account of incident
5.	General appearance of offender
6.	Sex and age of offender
7.	Scholastic attainment
8.	Practical handling of problems by offender
9.	Attitudes towards authority
10.	Routine and ritualized behaviour
11.	Patterns of emotionality
12.	Offender's reactions to recognition and approval
13.	Degree of offender's dependency
14.	Sibling court contacts
15.	Routine intelligence tests
16.	Psychologist's recommendations
17.	Psychologist's diagnosis
18.	Health habits – Medical reports
19.	Mother's expression of offender's attitude at home
20.	Psychiatrist's comments

Ref. No.	Description
21.	Father's occupation
22.	Family income
23.	Teacher/counsellor evaluation
24.	Employment record of offender
25.	Attendance record
26.	Offender's religious training
27.	Offender's religious attitudes
28.	Interests and activities of offender
29.	Employer/offender relationship
30.	Adjustment reaction to detention
31.	Peer group relations
32.	Offender's perception of parental roles
33.	Mother/father relationship
34.	Residence (home conditions)
35.	Neighbourhood
36.	Previous conduct difficulties
37.	Offender's statement indicating attitude to school
38.	Indication of effectiveness of parental supervision and control
39.	Indication of leadership ability of offender
40.	Conformity and standards of behaviour
41.	Offender's involvement with community activities
42.	Parents' community interest and involvement
43.	Imitation or contagious behaviour
44.	Offender's self-ideal
45.	Offender's self-concept
46.	Offender's manner of self-expression
47.	Investigator's impression of offender's insight
48.	Profile of mother
49.	Profile of father

Results

The main results are summarized in the battery of charts which follow. Changes in decisions are indicated, together with the value given to the rating of confidence and the total number of cards studied; the sequence in which the information was considered is shown in *Table 2* below.

It seems that the ways in which probation officers seek and utilize information in the course of the making of decisions as to action regarding their cases are characteristic of the officers rather than the nature of the information. The methods for seeking and utilizing information would

FIGURE A

Relationship between confidence ratings and ratings of difficulty, with decision change points

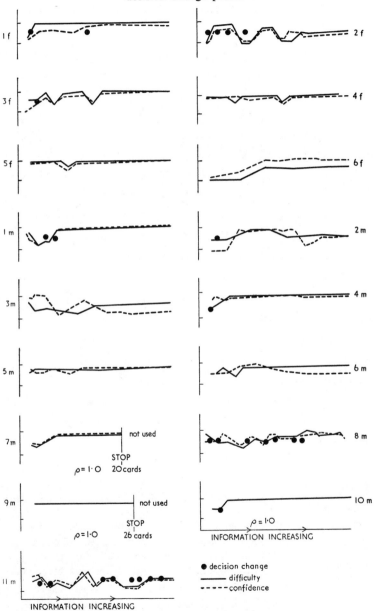

seem to be unrelated to the type of decision arrived at. The reversal of a decision does not appear to be related to any particular items of information. It is clear, however, that the probability of a reversal of a decision decreases rapidly as the number of items of information examined increases.

TABLE 2

Sequence of information reference by subjects, and items related to changes of decision

1	2	1	1	1	1	38	15	38	1	6	1	1	25	17	1	1
4	4	4	5	2	2	16	33	19	2	1	2	4	1	20	2	33
2	33	3	11	4	9	13	22	9	4	36	4	2	2	9	3	48
3	16	9	15	19	16	14	18	4	17	33	23	23	4	8	4	49
5*	11*	36	19	5	25	6	21*	23	36*	17	19	48	38*	19	7	36*
7*	32*	26	20	7	19	7	9*	15	19*	20	6	49	36*	7	14	16*
25	37*	40*	23	9	20	1*	7	17	40	15	32	36	20*	37	9*	20*
23	7*	23*	25	8	23	6*	23	22	10	5	36	7	30*	2	8*	34*
35	15*	31	26	10	31	25*	5	26	9	4	14*	25	15	4	5	35
34	23*	16	27	11	35	32*	35	45	16	41	17*	28	9	3	11	7
35	22	17	28	13	33	31	1	31	31	45	16	42	19	28	15	8
41	34	20	31	15	36	18	2	6	6	44	20	38	6	48	18	15
33	35*	35	33	20	40	39	4	3	20	31	38	11	39*	33	13	25
6	5*	32	34	28	21	48	6	29	38	30	47	22	43*	23	48	28
22	8	33	35	33	22	38	24	31	46	21	44	6	33	32	49	31
21	12	13	38	38	15	28	20	42	8	14	45	15	21	36	22	37
32*	19	20	39	36	34	22	36	11	41	39	48	5	47*	5	24	38
9*	31	18	40	40	10	4	39	10	43	12	49	34	31*	25	21	40*
10*	38	8	41	41	8	5	34	47	48	11	31	35	8*	43	19	22*
37*	24	25	44	44	26	19	23	28	49	24	9	14	37*	26	17	24*
13	29	38	46	47	27	17	11	14	14	19	25	—	7	24	16	29*
15	45	11	48	46	28	20	8	13	11	13	33	—	15	44	31	45
17	39	47	49	3	4	31	6	4	23	9	24	—	40*	45	32	41
16	40	30	2	12	2	47	10	39	18	32	35	—	24*	34	42	3*
28	13	13	3	23	3	34	17	35	33	48	37	—	29*	6	41	2*
38	42	28	13	6	30	35	32	5	44	49	38	—	44*	14	47	4*
18	48	19	18	22	18	38	40	49	22	43	8	—	49	—	44	11*
11	49	34	21	31	32	42	38	48	13	38	10	—	48	—	45	15*
12	44	35	29	32	17	3	43	40	47	34	29	—	32	—	6	18*
28	46	33	24	34	16	12	48	33	35	35	28	—	41	—	10	14*
31	47	19	32	35	41	32	49	27	29	47	26	—	26	—	23	19*
39	14	18	30	37	38	29	15	18	12	46	21	—	18	—	25	23
40	12	7	36	39	37	40	40	11	7	42	22	—	5	—	26	32
43	18	5	47	45	44	43	43	37	39	28	5	—	12	—	27	—

* Decision change points.

Very considerable individuality is revealed in the types of information sought at different times, but some uniformity is to be noted in that just over half of the officers referred to the details of the offence behaviour at an early stage, whereas others did not do so. Some officers did not refer to this item of information at all. Some items seem to be referred to quite early if they are likely to be sought, and their probability of reference decreases rapidly with increase in information.

It has been demonstrated in other studies that too much information obscures the problem and instead of decisions improving with increasing information the increased complexity leads to less effective decisions; but in this study only two officers indicated that they had had enough information before the experiment was terminated. It has also been shown that the sequence of information can cause persons to change their opinions (where the type of information is constant), but in this study the sequence of the information was at the will of the subject. It seems that where subjects may select the sequence of information – as indeed people usually do in practice – some persons will not select the optimum sequence, or may select a sequence which is likely to confirm their stereotypes.

A study of the charts will reveal that the reversal of a decision does not appear to be related to the degree of confidence in the decision preceding or following the change. A high rating of confidence may be given for the decision at point (n), the decision may be changed at $(n+1)$, and the degree of confidence remain unshaken or even increase. But the rating of confidence in decisions is directly related to the rating of the ease of the decision – an easy decision is one in which confidence is normally expressed, and conversely, a difficult decision is regarded as one in which little confidence is felt. The correlation between the 'ease-difficulty' scale and the confidence rating scale is so close that it appears unnecessary to use both. Subjects found the confidence rating scale unsatisfactory but were quite happy with the rating on the 'ease-difficulty' continuum.

TABLE 3

Importance of items of information as indicated by sequence of selection and decision change

Item No.	First 4			First 8	First 10	Charge items		
	+	—	Σ			+	—	Σ
1	5	7	12	13	13	1		1
2	3	6	9	10	10			
3	—	3	3	3	3			
4	3	7	10	10	11			
5	1		1	4	6	2		2
6	1		1	4	5	1		1
7	—		—	8	8	2		2
8	1		1	3	3	1		1
9	1	3	4	7	9	2	1	3
10	—			1	2			
11	1		1	2	4		1	1
12	—			—	—			
13	—	1	1	1	1			

TABLE 3—*continued*

Item No.	First 4			First 8	First 10	Charge items		
	+	—	Σ			+	—	Σ
14	—	1	1	2	3	1		1
15	1	1	2	4	6		1	1
16	1	2	3	4	6			
17	1	1	2	4	5	1		1
18	—	1	1	1	1			
19	1	1	2	7	7	1		1
20	1		1	5	5			
21	—			1	1	1		1
22	—	1	1	1	1			
23	1	1	2	8	10	1	2	3
24				—	—			
25		1	1	4	6		1	1
26				1	3			
27					1			
28				1	1			
29				1	1			
30					1			
31				2	2			
32	3	1	4	4	2		2	2
33				1	4			
34					2			
35					4	1		1
36	1		1	7	7	1		1
37				2	2	1		1
38		2	2	3	3			
39					—			
40				2	2	1		1
41					1			
42								
43								
44								
45					1			
46								
47								
48	1			2	2			
49	1			2	2			

An interesting suggestion from these data, but unfortunately one which may be unsound, is that there are types of information which are 'important'. That is to say, after an *important* item a person is likely to change his mind, but not in any specified direction. After taking in an *important* item it may be that the person relates it to his background or personality, and this item makes an impact, but the nature of the impact is in terms of an interaction leading to an uncertain outcome. There were items which were associated with more than chance frequency with a change of decision, but if the direction of the change is taken into account, there is no significant distribution of the items. Presumably no item referred to by subjects (at least in the early stages when they were likely to change their minds) was regarded by them as unimportant, since if they thought it unimportant they would not refer to it in the conditions of the experiment.

Discussion

The apparatus described is simple to make and is adaptable to many types of situation. If, for example, it is known that some persons are better assessors than others, it is possible that one of the main reasons for their success is that they have found a method of programming the sequence of their information input, and are more aware than others when they have reached a sufficiency.

It is clear that the amount of information which can be processed effectively by the human mind is quite small.

Perhaps the most valid use of the information board is in the identification of types of decision-maker. It does not seem unreasonable to suppose that the way people go about their search for information is related to the way they go about their work in dealing with the problems to which the information relates. If different types of probation officer are more successful in treating different types of case, one way in which the different types of officer might be identified is by means of their *information search profiles*. The apparatus would also be useful in certain problems of evaluation of training programmes.

The apparatus is described and the methods of analysis suggested only as one simple illustration of the ways in which information processing may be studied. It is put forward because it is believed that information is a key variable in the measurement of human behaviour.

If the sample size were larger, the data provided by this approach would have been amenable to sundry statistical analytical procedures. Officers who were most different from or most similar to each other might be identified by a generalized distance function, using the type of information and the sequence in which it was sought as the basic data. Types of datum might have been assessed in terms of the likelihood of pairs or triads of information being taken together.

The items of information used in the construction of the information board will derive from populations, and it is possible to ascertain for such populations the correlations between items of information. It would be interesting to examine the ways in which decision-makers using the information board dealt with correlated and uncorrelated information. The sequences in which items were studied would, if related to correlations in the 'real world' (population), indicate the possible power of different strategies for information-seeking. It might be expected, for example, that efficient decision-makers would select items in the initial stages which were uncorrelated with each other but correlated with the criterion.

Standard information boards have been prepared for the study of delinquency and its treatment by the University of California, Department of Criminology, Berkeley, and are copyrighted.

Index

NOTES

NOTES